The Suburban
Environment

Studies of
Urban Society

David
Popenoe

**The Suburban
Environment**

Sweden and
the United States

The University of
Chicago Press

Chicago
and London

781823

The University of Chicago Press, Chicago 60637
The University of Chicago Press, Ltd., London

DAVID POPENOE is associate professor of sociology at
Rutgers University. He is the author of *Sociology,*
editor of *The Urban-Industrial Frontier: Essays on
Social Trends and Institutional Goals in Modern Com-
munities,* and coeditor of *Neighborhood, City and
Metropolis: An Integrated Reader in Urban Sociology.*

Library of Congress Cataloging in Publication Data

Popenoe, David, 1932–
  The suburban environment.

  (Studies of urban society)
  Includes bibliographical references and index.
  1. Suburbs—Sweden—Case studies. 2. Suburbs—
United States—Case studies. 3. Levittown, Pa.—
Social conditions. 4. Vällingby, Stockholm—Social
conditions. I. Title.
HT351.P66 1977   301.36'2'09485   76-8091
ISBN 0-226-67542-4

Contents

Preface

After the Second World War, the two most "modernized," economically advanced, and affluent nations in the world—the United States and Sweden—faced a serious housing shortage. The shortage was particularly severe in urban and metropolitan areas. Each of the two nations dealt with its urban housing problem in a very different way but one that was in keeping with the character of its political and economic institutions. In the United States, the mass building of suburban housing was undertaken by the private home building industry, with the assistance of financial subsidies of various kinds from the federal government. In Sweden, national and local governments became involved directly in the building of mass suburban housing, often on land which was already government-owned. These dissimilar approaches have been the subject of a lively interchange among planners, public officials, and social scientists over the past two decades.

The difference in approaches, however, was no greater than the difference in results. The suburbs built in Sweden were high-density (mostly apartments), compact and relatively self-contained yet closely tied to the city, and oriented to public transportation. The U.S. suburbs were low-density (exclusively single-family, detached houses), "sprawling," often detached from the city and oriented to the automobile. Swedish suburbs are a true extension of the city; the U.S. suburbs are a world apart from the city. Thus, the postwar suburbs in each nation are, as residential environments, virtual opposites of one another.

Though the environments were very dissimilar, the people who came to inhabit them were quite similar in major sociological respects: they were middle- and working-class families, typically with young children; their work tied them to the city; they were moving to get a dwelling unit of their own. Thus a comparison of social outcomes is suggested. Have the differences between the two environments made any real and lasting impact on the lives of these families? Has one environment proven itself to be "socially superior"?

The personal and social consequences of suburban living have been the subject of much intellectual controversy in both nations over the last few decades. Some intellectuals, architects, and social scientists have heaped scorn on American suburbs for generating a long list of undesirable characteristics ranging from conformity to alcoholism to neurosis in housewives. Others, however, especially sociologists and economists, have come to regard these suburbs as smoothly functioning products of consumer choice which the residents desire and appreciate. Swedish suburbs, on the other hand, have been widely praised, particularly by architects and planners in both countries, for providing aesthetic delight, human contact, and social efficiency. It recently has become popular in Sweden, however, to deride the planned Swedish suburbs as inhuman, unattractive, and undemocratic. This point of view is particularly common in journalistic and radical social-science circles.

The postwar suburban building boom in each nation has now come to a close. As the last quarter of the twentieth century begins, and as each country prepares to go off in perhaps new directions of urban growth, the time seems ripe for a careful comparison of the two suburban experiences. The purpose of this inquiry is to provide, from a socio-logical perspective, such a comparison. Through this cross-national inquiry, I hope to make a con-tribution to our understanding of the influences which residential environments have for human behavior and social organization.

The study focuses on two suburbs which seem very typical of their nations, their era, and their genre: Vällingby, a suburb of Stockholm, and Levittown, Pennsylvania, a suburb of Philadelphia. These two suburbs, the products of Western culture and postindustrial affluence, provide an unusual opportunity for a natural comparison. Both are "packaged" suburbs containing about the same number of dwelling units, both were built in the early 1950s, both were designed to house working- and middle-class families. Each suburb has now been in existence for more than twenty years, time enough to have established solid identities.

The data on which the findings, interpretations, and judgments of this book are made come from five main sources: first, intensive interviews with a small sample of families in each community; second, interviews with leaders, decision-makers and experts in each community who had a special knowledge of that community's social structure and problems; third, discussions with scholars and experts in both countries in the fields of housing, planning, and the social sciences (in all, over 250 persons were personally interviewed by me in the course of the study); fourth, the available second-ary data about the two communities, especially that from national and local censuses; fifth, many weeks of direct field observation in both suburbs. The interpretations and judgments were enriched by the scholarly literature on the suburbs, and on the residential environment in general, which exists in each nation. Data collection took place over a three-year period that included three visits to Sweden, one of which was a year's stay as Senior Fulbright Research Scholar at the University of Stockholm.

Because cross-national research in environmental sociology is in its infancy, this inquiry is necessarily an exploratory one. My intention has been, using a cross-national framework, to suggest new hypotheses, challenge some common assumptions, and bring greater intellectual order to the field of man-environment relations. The practice of sociology moves in two complementary directions: the development of increasingly perfected theoretical and policy interpretations of its subject matter, and the discovery of increasingly refined empirical generalizations. My approach here lies more in the former direction. I have sought especially to cast light on the complex issues in the social quality of residential environments.

This work is directed principally to social scientists, and to planners, architects, builders, and others who seek a broader base of knowledge for the design of the urban environment. I have attempted to stay as much as possible within the realm of scientific theory-building and social-science rules of evidence. Yet, I also have tried to select variables and to investigate social situations and issues which commonly figure in public discussion, and thereby make the inquiry as relevant to the ongoing public debate about housing and urban development policies as possible. In the same spirit, I have added a final chapter in which the policy implications of my findings are discussed. Throughout the book I have sought to avoid unnecessary sociological jargon. Information from the social sciences is in too short supply, in this field at least, to keep it within the confines of the academy.

This inquiry would not have been possible without the support—both financial and intellectual—of a great many institutions and individuals on both sides of the Atlantic. Rutgers University granted a Faculty Research Fellowship which, together with a travel grant from the Fulbright Commission, permitted me to spend the year 1972–73 in Sweden with my family. The Swedish Institute for Cultural Affairs awarded a Swedish Kennedy Scholarship in 1974, allowing me to return to Stockholm for the summer. In 1975, my return for six weeks in May and June was made possible by an invitation to be a visiting professor at the National Swedish Building Research Institute and the University of Stockholm. During each of my stays in Sweden, office space, secretarial services and supplies were generously provided by the Sociology Department of the University of Stockholm and the National Swedish Building Research Institute. Finally, Svenska Bostäder, the principal builders of Vällingby, graciously provided unlimited access to their community, and the assistance of their staff. To each of these institutions I express deep gratitude.

So many individuals have played a role in this inquiry that it is impossible here to thank them all separately, as I would wish. But I cannot fail to mention some, without whom this inquiry might not have been completed. In Sweden, Professor Carl-Gunnar Janson and his wife Ann-Marie generously provided me with support of all kinds, including their close friendship and intellectual companionship; Åke Daun, Ulla Bergström, and Göran Sidenbladh consented to read and comment on portions of the manuscript; Birgitta Lundberg assisted me with the household interviews; Karin Wiklund and Nils Johansson helped with housing arrangements; Olaf Hirn arranged interviews with Swedish housing officials; Jan Ericson, Anna Holtz, and Lennart Widgren were, together with Nils Johansson, faithful friends and guides on field trips to the Stockholm suburbs; the faculty and staff of the Sociology Department of the University of Stockholm, together with my graduate students there, provided me with continuing education, counsel, and guidance in matters Swedish.

In the United States Harriet Kneller assisted me in finding data on Levittown, Professor David Crabb kindly permitted me to use the anthropological materials collected in Levittown by his students, and the Reverend John Spahr helped to arrange Levittown interviews. I cannot begin to express to all these individuals, and to the many others not mentioned, the depth of my gratitude.

Finally, this book would not have been possible without the wise, diligent, and immensely helpful assistance of my wife, Kate. To her, though it cannot begin to express my debt, this book is lovingly dedicated.

1 Introduction

The suburb—a community which lies apart from the city but is adjacent to and dependent on it—is not a latecomer in world history. Its origins go back almost as far as the city itself. Traces of suburban development can be found at the sites of the earliest Mesopotamian cities, where scattered buildings were unearthed outside the main city boundaries. There is substantial knowledge about suburbs in the Middle Ages. The wealthiest city dwellers then were able to establish small settlements of country homes in the urban hinterland; their work tied them to the city, but they were able to avoid the city's ills in much of their residential life. As Lewis Mumford has put it, "one might say that the modern suburb began as a sort of rural isolation ward";[1] it became in time "the collective urban form of the country house."[2]

So long as means of transportation remained primitive, suburbs were limited to the wealthy— the ordinary urban worker had to live within walking distance of his place of employment. The city began to decentralize in earnest with the coming of the first vehicles of mass transportation, and the process of suburbanization intensified with the advent of the steam locomotive and later the suburban trolley line.[3] These means of transportation were expensive, however, and relatively inflexible. The nineteenth- and early twentieth-century suburbs were well beyond the means of even the middle-class worker, and suburban development was restricted to small neighborhoods on land adjacent to metro-politan rail lines.

The widespread movement of urban residents to the city's edge depended on the mass production of automobiles and on the growth of personal incomes, conditions which made it possible for many families to afford a private means of transportation and a single-family house. Growing use of the automobile also signaled what is aptly called the scatteration of the city; no longer did urban growth have to be tied to fixed transportation paths. At the same time that opportunities to live in suburbs were provided by these advances, the older cities, built mostly in the nineteenth century, were becoming more congested, polluted, and less desirable as residential environments. The ordinary city man wanted out—in the suburbs he had visions of "withdrawing like a monk and living like a prince,"[4] as the wealthy before him had done.

What followed in the United States was the emergence of the low-density suburb, organized around the automobile and the single-family house, as the principal type of residential environment. The middle classes and then the working classes left the older cities in large numbers, abandoning them to the poor and, unintentionally but inevitably, to a spiral of decay and neglect. Unlike their predecessors, many migrants from small towns came to settle in the suburbs without ever passing through the cities. In the newer cities of the nation, built after entry into the automobile era, most of the urban area was developed in a pattern similar to the suburban extensions of the older cities. By the last quarter of the twentieth century, a majority of Americans were living in an environment which was once the exclusive habitat of the urban rich.[5] It is not always recognized, however, that this type of residential environment is atypical of much of the world outside of North America. Other nations, just as modern, affluent, and advanced as the United States, have chosen different paths of urban growth.

Studies of the American Suburb

Informed opinion about the American suburb has had a fascinating career in the last two or three decades. The suburb has been the focus of a lively intellectual debate, with issues which have spanned the social sciences, the popular press, and even the humanities. The literature has been filled with charges and countercharges. Some of the debate has been scientific, grounded in research findings; most of it has not.

Before World War II, the suburb and suburbanization were seldom studied or even discussed, though one estimate put the 1940 suburban population in the U.S. at 17 percent.[6] The pioneering social science work on the suburb, by

H. P. Douglass, appeared in 1925, but it was mostly a discussion of demographic trends.[7] A few studies of suburbs were made in the thirties and early forties,[8] but as late as 1952 one urban sociology textbook devoted only two pages to a discussion of the subject.[9] There was great interest within sociology in big cities,[10] and in small towns,[11] but in very few other community types. The intellectual controversies in the field of urban sociology revolved mostly around the evils of the big city. Even this controversy was muted, because the big city had few defenders.[12]

After the war, the rush to the suburbs began for millions of Americans. By the 1950s, America's journalists, intellectuals, and social scientists had had a chance to take careful note. The mid-fifties saw an outpouring of popular literature on the suburbs that one author has called "a critical onslaught of monumental, and largely nonsensical, proportions."[13] The best-known books were: Whyte's *The Organization Man,* and Keats's *The Crack in the Picture Window,* and later, *The Split-Level Trap,* by Gordon, Gordon, and Gunther.[14] These were accompanied by a spate of articles in such magazines as *Better Homes and Gardens, Fortune, Reader's Digest, Harpers,* and *The Saturday Evening Post.*[15] The bulk of this literature, as one could surmise from the book titles, was highly critical of suburban life. A move to the suburbs was alleged to foster overconformity, hyperactivity, anti-individualism, conservatism, momism, dullness and boredom, and status seeking, as well as a host of specific psychological and social ills including alcoholism, sexual promiscuity, and mental illness. Even the movies entered the act, and brought these themes to the big screen. The suburbs were portrayed as a kind of national scandal.

Sociologists also entered the fray in the fifties, but mostly in a quiet and more unassuming way. A series of articles was written by different scholars with such titles as "The Structuring of Social Relationships Engendered by Suburban Residence"[16] and "Suburbanism as a Way of Life."[17] While articles such as these contributed greatly to our empirical knowledge about the suburbs, they did not directly enter the popular debate. There were two major exceptions, however. The influential Harvard sociologist David Riesman wrote an article in 1957 for *The Annals* entitled "The Suburban Dislocation,"[18] in which he sided with the popular criticism of the suburbs through a sophisticated discussion of the way in which suburban living causes a loss of "diversity, complexity, and texture" in life.[19] In addition, he wrote the preface to the one major sociological study of a suburb in the 1950s that tended to confirm the popular image: *Crestwood Heights.*[20] Written by a team of social scientists headed by a psychoanalytically oriented sociologist, John R. Seeley, this book examined an upper middle-class, inner suburb of Toronto and found in the culture and social structure of suburban life a considerable number of factors that the authors concluded to be pathogenic for mental health and personal maturation.[21]

By the end of the 1950s, however, most leading sociologists in this field were attempting to meet head-on the popular view of the "effects of suburbia." The first major effort was by Bennett M. Berger in the book *Working Class Suburb*.[22] Most of the popular suburban images concerned middle-class values and characteristics; Berger wanted to establish what social effects the suburb itself, apart from social class, might have on its residents. Moreover, Berger stated, "the burden of the study has been to call into question certain commonly accepted facts of life in 'suburbia,' as these facts have been presented to us both by popular writers and by some professional social scientists."[23] He came upon a unique natural experiment in process: a large group of Ford Motor Company workers was being moved from Richmond, California, to a new suburban area fifty miles away. Would the new environment change the lives of these urban-dwelling members of the working class in the direction of the popular image? Berger studied them after they had been in their new homes for two years.

What did he find? In a review of the study several years later, he put it this way: "as the interview evidence piled up, it became clear that the lives of the suburbanites I was studying had not been profoundly affected in any statistically identifiable or sociologically interesting way."[24] This finding led him to refer to the "commonly accepted facts" as "the myth of suburbia"—a phrase which quickly became popular and was to linger on to the present time.

Berger not only helped to destroy the myth, however. He also may have helped unwittingly to undercut the study of man-environment relations with such conclusive-sounding statements as "the variety of physical and demographic differences between cities and suburbs . . . bears little significance for the way of life of their inhabitants."[25] In fact, some social and cultural changes were reported in *Working Class Suburb* (the changes for women were greater than for men; women tend to be more affected by the residential environment), but Berger did not feel at the time that these changes were especially significant. In any event, as he later was to say about suburban studies in general, "the reported changes in the lives of suburbanites were not *caused* by the move to suburbia, but were reasons for moving there in the first place"[26] (this reasoning applies especially to such traits as sociability and home-centeredness). Yet, in view of the presumably subtle nature of suburban differences, one can ask if the social effects of suburbia would show up in full force after only two years. A negative answer seems eminently reasonable.

Berger's work made ripples which lasted through the sixties, and the field of interest was further developed by many other scholars. The "myth of suburbia" became standard fare in many introductory general and urban sociology texts. Berger himself continued to write articles more or less in praise of suburbia and suburban trends.[27]

The landmark suburban study of the 1960s was *The Levittowners*, by Herbert Gans.[28] Educated as both a sociologist and a planner, Gans had already completed some of the pioneering suburban investigations when he decided to do a major participant observation study in the new Levittown, New Jersey.[29] *The Levittowners* is very similar to *Working Class Suburb* in both structure and conclusions. Gans studied the first few thousand arrivals to Levittown for the initial two years of their residency. Like Berger, he was primarily interested in changes in interests and life-style that may have resulted from the move. He carefully interviewed people about life in their previous communities, as well as about their adaptation to the new one. Most of the residents had come from the city, so Gans's analysis focused on city-suburban differences.

Gans's investigation is more systematic and detailed than Berger's, though with the same limited two-year time frame. Like Berger, he concluded that "few changes can be traced to the suburban qualities of Levittown."[30] Perhaps partly as a result of this finding, the bulk of *The Levittowners* deals with other issues: a description and analysis of the development of a new community and its institutions—churches, schools, organizations, and especially political life.

Gans firmly joined the growing chorus of "demythologizers": "The findings on changes and their sources suggest that the distinction between urban and suburban ways of living postulated by the critics (and by some sociologists as well) is more imaginary than real."[31] But he also offered an explanation for what changes did occur. "The crucial difference between cities and suburbs, then, is that they are often home for different kinds of people."[32] In emphasizing this fundamental, but often overlooked, fact, Gans made two important sociological points: it is difficult to compare the effects of dissimilar residential environments when the people who reside in them are also very different; and, the characteristics of the residents are more important than the characteristics of the environment in accounting for human behavior and social organization in any community.

The latter point ("people are more important than buildings" is its popular form) became a major theme of Gans's later work. In reaction to the ideology of environmental determinism which was dominant in the world of planners and architects of the time, he heavily emphasized the social and cultural components of behavior over the environmental. This emphasis was undoubtedly salutary for architects and planners, but, like the views of Bennett Berger, and despite Gans's intentions, it may have helped to undercut the study of man-environment relations within sociology. Gans states: "Plans and policies aimed at changing people's behavior can therefore not be implemented through prescribing alterations in the physical community or by directives aimed at builders."[33] So much for architecture and planning and their supposed social effects! A generation of sociologists came to accept this kind of statement at face value—the residential environment has little or no effect on behavior.[34]

Like Berger, Gans emerged from his Levittown study with quite positive views about suburbs in general and Levittown in particular. "Levittown permits most of its residents to be what they want to be."[35] "Whatever its imperfections, Levittown is a good place to live."[36] His deep concern for equality, good housing for all, and the redistribution of income came to override any negative opinions of the suburbs that he might have emphasized: "it is much less important to plan for new and improved suburban communities than to make sure that more people are able to live in suburbs like those now being built."[37] The positive view of the suburbs in explicit opposition to the negative "myth," together with the attack on "environmental determinism," became hallmarks of much of the U.S. sociological literature on suburbia of the 1960s.[38]

By the late 60s, the suburbs had become a serious focus of scholarly efforts not only within sociology but also in the allied disciplines of political science, economics, and geography.[39] A large amount of empirical evidence, typologies, and theoretical perspectives was accumulating. Just when the accumulation was beginning to add up to some solid and refined knowledge about this new environmental form, however, scholarly interest in the suburbs suddenly all but vanished.[40] The field of urban studies was overcome by the events of the late 1960s, and the problems of the big cities again gained hegemony over the interests of the urban-suburban scholar. The pressing concerns were race and poverty, riots and rebellion, welfare and slums. The quiet world of the suburb was all but drowned out by the sea of scholarly, downtown-oriented efforts which marked the maturation of urban studies— the study of urbanization, urbanized communities, and urban problems—as a major field of academic life.[41]

The spirit of the late 60s, which dominated the university campus not only in politics and life-style but also in urban studies, faced away with the end of the Vietnam War. Today, the problems of the large cities remain unremedied and poorly understood, and the amount of ongoing urban research remains fairly large. But the pressure "to do something" about the cities has declined, and urban research is again able to venture into somewhat less politically pressing but nonetheless intellectually rewarding areas of investigation such as the suburbs.

As quickly as interest in the suburbs vanished, it has suddenly reemerged within the last several years as an important area of scholarly activity within the social sciences. Since 1972, no less than five suburban readers have been published—collections of articles on the suburbs for the use of students and scholars.[42] Many serious studies of suburban areas are now underway in North America, some at new centers for suburban studies which have been established in several universities. It was also in 1972 that a new, popularly written attack on contemporary suburban living was published: Vance Packard's *Nation of Strangers*—which deals with the "rootlessness" in the suburbs caused by high residential mobility.[43] The rather negative view of the suburbs in this book has not been well received within sociology,[44] in contrast to the book's warm reception in the popular media, but the "evaluation gap" between scholar and popular commentator has diminished somewhat over the years as social scientists have become harsher in their suburban evaluations. This is suggested by the title of one of the recent books: *The End of Innocence: A Suburban Reader*, which stems from a federal task force which was set up to study suburban problems.[45]

The renaissance of suburban social science research has almost certainly been triggered by the fact that "real" problems have finally come to the suburbs: crime and delinquency, drugs, political corruption, racial conflict. The new problems in the suburbs are very different from those studied in the 1950s and 1960s. The city has by now spilled over into the suburbs, bringing its problems with it; the line between city and suburb has become blurred.[46] Moreover, the perspective on the suburb has changed. More Americans now live in suburbs than in either cities, small towns, or rural areas. The suburb is no longer a curiosity; it is where the middle American lives—and where many of our present urban dwellers would like to live.[47] To study the suburban environment now is to study the most typical environment in America.

Most suburban studies have found the residents quite pleased with their environments. This is especially true of those who came from the city; very seldom do they express a desire to return. And many investigations have verified that most suburbanites are in fact much "better off"—in many ways—than their urban counterparts.[48] Yet, is the comparison of the suburb with the American city still useful and relevant? In many ways it is not, because the two environments are not real alternatives for most people. The older American city is no longer regarded by the overwhelming majority of working- and middle-class persons as a viable residential environment—a place where they might live of their own free choice. Further, the newer cities of America—Fort Worth, Phoenix, Saint Petersburg, San Diego—are built in the environmental form which has traditionally been called suburban—low density and automobile-oriented. The urban-suburban comparison does not speak to the real issues which confront the future of urban development in this nation. The main issue is, What kind of *suburban* environment is best? Or more generally, What kind of metropolitan residential environment is best among those that are realistic alternatives for most people?

The sociological study of suburban environments has been developing in two directions. First, the last few years have seen the emergence of some major comparative investigations—a mark of scientific maturation. Second, as it has become clear that suburbs are much too amorphous to study as discrete entities, research has increasingly become focused on selected characteristics of those environments. Sometimes the selected characteristic is political structure, sometimes economic base, sometimes class or ethnicity, or sometimes—as in the case of this investigation—ecological structure and the built environment. In other words, sociological work in this field has become far more specialized than it was even a few years ago.

Within sociology as a whole, one of the rapidly growing areas of interest at the present time is the study of man-environment relations—the interaction between the natural and man-made environments and human behavior and social organization. One aspect of this emerging interest concerns the social consequences of living in different man-made, or built, environments. This has helped to stimulate research in suburbia as an environmental form. As was mentioned above, many sociologists of the 1950s and 1960s tended to downplay the social importance of the environment in reaction to the environmental determinism of the time and because they encountered factors like social class and ethnicity that are much more important determinants of behavior. Unfortunately, they left a vacuum. As sociologist Robert Gutman stated in a review of the literature of this period which related site planning and social behavior:[49]

> It has been estimated that in the next forty years, this nation will have constructed as many new dwelling units as were built in the previous two centuries of United States history. It is difficult to accept the conclusion, that it makes no difference how these houses are built, where they are located, and how they are arranged in space. Surely, there must be better and worse methods of planning a site, and hopefully the social sciences will be able to guide us in deciding what these methods are.

Sentiments such as these were instrumental in initiating the present investigation. Can it be that the residential environment really makes no difference?

The Comparative Analysis of Residential Environments

Comparative analysis within sociology is not a distinct method or technique; in the broadest sense, it suggests simply the process of discovering similarities and differences among social phenomena. It is even reasonable to think of sociology as, by its very nature, comparative. Emile Durkheim once stated: "Comparative sociology is not a particular branch of sociology; it is sociology itself, insofar as it ceases to be purely descriptive and aspires to account for facts."[50]

In practice, however, the difference between comparative and noncomparative sociology lies in the range of social variation considered. The term "comparative analysis" is used mainly to refer to "social science analysis involving observations in more than one social system, or in the same social system at more than one point in time."[51] By no means does all sociological research match this description; most research consists of cross-sectional analysis within a single social system, an observation that holds for research on the sociology of residential environments. Yet there has been some important comparative work in this field, and it has been influential in the present inquiry. The studies to be briefly reviewed here are the major investigations in which two or more environments have been compared to determine their differential effects on social behavior. In every case but one, the studies compare environments within a single nation or social system. Cross-national comparative research would appear to be a major need at the present time.

When the principal goal of research is a better understanding of the consequences of a residential environment for human behavior and social organization, the comparative research design often thought to be most adequate is one in which the same people live successively in two or more dissimilar environments in the same geographic area and society. The significance of this design is that as many things as possible, other than the residential environment, are held constant—especially the residents. Their behavior can then be carefully monitored to see what effects, if any, the environmental differences have made. This is not a commonly found situation, however. When it is found, there are inherent problems: the people will probably have lived much longer in one environment than the other, and have lived there at a different stage in their life cycle (Are they still the same people?). Further, it is difficult to carefully monitor people over a long period of time. It is more common, as in the suburban studies of Berger and Gans discussed in the last section, to ask residents to recall their experiences in the earlier environment.[52]

The longitudinal research design, utilizing the same residents in two different environments, is not unknown in the field, however. The two most important are D. M. Wilner et al., *The Housing Environment and Family Life,*[53] which "followed" families from Baltimore slums into near-by public housing projects, and Morris and Mogey's *The Sociology of Housing,*[54] which followed English families from slums to suburban project housing. Both of these studies were able to use the panel approach, in which households are interviewed several times over a period of years, both before and after the move.

For comparison with those who moved, Wilner and his associates used a matched group of families who stayed in the slums. They found among the movers, as compared to the control group, some improvement in physical health and in social and psychological adjustment. It was impossible to determine, however, because of the very brief period the families resided in the public housing (the time lapse of the study was three years), how long-lasting these improvements might be. It also proved difficult to isolate as causal factors specific environmental elements, from other life changes which took place.

Morris and Mogey utilized a very similar research design, including a matched sample of families who remained in the slums as a control group. They found comparable, though perhaps even more modest, improvements in the social and psychological adjustment of those who moved, concluding that "changes in family and neighborhood behavior can be achieved through rehousing, although the scope for such changes is usually exaggerated."[55]

Each of these studies looked at the effects of the new environment after the residents had lived there for, at most, two or three years. This brief time span has been a pervasive problem in studies of the residential environment, including most of the noncomparative, single-case investigations of suburban areas that have been done over the years. Due to the very subtle nature of environmental influences on behavior, it is quite likely that whatever influences there are become manifest only after a relatively long period of time. Moreover, there is a substantial body of evidence that the "newcomer effect" is quite significant in accounting for changes in the behavior of persons in new environments—that is, behavior is modified simply by the fact that people are newcomers to an area. These newcomer behavior patterns change in time and can not be attributed to changes in the residential environment. One area of behavior which has been shown to be heavily influenced by the newcomer effect is neighboring, which is relatively extensive in the early years of a new community (because neighbors are the most available source of friends), but declines over time.[56]

One of the few studies which has looked at a "new" housing development after a time lapse of many years is Peter Willmott's *The Evolution of a*

Community.[57] This study examines working-class life on the London housing estate of Dagenham, some thirty to forty years after it was built. Willmott concluded that the traditional life styles of working-class families didn't change much over the years in what was at first a strange new environment to them. Nevertheless, he found many environmental effects of a more subtle nature—effects on privacy, children's aspirations, and friendship patterns.[58]

Most comparative studies of residential environments are cross-sectional; they compare different people living in different environments at a single point in time. The earliest such studies compared two neighborhoods that differed in physical characteristics, with class held constant;[59] or that differed in distance from the center of the city.[60] Later studies compared a wider array of neighborhoods within a metropolitan area. Often, the neighborhoods were differentiated by the use of social area analysis, a technique which uses census data to distinguish the demographic composition of neighborhoods.[61] Studies based on social area analysis have usually not had much to say directly about man-environment relations (because they focus on demographic rather than physical structure), but their findings have been substantial and have become important components of all urban sociology texts.[62]

The most ambitious comparative neighborhood study was done in San Juan, Puerto Rico, by Theodore Caplow and his associates. Published under the title *The Urban Ambience,*[63] the study compared twenty-five residential areas which were selected to represent a variety of ecological and demographic characteristics. Wide variations in neighboring and friendship patterns, and levels of community satisfaction, were found. These variations were most highly correlated with social-class level. The environmental differences among the neighborhoods didn't emerge as prominent factors; this was partly due to the fact that they were "overwhelmed" by the tremendous sociocultural variation which existed.

Two of the most influential studies of residential environments were conducted several decades ago by Michael Young and Peter Willmott of the Institute of Community Studies in England. *Family and Kinship in East London* compares an older working-class district in London with a new, working-class housing estate on the city's edge, most of whose residents came originally from the inner-city area.[64] They concluded that the residents in the "slum" were better adapted and more contented, by and large, than those in the new housing. The principal reason was that those who moved to the new estate were forced to curtail or sever many of their traditional ties to kin and neighbors.

In *Family and Class in a London Suburb,* these same authors examine a middle-class suburb and compare it with the inner-city district looked at in the earlier book.[65] A major finding was that kinship ties in the suburb are much looser than in the inner city; "kinship matters less—friendship more."[66] Because the research design included a major social class as well as environmental difference, however, the book is not as significant for the field of environmental sociology as the first one. It points up what has long been an important problem in the field: the effects of class almost invariably overshadow the effects of the environment, so it is necessary in most environmental studies to hold class constant.

Not all contributions to the sociology of residential environments are necessarily *directly* concerned with the effects of the environment. Sometimes, researchers will pick a comparative-communities research design not because of any particular interest in the communities but merely to get a wide array of some social phenomenon or characteristic. Such investigations may provide valuable insights into the effects of the communities themselves, however. One example is James S. Coleman's *The Adolescent Society.*[67] Designed to be a comparative analysis of adolescent peer groups, Coleman picked his sample from nine communities in northern Illinois ranging in size from a small village of a thousand population to the city of Chicago. Coleman developed some significant insights into the relationship between adolescent peer groups and such community-structure characteristics as population size, heterogeneity, and economic base.

Another example is Helen Z. Lopata's study, *Occupation: Housewife,* in which she interviewed 299 middle-class women in twelve Chicago suburbs.[68] While concerned mainly with the changing roles of young suburban housewives, the work also makes a major contribution to our understanding of suburban neighboring.

The first large-scale comparative study of suburbs was S. D. Clark's *The Suburban Society.* Clark conducted interviews in fifteen suburbs in and around the Toronto area; he was rather more interested in a comparison between suburban and urban living than in differences among the suburbs, however. He concluded that "people were made into different beings by the demands of suburban living, with tastes that were inevitably simpler, standards of judgment that were lower, and social interests that were narrower and more self-centered."[69] But, "there was nothing 'sick' about this society. If anything, it would have to be described as disturbingly healthy."[70]

In the last several years, cross-sectional comparative studies of residential environments have become more methodologically refined, with the use of sophisticated regression models, survey research instruments, and the use of time and activity budgets. One British study, *The Sociology of Planning,* carefully analyzed "visiting" patterns in eight newly built private housing estates which differed in their physical arrangement. It concluded that the physical arrangement of the housing had very little effect on visiting patterns.[71] The conclusion must be interpreted with caution, however, because the physical differences among the housing estates were quite minor.

In the United States, planned new communities were compared with ordinary suburbs in a recent monograph, *Planned Residential Environments*.[72] Very few differences were found in people's attitudes and life-styles, although those who lived in the planned communities expressed a higher overall level of satisfaction. Again, the physical differences among the communities were not great, with the exception of two inner-city renewal areas of higher-income apartments (where the character of the population was very different from the suburban areas).

The most refined and sophisticated comparative analysis in the field of environmental sociology at the present time is that being undertaken by William Michelson in Toronto.[73] The project is both cross-sectional and longitudinal; it is designed to study "the social consequences for a family of living in some of the polar choices in housing available to them in contemporary metropolitan areas."[74] About eight hundred middle-class couples or families were interviewed at the time they moved into one of four housing arrangements: high-rise apartments in downtown Toronto, high-rise apartments in the suburbs, single-family houses in town, and suburban single-family houses. They were then reinterviewed at various intervals over a six-year period.

This study is the most promising single piece of research in the emerging field of environmental sociology; its conclusions are eagerly awaited. Like every other comparative study in the social sciences, this one has its limitations, which one should be aware of. In this case, there is a large amount of self-selection by the residents to each environmental and housing type. Each type is freely chosen, often with the other alternatives in view, and thus each environment is selected by persons with differing characteristics. Young families with working wives and few children are attracted to city apartments; higher-income families with many children are attracted to suburban houses; older families with higher incomes are attracted to inner-city houses; and small, lower-income families are attracted to suburban apartments. As an examination of the factors involved in such self-selection, together with the consequences of the choices, the study is difficult to fault; indeed, this was its principal goal. As a comparative analysis of environmental effects, however, the study faces the recurrent problem: the people who live in each environment are as different as the environments themselves.

None of the comparative studies mentioned so far has been cross-national. I am aware of only one cross-national study extant in this area of investigation, an overlooked study by the Englishman H. E. Bracey, entitled *Neighbors: Subdivision Life in England and the U.S.*[75] Bracey compared a new housing estate near Bristol, England (interviews conducted in 1957) with several new suburban subdivisions near Columbus, Ohio (1958–59), reaching conclusions which are favorable to the American suburb. He found that in the U.S. there is much more neighborliness, fewer lonely women, more voluntary organizations, and a greater concern for community change. He did not attempt to relate these differences to specific characteristics of community or environmental structure.

Because of its cross-national, exploratory character, the present Swedish-U.S. environmental inquiry differs from most of those just discussed. Nevertheless, I have tried to incorporate in it some of the lessons learned from comparative research in this field. For comparison with a typical postwar U.S. suburb, I sought a suburban residential environment which differed in many significant respects but whose residents were sociologically as similar as possible, especially in social-class level and stage of life-cycle. It was important for both suburban environments to be more than a decade old, owing to the likelihood that much environmental impact on behavior becomes manifest only after a relatively long time-period. Because environmental effects on behavior are notably weak, I wanted to emphasize in the research design the simultaneous and cumulative effects of a variety of environmental differences, an emphasis which suggested a holistic approach utilizing several of the more qualitative methodologies.

Public Policy Alternatives and the Selection of Cases

It is likely that much of the urban growth in the United States in the next twenty-five years will take place within existing metropolitan regions and will take the form of further suburban extensions of the nation's urban places. The development of more than a handful of totally new urban places appears to be beyond the fiscal and political capacity of the American system. Thus a major question of public policy is: what community and environmental forms should the new suburban housing take? The search for answers to this kind of question has become much more than an idle academic exercise in view of the fact that urban development in the years ahead will probably have a larger input of public planning, decision-making, and financial support than the urban building programs of the past.

While the subject matter of this inquiry derives from sociological curiosity about low-density American suburbs, and the inquiry's comparative design was dictated by considerations of scientific research, the choice of a Swedish residential environment for comparison developed out of an interest in such questions of public policy. A social scientific interest in comparative analysis is not far removed from the policymaker's search for "alternatives." The two interests may be combined through the comparison of cases which not only have scientific importance but which also represent real alternatives of public policy. At the same time that it contributes to our understanding of a phenomenon, the information gained in such a comparison can assist policymakers in making the difficult decisions which they face. It was this concern, then, which led me to seek an environmental alternative to the low-density U.S. suburb, an alternative which differs greatly in visual and planning characteristics but which is meant to serve similar functions for its residents and its society.

Just a few years back, alternatives to the low-density suburb were seldom entertained seriously outside of academic circles. Most public officials and private builders felt that the American suburb was almost as permanent a national fixture as the large business corporation, the skyscraper, or the high-speed expressway. People wanted it, it worked, and it could not be changed. The "energy crises" set new forces in motion, however, and the suburb has become the focus of growing public concern and even condemnation. It is now frequently attacked by environmental and consumer groups, responsible journalists, and many politicians and public officials as a despoiler of the landscape, a waster of energy resources, and a destroyer of the city. For the first time, there seems a willingness among the nation's decision-makers to seriously consider alternative environmental forms of urban growth. [76]

The most obvious and significant alternative to the U.S. suburb is the higher-density residential environment of attached houses and apartments, built around public transportation and offering a wider array of community services. A tradition of apartment living, while by no means absent elsewhere in the United States, is the almost exclusive property of the very large cities of the East and Midwest (which are generally considered to be among the less desirable areas to live in the U.S.). The typical and predominant dwelling, even in most of the towns and cities of America, is the single-family house. Among middle-class suburban residents, apartment life has been known only in a few of the largest Eastern metropolitan areas.

Yet at the same time that alternatives to the low-density suburb are becoming more seriously entertained in public discourse, there are strong indications that movement toward a higher-density suburban alternative is in fact already underway, brought about not by public design but by private economics. One of the most significant housing trends in the last few years has been the sharp increase in suburban garden-apartment construction. From 1960 to 1970, the percentage of multifamily units in America's suburban areas climbed from 15 to 22 percent. [77] The 1970s will see this figure climb even higher. At the present time there are almost as many new multifamily as single-family dwellings being built each year in the U.S., and there is little doubt that this trend toward higher density and multifamily housing will continue. The reasons are almost exclusively economic; the price of a new, single-family house is now so high that coming generations of young, lower middle- and working-class Americans may have to settle for housing which has never been a part of the American dream—a suburban apartment.[78]

Since large numbers of suburban Americans seem already destined to live in high-density residential environments, it is doubly important to have a fuller understanding of the social effects of this environmental form. Much of the recent information sounds ominous; the increase of some social pathologies in the suburbs, such as crime and delinquency, seems to occur at about the same rate as the increase in suburban high-density housing. Many suburbs have become very resistant to this type of housing; the typical suburban resident is thought to abhor it.

It would be a mistake, however, to draw many conclusions about higher-density suburbs in general from the recent U.S. experience with garden apartment developments, even if some negative social consequences could be proven. Many garden apartments in recent years have been designed and built with less care than even the worst of postwar tract housing; construction has been poor, essential services like public transportation are inadequate or nonexistent, and broader environmental planning is lacking. Moreover, the garden apartments have attracted residents who are very different from the residents of the single-house suburb in age, stage of the family life-cycle, and degree of transiency. The experience of America's suburban garden-apartment developments is a poor basis on which to base any major and long-range change in urban growth policy.

Higher-density residential environments that are more realistic alternatives to the low-density suburb do exist in the U.S., but they are few in number, very recent in development, and often small in scale. America's handful of suburban "new towns" and "planned unit developments" can provide many useful lessons as pilot experiments. These lessons have not been totally overlooked or unheeded.[79] Because they are new and experimental their residents have tended to be, compared to the typical suburban family, of higher income, better educated, more liberal politically, and more cosmopolitan in life style.[80] This demographic dissimilarity, together with the newness of the developments, limits the usefulness of these planned environments as targets of scientific investigation for policy purposes.

Because there does not exist in the United States a higher-density suburban alternative which is entirely suitable for comparison on both scientific and policy grounds, I was prompted to look abroad, toward those nations which have had a long and apparently successful experience with higher-density forms of living. Some of these foreign experiences, I felt, could be more indicative of what might lie ahead for America, or what should lie ahead, than the experiences found closer to home. The importance of limiting the comparative differences as much as possible to environmental as distinct from social factors led naturally in the direction of what is sometimes called a "most similar systems" comparison, an approach commonly used in comparative research. As Niel Smelser has stated: "The more similar two or more societies are with respect to crucial variables, the better able the social scientist is to isolate and analyze the influence of other variables that may account for the differences he wishes to explain comparatively."[81]

The search turned to Europe, therefore, and then to Sweden. Sweden is commonly regarded by Europeans as the European country most like the United States. They single out its high standard of living (in the summer of 1973 Sweden surpassed the U.S. in per capita income to become the world's richest nation), its high percentage (94 percent) of *private* ownership of the means of production, and its emphasis on efficiency and rationality. Of particular importance to this study is the fact that Sweden, like the U.S., has had abundant land for urban growth, and it has Europe's highest per capita rate of automobile ownership—factors important in urban development. Moreover, there has been a strong U.S. influence on Sweden in recent years, in such areas as business practices, education, and the arts, building on a common tradition of political democracy and egalitarianism. (There are other similarities and, of course, some notable differences; these will be explored in the next chapter). The selection of Sweden was assured by the fact that, in addition to its status as a "most similar system," after the war it had built planned, high-density suburbs which have become world famous—the destination of pilgrimages by architects, planners, and social scientists from many nations.

Sweden's best-known postwar suburbs are located in the capital city of Stockholm, whose metropolitan area is comparable in population size (1.3 million) to the medium to large metropolitan areas of the U.S. Vällingby was selected because it was the first postwar suburb of Stockholm to be developed, and it is considered to be one of the most successful. Further, the Stockholm Planning Commission had undertaken intensive studies of the use of residential facilities and services in Vällingby, thus providing an important source of data. The Vällingby environment is typical of the early postwar suburbs built in Sweden, though the later suburbs have been built at higher densities. (A comparison between Vällingby and the later suburbs of Stockholm—considered by some Swedes to be less desirable—is made in the final chapter of this book.)

The U.S. suburb was chosen on the basis of criteria specifying a typical American suburb built at the same time as Vällingby (early 1950s), housing people of the same income and occupational levels and life-cycle stage (skilled blue-collar and lower white-collar families), with approximately the same number of dwelling units (about 18,000), and built, like Vällingby, at one time as a single environmental unit (a "packaged" suburb). Levittown, Pennsylvania, fit these specifications almost to perfection. Further, its name has justifiably become closely associated with suburban living in the United States.

Of the three early and well-known Levittowns, the Pennsylvania branch is the only one which has not been the subject of a major investigation by sociologists. The first Levittown, built on Long Island in the late 1940s (some four to six years prior to Levittown, Pennsylvania) was the focus of much of the early suburban research and popular debate. The third Levittown, in New Jersey, was completed in the late 1950s and early 1960s and houses a population which is somewhat higher in class level than its earlier Pennsylvania counterpart. It was the subject of Herbert Gans's well-known book, *The Levittowners*. These prior sociological studies were a great advantage, something on which I could build and compare.

Both of the other Levittowns were studied in their infancy—the first several years of their existence. Does the behavior and social organization of the Levittowners change over twenty years? How have these communities stood the test of time? Have they become suburban slums, as many predicted? Do the residents still like them? I felt that picking a Levittown might provide the added bonus of finding answers to these interesting questions. While it was not the same Levittown after twenty years, the Pennsylvania Levittown was quite similar to the others.

Data Collection

The research approach used in this inquiry is the field study, the observation of subjects under their usual environmental conditions of life. Each community was investigated for many months over a three-year period, with the goal of assembling a detailed description of the environment, the residents, and the interrelationships between the residents and their environment. How is the environment used; what parts are used more than others; what are the residents' attitudes about the environment; in what ways does the environment support or impede different patterns of behavior and life styles; is there any evidence linking the environment to such personal or social pathologies as boredom, delinquency, alcoholism; how has the environment changed over time; how has the residents' use of the environment changed over time? These were the kinds of questions to which I sought answers.

The data come from four main sources:

Respondent Interviews

In each community the residents of twenty-five selected households were intensively interviewed by me, a total of 119 respondents. The interviews were semi-structured; I used but did not limit myself to a fixed set of questions. With a few exceptions, the same questions were asked of the interviewees in both countries. In most cases I succeeded in interviewing each householder over the age of about ten or eleven. Typically, the interviews were conducted in a "family setting," with each person helping to corroborate or question the others' factual answers. In addition, I requested and usually succeeded in interviewing the teenagers apart from their parents, suspecting that this might enable them to be more open about their attitudes and opinions. The average length of each interview was about an hour and a half.[82]

Informant Interviews

The purpose of informant interviewing is to get factual information from persons especially knowledgeable about a situation, when the researcher has no direct access to the information. Unlike in the respondent interview, the interest is not in the interviewee but in the situation about which knowledge is sought. The informants, in this case community leaders and professionals, have characteristically been participants in important events or activities in the situation being analyzed. In each community I interviewed about twenty such informants, using a snowball sample (one informant suggests another); each interview lasted a minimum of about one hour. Almost every major institutional area of community life was looked into—education, religion, mental health and welfare, recreation and leisure, government, planning and housing, and police (the field of medical care was not investigated due to lack of time and money). Factual information from the informants was continuously cross-checked with other sources of data and between the informants themselves. The information from direct participants in the Vällingby community was supplemented by interviews with fifteen other persons knowledgeable about Swedish housing, urban development, and Swedish suburban life in general. In the United States, I felt that my own knowledge was sufficient to provide this intellectual backstopping.

Available Data

In each country there existed data (sometimes called secondary data) about the two suburbs which had already been collected for other purposes. The major sources of available data were the national censuses of population and housing, governmental studies of planning, housing, and welfare, and institutional reports and records, such as those from police or recreational agencies. In Levittown, in addition, I was able to draw on respondent interview and observational data which had been gathered by a dozen Levittown teachers in an anthropology field project conducted under the auspices of Princeton University in the late 1960s.

Sociological studies of other suburbs in Sweden and the U.S. were very helpful in determining the typicality of Vällingby and Levittown in their respective metropolitan areas and parent societies and in providing leads for investigation. These studies are cited at appropriate places throughout the book.

Direct Observation

Many weeks were spent in both suburbs observing the life of the community. Each major type of facility used by the residents was visited—shopping centers, parks and play areas, bars and indoor recreational facilities, libraries and schools, churches and day-care centers. Each neighborhood type was traversed on foot, with observations being made of children's play and teenage activities. The daily rhythms of the community were determined by returning at regular intervals to the same location during a twenty-four-hour period, and seasonal variations were noted through visits made during each of the four main seasons of the year. To record these observations, a detailed field diary was maintained.

The field study is an exploratory approach in the social sciences; its purpose is not to test existing hypotheses and theories but to develop new hypotheses and bring fresh insights into theoretical issues. The end product of a good field study is an analytical description of one situation or event—a description which is systematic, which identifies significant variables and relationships between the variables, and which is organized in terms of concepts and generalizations permitting a comparison with other cases. The data sources used in this inquiry were felt to be adequate for making a realistic analytical description of man-environment relationships in both of the communities investigated, including the identification of key variables and relationships. In addition, through a comparison between the field-study findings (analytical descriptions) of two cases picked so as to highlight man-environment relationships, this inquiry was able to go beyond the limitations of a single field study. The comparison led to a further refinement of variables, hypotheses, and generalizations, and, one hopes, it also led to a greater contribution to social theory.

Practical Arrangements

The fundamental problem in cross-national research is comparability. Are the events and situations for which explanations are sought comparable from one sociocultural context to the next? Do they have the same meaning for the participants, the same functions for the society? The solutions to this problem are based on a thorough understanding of each sociocultural context that is being compared. Because the Swedish culture was foreign to me, my research schedule was arranged so as to provide the opportunity to gain such an understanding.

I was fortunate to be able to spend the 1972–73 academic year in Sweden with my family, on sabbatical from Rutgers University, as a Senior Fulbright Research Scholar at the University of Stockholm. The year was spent laying the foundations for, and initiating, this inquiry. A large part of the year was devoted to studying Swedish language, culture, history, and contemporary social structure; getting the lay of the land by traveling throughout the populated parts of the country; making contact with Swedish social scientists, architects, and planners; and familiarizing myself with Stockholm and its suburbs. My family's participation in Swedish life, including my children's year in the Swedish school system and our residential experiences in a Stockholm garden apartment, brought many additional insights and contacts. Also illuminating were my contacts with graduate students in sociology and urban planning at the University of Stockholm, where I gave a graduate seminar on the sociology of residential environments, and with students I met while giving lectures at several other universities and colleges in the nation. During the year, I familiarized myself with most of the important Swedish social science literature on residential environments.

To gain perspective on the Swedish experience, I visited each of the other Scandinavian countries except Iceland—Norway, Denmark, and Finland—looking especially at their housing and planning efforts. I also was able to make excursions to the U.S.S.R., Germany, and Great Britain (where I visited ten English and Scottish new towns), and to Greece, Israel, and Spain as a visiting Fulbright lecturer. On an earlier trip abroad, I had visited planned suburbs and new towns in France and additional new towns in England.

Early in 1973, after looking into most of the major Stockholm suburbs, I began the field work in Vällingby. In the late spring of 1974 I returned to Sweden, conducted interviews with the Vällingby household sample, and completed the informant interviewing, secondary data collection, and field observations. My initial investigation of Levittown took place during the fall, winter, and spring months of 1973–74. The household interviews were not conducted until the early fall of 1974–75, after I had returned from my second trip to Sweden; during this time the collection of data from the other main sources also was completed. Finally, in the summer of 1975, I made a third trip to Sweden to gather information on the recently completed Stockholm suburbs and on changes in Swedish housing policies, material which forms the basis of Chapter 9.

Conceptual Orientation

An earlier generation of sociological ecologists, together with most present-day social geographers and regional scientists (regional science is a hybrid discipline made up of economists and geographers), was concerned mainly with accounting for the way in which the built environment, together with the spatial distribution of population, are *shaped* by the natural environment and by social and cultural factors (typically giving a heavy emphasis to economic considerations). The thrust of contemporary environmental sociology is to account for the ways in which the natural and built environments *shape social behavior*—almost the reverse of the prior concern.

Basic to the understanding of any sociological work is a comprehension of the author's conceptual frame of reference, which differs widely among sociologists and among fields of sociology. The conceptual scheme of this inquiry emphasizes the environment as a social force and is organized in the following way. At the center of the scheme is *the individual,* usually the individual in a *family setting*—because that is the microsetting in which most persons are found.[83] Many planners and other social scientists take as their main point of grounding a social system such as a city, political system, or the market. Taking the individual as the main point of reference, however, is basic to an approach which attempts to deal with the social quality of various modes of living. Taking the individual *in family* is essential if children and teenagers are not to be overlooked. In the environmental sociology field, as noted above, children and teenagers are studied far less than adults, yet the residential environment probably affects their behavior to a much greater extent than it affects adults.[84] The relationship of the environment to children and teenagers is a particular concern and focus of this inquiry.

Outside the individual and family lies the residential setting, or *residential environment.* The basic unit of this environment is the residence unit or *household,* and the environment is spatially organized in terms of the daily patterns of interaction of the persons who make up these households. Residential environments thus range from a small group of neighbors to a vast metropolis, or perhaps an area even larger for a few wide-ranging professionals and business men.[85]

The residential environment, in turn, consists of four major components.

The *natural environment* (climate, geomorphology, soils and vegetation, and natural resources—the subject matter of the natural sciences and physical geography); the *population* (the primary subject matter of demography); *the built environment* (physical, man-made, created—the achievement of builders, planners, and architects); and the *social environment* (social and cultural structure, often called the local community or local social system—the subject matter of community studies in the fields of sociology and anthropology). These are four "fields" within which, and with reference to which, behavior in a residential environment takes place.

To add further complexity, a local residential environment exists in its own larger environments of regions, states, nations, and the international or world system. The larger environments can also be divided analytically into the same four components as the residential setting (natural, built, population, social). The behavior of individuals in a residential environment may be explained partly with reference to that setting and partly with reference to the regional, national, and world settings. This is especially true in regard to the social environment where, for example, behavior may be influenced as much, if not more, by national as by local cultures, politics, and events.

The built environment is usually the weakest of these components in its influence on social behavior. This magnifies the need for researchers in this field to develop a broad knowledge of the ways in which behavior in the residential environment is shaped by social forces in both the society and the local community, as well as by strictly environmental factors. An example will help to clarify this point. How is one to account for the neighboring behavior among a group of coresidents in a housing development? There are three general directions in which to turn: First, to the societal sociocultural system, to look at such things as "national character," social-class variations in neighboring patterns, or religious factors. Next, to the local social system, to determine any unique ways in which these national sociocultural patterns may be expressed in the particular local setting. Third, to the built environment, to examine the effects of such factors as different housing types, residential patterns, and distance from services. Knowledge of the first two sets of relationships is essential for a full understanding of the third; all three are intricately interrelated in the neighboring phenomenon.

It was noted that the conceptual scheme centers on the individual. It is important to mention a limitation of sociology in this respect. Scientific disciplines hypothetically divide the individual into three components: his physiological being or organism (the focus of the medical doctor and physiologist); his mental being or personality, including such elements as needs, drives, motives, attitudes, and satisfactions (the subject matter of the psychologist); and his social behavior or social relationships in such areas as organizational ties, work performance, social control and socialization, family functioning, and neighboring and friendship relationships (the subject matter of the sociologist). Although there are no hard and fast boundaries between the disciplines (and there are many important interdisciplinary fields like social psychology), the knowledge gained through each discipline is inherently limited by virtue of this specialization.[86]

The distinctions between sociology and psychology are especially important to keep in mind when using sociological materials for qualitative and policy judgments. Many value judgments in the field of human affairs rest ultimately on knowledge about such phenomena as mental health, self-actualization, and personal happiness. While direct investigation of these phenomena is for the most part outside the range of the sociologist, in the field of environmental sociology social relationships may usefully be considered as intervening variables between the built environment and psychological states of well-being. For instance, there is some evidence that cul de sac streets promote neighboring and friendships among those who live around them. This evidence stems from a number of sociological investigations.[87] Are cul de sac streets therefore "good"? Should we build more of them? These judgments rest on many different factors, but the most salient social scientific information which is needed is in answer to such questions as: Do people "need" more friendships? Does neighboring promote human happiness, psychological well-being, and mental health? The development of knowledge in these areas depends rather more on the psychologist and psychiatrist than on the sociologist.

The concern of this inquiry, then, and of much of environmental sociology, is limited to the relationship between the environment and social behavior (taking into consideration at the same time the relationships between social behavior and local and national-level social systems, as noted above). The bulk of social science knowledge has indicated that, to a large extent, an individual's social behavior can be explained by such "background" factors as income, occupation, education, family structure, age, religion, sex, ethnic group. The question raised by environmental sociology is, To what extent can an individual's behavior be explained by his geographic location—by who and what is around him, affecting his daily life by virtue of the fact that these persons and things and not others are in his presence? Most people have as their "home base," the place around which their daily life revolves, a residence, and this gives rise to the concern for the ways in which differences in *residential environments* affect social behavior and social structure. If a person of a given age, sex, class, religion, and ethnic group moves from one residential environment to another, what major changes will occur in his life?

The interests of environmental sociologists are closely allied with those of environmental planners, architects, and urban designers. The environmental components which these professionals are most able to shape, for example in the design and building of new communities, are the ones emphasized in this inquiry: the *built environment* (together with some aspects of the natural environment); the *demographic structure* (which can be indirectly shaped through housing types and prices, and the provision of special services), and the *structure of residential services* (such as recreation, employment, education, and shopping). Because of this emphasis, the inquiry may be regarded as an effort to advance our understanding of urban design and physical planning.

The Organization of This Book

The chapters in this book, and the subdivisions within the chapters, follow closely the conceptual scheme outlined in the last section. In chapters 3 and 5 each of the two suburbs is analytically described as a residential environment. The presentation is divided into (1) the built and natural environments, (2) the demographic structure, and (3) community system characteristics, with emphasis on the structure of residential services. These descriptions are followed by discussion, in chapters 4 and 6, of the life-styles, attitudes, and environmental usage of the residents of the respective environments, using the concept of environmental fit or congruence—the extent to which values, needs, and behavior patterns mesh with environmental characteristics.

In chapter 7 the structural similarities and differences between the American and Swedish suburbs are summarized, drawing on data presented in the earlier chapters. Chapter 8 pulls together the behavioral similarities and differences between the residents in each community, emphasizing the ways in which living patterns may be shaped by features of the environment. In a final chapter, some implications of my findings for housing and urban development policies in the United States and Sweden are considered.

Since the aim of this study is to develop a better understanding of the relationship between social behavior and elements of the residential environment, it is mainly directed to the environmental social scientist and to the planner, architect, builder, and others who desire a stronger base of knowledge for the design of the urban environment. Although the orientation of the book is academic, social situations and issues have been investigated which commonly figure in public discussion. My intention was to make the inquiry as relevant as possible to the ongoing public debate about housing and urban development policies. Some social scientists may criticize me for "pushing" the data too far in reaching judgments and conclusions that have practical importance. I am more willing to face this charge than the charge from the other side—that sociologists are irrelevant and have nothing to contribute to the arena of social policy. For while knowledge in environmental sociology may be quite small in amount, there is certainly more known at the present time than is put to use in the design of cities. This is a gap which must be closed if the social sciences are to continue to have public appreciation and support and if urban environments are to become more responsive to human needs and aspirations.

Sweden   Urban
Development
and Planning

It is difficult to understand and appreciate a suburb
like Vällingby without some knowledge of *its*
environment—the city of Stockholm—and the processes through which urban growth and development in Sweden take place. Further, it is important
to have a general understanding of Swedish
society, especially its patterns of urban living.
These are the concerns of the present chapter.
After a preliminary discussion of Sweden as a
society, the history and present structure of Stockholm are surveyed. The chapter concludes with
an analysis of the decisions which led to the
development of Vällingby.

Sweden and the United States: Some Basic Similarities and Differences

Scandinavia is off the main European tourist track
for Americans, but those tourists who do get there
often cite Sweden as one of the least interesting
countries in Europe. The comment is frequently
heard among Americans that Sweden is the European country, except for England, that looks and
feels most like the U.S., and that a visit to
Sweden, therefore, is too much like staying home.
It is said that traveling through Sweden is like
a trip across Indiana or Minnesota. The main
factors which account for this apparent similarity
between the two nations are the following.
    1. The high Swedish standard of living, which
on a per capita basis is now higher than that of

the U.S.[1] This means that the quality of clothing and other consumer goods is comparable to the quality of those goods in the U.S., that the life-style is similar insofar as it is caused by high material living standards, and that prices are high.

2. The Swedish rate of automobile ownership, which in Europe is the rate most comparable to that in the U.S.: 1 passenger car to 3.1 persons in 1971, compared with 1:2.3 for the U.S. and 1:5 or 6 for Great Britain. The automobile has, of course, widespread impact on society, especially those aspects with which a casual observer comes in contact.

3. The Swedish countryside, which is more similar to the American than the continental European pattern, in that rural residences are separated from one another on individual farmsteads instead of clustered together in small villages, the common pattern in Germany and France.

4. The appearance of Swedish towns and cities, which were built for the most part in this century, and often lack the very old historical tradition and architecture of many other places in Europe.

5. The Swedish people, who are "middle class" in temperament, outlook, dress, and manner, and thus lack the "charm" and "spontaneity" of the southern European peoples—the traits that many Americans go to Europe to seek.[2]

As national social systems, Sweden and the United States are both advanced, urban-industrial societies with high standards of living, mostly middle-class populations, democratic forms of government, and largely capitalist economic systems.[3] Contrary to popular notions in the U.S., the Swedish economy is more that 90 percent under *private ownership,* a percentage similar to that in the U.S. and much higher than in such countries as France and Italy, which are commonly regarded as "non-socialist."[4] Further, most of the public ownership in Swedish industry predates the political dominance of the Social Democratic party, having been instituted early in this century.[5] It is not accurate to describe Sweden as a socialist state in the economic sense therefore. The economy *is* subject to a higher degree of *public control* than in the U.S.

Sweden comes closer to being a "socialist" state in the social sense, with one of the most comprehensive public welfare systems in the world. Politically, the society was governed uninterruptedly by the Social Democratic party from 1932 to 1976, with the exception of a three-month agrarian government in the mid-thirties.[6] Fundamental differences between the American and Swedish systems, then, are Sweden's more left-wing political coloration, though during much of their long reign the Social Democrats commanded the allegiance of *less* than a majority of the population, and Sweden's comprehensive welfare provisions.[7]

Even more basic are the differences in population size and composition. Sweden's eight million population is smaller than many states in the U.S. (total U.S. population is over two hundred million). And Sweden is one of the very few modern industrial nations with a homogeneous population. Only about 8 percent of the total population is made up of foreign-born citizens and foreign nationals, most of whom have arrived in the past few decades from neighboring Scandanavian countries, especially Finland.[8] Whereas the United States is characterized by high ethnic, religious, racial and regional diversity, Sweden has almost no ethnic or racial or religious diversity (95 percent of the population is allied to the state Lutheran church) and very little regional diversity. Population size and composition surely have a marked effect on other aspects of the social system. They help to account, for example, for the great social solidarity and political stability which have long existed in Sweden.

Swedish Social Development and the Rise of Urban-Industrialism

Sweden and the United States are quite dissimilar in historical development, however similar in social structure they may be at the present time. The two nations were born under different circumstances and have shown divergent patterns of modernization.

Modern, democratic, urban-industrial societies are sometimes divided into two categories: those which were born free, so to speak—they have had from the very beginnings of nationhood relatively free, democratic institutions—and those whose freedom emerged from a feudal past. The United States as "the first new nation,"[9] is the best example of the first category; most of the countries of Europe belong to the second category. Sweden, as noted by sociologist Richard Tomasson, lies midway between these two poles. European feudalism was never characteristic of Sweden's past; Swedish peasants were never serfs, and they had an important role in the government as early as the 1400s.[10] Further, the peasants generally gave solid support to the royalty; the violent and sweeping revolutions which dominated European society in the eighteenth and nineteenth centuries were virtually absent in Sweden and the other Scandanavian countries. Indeed, the road to the present Swedish political structure has been even less rocky than that of the United States.[11]

The emergence of Sweden as a nation-state usually is dated from the sixteenth century, when Gustav Vasa unified the Swedish population, ended the political domination of Denmark, and severed the tie to the Roman Catholic church. The next hundred years saw Sweden as one of the great powers of Europe, with Sweden controlling the Baltic states and areas of present-day Germany. After a series of military defeats, Sweden settled down during the eighteenth and nineteenth centuries into a relatively peaceful period which some historians describe as dull.[12] It probably was, compared to the times of military and political conflict in the United States, Europe, and England during this period.

Sweden was the first nation not engaged in the Revolutionary War formally to recognize the new United States after the revolution, in 1783. At the time, Sweden was ruled by Gustav III, who is credited with having culturally enriched Sweden through establishing strong ties with the continental European worlds of art and literature. Sweden has tended throughout its history to be cut off from the major cultural events of the continent. Developments in European art, for example, would get to Sweden some hundred years after their impact elsewhere. This geographic and social fact means that Sweden was removed also from many of the turmoils in Europe such as the Napoleonic wars, although a Napoleonic general was selected as Swedish monarch in the early nineteenth century (his descendants are still on the throne).

Until the late nineteenth and even early twentieth century, Sweden was one of the poorest countries in Europe. The great poverty, together with related agricultural problems, caused some one-quarter of the Swedish population (about one million persons) to emigrate from Sweden during the period from 1850 to 1930. Most went to the United States, where they seem to have adjusted to the American pattern with particular facility and rapidity.[13] The effects of this large-scale emigration on the rest of Swedish society are not clear, but it is reasonable to believe that the population decline eased the path of eventual urbanization and industrialization through removing surplus labor—labor which no longer was needed in agriculture but for which there were not yet sufficient industrial jobs. Further, it diminished the uneconomic partitioning of agricultural land and solidified the landholdings of those who remained. Sweden's economic development also benefited because, like the United States but unlike most European countries, Sweden has not been involved in foreign wars on its own soil for over 150 years.

Among the highly modernized European countries, the Scandanavian nations are unique in how late industrialization came and in how rapidly it developed once it began. In the 1880s more than three-quarters of all Swedes were still living on farms (compared to about one-half of the U.S. population), and the economy and the cities were quite primitive and backward. Yet by 1930, only a little more than a generation later, Sweden had achieved urban and industrial maturity. During this same period, Sweden also developed the system of parliamentary democracy and social welfare which much of the world looks to as a model.

Urbanization since the turn of the century has been swift, but it has also been quite placid in its consequences. The pressures of overurbanization have not been felt in Sweden in anything like the degree to which they are felt today in most Third World nations, or even in the Chicagos, New Yorks, and Pittsburghs of nineteenth- and early twentieth-century America. Rather than in a mass exodus to large cities, the Swedish people have tended to migrate in step-wise fashion from rural areas to small semiagricultural towns, then to larger regional centers, and later to large metropolitan regions. This population movement has been instrumental in generating Sweden's present pattern of dispersed small and medium-sized urban localities. It has also helped to ease the problems involved in the transition from rural to urban living.[14]

The rural-urban migration patterns of Sweden may be accounted for in large part by the fact that a high percentage of Swedish industry is decentralized. The Swedish government has long had policies which promote industrial development in the smaller towns and more remote regions. For example, the first railroads were laid out in a way calculated to open up the undeveloped areas and to provide greater accessibility to the already populated places. Some of the characteristic Swedish industries, such as glass manufacturing or those based on wood production, are quite profitably located in smaller towns. Moreover, industrialization came so late to Sweden that much of Swedish industry was geared initially to electric power, the most mobile energy source. Even today, large subsidies are given by the Swedish government to encourage business and industry to locate in small towns or cities.[15]

Swedish Urban Structure

Though Sweden is one of the largest countries of Europe in land area, 90 percent of its population lives in the southern half of the country. Population densities range from 229 persons per square kilometer in Stockholm County to 3 persons per square kilometer in Norrbotten County in the far north.[16] Sweden's large amount of available land contrasts sharply with most European countries; the overall density of 19 persons per square kilometer is about the same as in the U.S. (22 per square kilometer), and very different from the situation in West Germany (240), the United Kingdom (228), and even France (93). There is no land pressure in Sweden of the kind which, for example, marks the culture of the Netherlands.

In 1970, 81 percent of Sweden's 8.1 million people lived in what are classified as urban areas. Sweden's figure of 200 persons as constituting an urban area, however, is somewhat at variance with the common international standard of 2,000 to 2,500 (and both are at variance with the popular image of what "urban" signifies!). Half of all "urban" settlements in Sweden had between 200 and 499 inhabitants, and all but 100 had under 10,000 persons—statistics characteristic of a sparsely settled nation. Yet the low figure of 200 persons constituting an urban settlement does not mislead as much as one might suspect. Eighty-six percent of the urban population lives in towns of more than 2,000 persons, and Sweden is slightly more urbanized than the U.S. (70 percent of the total Swedish population live in places with 2,000 or more residents, compared to the U.S.'s 66 percent).[17]

Nevertheless, most of Sweden's urban population is best thought of as a medium-sized town or small-city population. There are only six metropolitan areas in Sweden, and three of these, Västerås, Uppsala, and Norrköping, barely met in 1970 the standard of "an area of 100,000 or more inhabitants."[18] Somewhere between 25 and 40 percent of Sweden's population, depending upon which boundaries are used, live in the other major metropolitan regions, Stockholm, Göteborg, and Malmö,[19] but both Göteborg and Malmö are under 500,000 in population and the population of the Stockholm region is less than one and a half million.

By American and even international standards, Sweden's cities and metropolitan regions are quite small. Moreover, they are spaced well apart from one another—there are no megalopolitan complexes. When one flies into Stockholm, over the forests and lakes, there is no hint of an approaching city. Suddenly the forests and farms vanish and the city begins, abruptly and emphatically, with a clearly demarcated boundary. Further, the cities themselves are very low-density, containing many fingers of park and open space which in some cases extend all the way to the surrounding countryside. A circle with a radius of twenty-five kilometers that had Stockholm at its center would contain about one million inhabitants. The same circle in Paris would contain five million inhabitants; in London, seven to eight million.[20]

The Growth and Development of Stockholm

The city of Stockholm was founded in the thirteenth century on the spot where the large and important Lake Mälaren empties into an arm of the Baltic Sea. It quickly became prominent among Sweden's towns because of trade advantages, and was established definitely as the national capital in the mid-seventeenth century, when the modern Swedish nation emerged. By the mid-eighteenth century it had a population of about 60,000, reaching 100,000 population only about one hundred years ago. For many centuries, the city consisted of a jumble of buildings on an island which separates the discharge of Lake Mälaren into two channels, an area now called Gamla Stan (old city). This area has an irregular, medieval layout with most streets ranging in width from two to five yards; its medieval character has been very well maintained.[21]

The development of modern Stockholm began about 1850 or 1860, when the island called Norrmalm took over as Stockholm's central business district. Housing was built mostly in large blocks of four- to six-story apartment buildings. Rich and poor were often combined in the same block, with the rich commanding the more desirable locations—those with more light and air, views, and quiet—while the low-income flats typically fronted on the dark, interior courtyards.[22] This pattern helped to prevent the marked segregation of working-class districts, and to this day the residential differentiation of income groups in Stockholm remains remarkably low compared to that of other major cities in the world.[23]

Working-class housing also developed on the city's outskirts, in areas of lower land-value where transportation costs were high—the traditional pattern of preindustrial cities. The well-to-do remained firmly in the central city until the late 1870s, when the building of suburban commuter railroads opened up the first Stockholm suburb of Sundbyberg. This did not survive as a place of suburban affluence, however, as proximity to the city caused it quickly to be overtaken by the city's normal industrial and residential expansion.

More successful in maintaining their protected suburban status were the wealthy communities of Djursholm and Saltsjöbaden, developed in the 1890s around two new commuter rail lines of that time. These developments with large Victorian mansions on substantial lots, situated in beautiful, wooded terrain, have many counterparts in the U.S. They were not especially influential as models for the further development of Stockholm, however, and stand today as unique testaments to a particular era.

The city of Stockholm has grown very rapidly in the twentieth century and has assumed a dominating role in Swedish society, though not nearly as socially and economically dominating as Paris or London in their respective societies. At the turn of the twentieth century, when the rapid growth of Stockholm began, the city, along with the other industrializing communities of Sweden, was still extremely poor. At that time 80 to 90 percent of Sweden's urban housing stock consisted of apartments of no more than one room and a kitchen; more than one-third of the urban dwelling units were overcrowded.[24] The worst features of European slum life did not develop in Stockholm, although the housing situation there was worse than in most other Swedish cities. The relatively slum-free environment was due in part to the strict control over land use and to other planning measures which have long characterized Stockholm's civic life. A municipal planning agency was organized in 1637, and has functioned more or less continuously for almost 340 years.

Like other expanding cities of the early twentieth century, Stockholm developed outward into its rural hinterland with housing densities which diminished with distance from the center of the city. But unlike many cities, especially those in the United States, the suburban development was middle and even working class, rather than exclusively upper and middle class. This was due partly to government policies and partly to the fact that the wealthier classes did not feel as strong a need to abandon the older parts of the city. Inner-city Stockholm maintained many comparative advantages over the outer-city areas as a desirable residential environment.

The period from 1905 to the 1930s is sometimes called the "garden suburbs" period in the development of Stockholm.[25] Heavily influenced by the garden-city movement in Britain, the early suburbs of the twentieth century were given over to small, owner-occupied homes, many of which were self-built. In 1904, the Swedish government set up a special loan fund to assist middle-class families in building their own suburban homes. As in other welfare measures of the time, a basic aim of the program was to discourage emigration through providing simultaneously work and residential accommodations. Over the years the price of this owner-built housing diminished, partly as a result of cost savings through prefabrication; some working-class families were thus able to join the middle class in having homes of their own in the new suburbs.

But the small-homes movement did not survive for long. As the vacant land near the jobs of inner Stockholm became scarce, and as the priority for workers' housing became paramount, the garden-suburb movement took a sharp turn toward the construction of workers' flats in large complexes of low-rise apartment buildings. These buildings of the 20s, 30s and 40s were usually three- or four-story walk-ups, and their physical design and layout were heavily influenced by the functionalism of the time, especially by a concern for sunlight and air.[26] In the 1930s, a uniquely Swedish type of high-rise apartment building was introduced—the point block (punkthus), about ten stories in height and rather slim and graceful in appearance against the often rock-strewn and undulating Stockholm landscape. For the perspective of today, the early garden suburbs appear as curious anomalies—their owner-built homes make up a very small percentage of Stockholm's housing stock, and they are surrounded by the looming apartment buildings of later vintage.

The suburban workers' apartment environments from the 1930s onward were a significant improvement over inner-city areas in their relatively low density, high standard of open space, and improved interior design and quality of household equipment. Yet they had few of the conveniences and services of the city and were not always well served by transportation. Unlike the housing developments after World War II, they were designed as dormitory areas rather than as partially self-contained, semi-independent settlements.[27]

These limitations of design helped to provoke in the 1940s a growing concern for the "human factor" in building and planning, a concern which took the needs of the residents into greater account. The "neighborhood unit" planning theory, which holds that neighborhoods should be relatively self-contained living units, was introduced into Sweden during this decade. Among the design innovations of the 1940s were the use of the Radburn Plan, facing residential buildings inward on a traffic-free common area, and the building of small community centers which were expected to enable people to "get back together" with one another.[28] World War II greatly diminished the production of Swedish housing, however, and the great shortages which developed triggered a postwar housing boom. The three decades following the war turned out to be what was probably the most extensive period of building in Stockholm's history.

Postwar Development of Stockholm: The New Suburbs

Prior to World War II, the general pattern of Stockholm's urban growth in the twentieth century was not essentially different from the pattern in American cities of the same period, except for the greater emphasis on apartment housing. The city grew with the aid of relatively limited planning through the accretion of dwellings added on more or less circumferentially around the existing developed area. Streetcars, buses, suburban railways, and the automobile were relied on to get workers into the downtown area, where most of the jobs and shops continued to be situated. (In 1945, there were only nine private cars per 1,000 inhabitants.)[29]

The war, in which Sweden remained neutral, provided a time to take stock of existing patterns and make plans for the future. The need for such plans became increasingly apparent with the prediction that there would be a heavy influx of persons into Stockholm following the war. This would add to an already serious housing shortage, which was generated by underproduction during the war years (one-tenth the level of housing starts reached during the late thirties), together with high rates of new-family formation and rising standards of living.

Based on the rather conservative standard of overcrowding of more than two occupants per room (including the living room but not including the kitchen), 21 percent of all Swedish households with children lived in overcrowded dwellings in 1945.[30] By this standard, however, a family of four in a one-bedroom apartment was considered not to be overcrowded, so the incidence of overcrowding by U.S. standards was actually much higher. Thirty-eight percent of the dwellings at this time were no larger than one room and kitchen, and an additional 31 percent were no larger than two rooms and kitchen.[31] Very often, the kitchen was used as a place for sleeping, and a major goal of Swedish housing policy was to make this practice unnecessary.

Within greater Stockholm in the early 1940s, 32 percent of the apartment units were only one room with kitchen (27 percent were two rooms with kitchen), but 20 percent were one and two rooms with no kitchen at all! For every 100 rooms, *including* kitchen and living room, there were 101 persons (1945). Only 76 percent of the flats had central heat in 1940, and just more than half had a bath or shower.[32] Thus the problem of housing in Stockholm was a very serious one, in spite of the fact that no houses in the city had been destroyed by the war.

In making the determination of the best development pattern for the immense amount of new housing which would have to be built, the Swedish planners faced two broad alternatives: to continue to expand Stockholm by accretion, or to cluster the new development into separate units, leaving open spaces in between. In either case, it was felt that the great bulk of the new housing should be apartments.

A great many considerations led to the final choice of the second alternative, the establishment of suburban clusters at relatively high density. These considerations are fully discussed in the following section and will only be introduced here. The most important factor, probably, was the prior decision to build a subway system in Stockholm. This was to a large extent dictated by Stockholm's unusual topographical circumstances: urban development spread over a series of islands connected by bridges. Suburban traffic to downtown Stockholm is necessarily concentrated on these few bridges, and complete adaptation to automobile modes of access would therefore be extremely costly. The subway system and the suburban "nodes" were mutually reinforcing. The clustering of surburban development around subway stops made the transportation system more efficient, and a subway system was to some extent dictated in the first place by the higher travel times which would be generated by including a great amount of open space in the suburban pattern, thus extending the distance of urban development from the central city.

It also was decided to localize business and industry in the suburban clusters, although true satellite towns were never intended. Thus it is not accurate to refer to the planned Stockholm suburb as a "new town," since that term typically refers to a more balanced, self-contained entity. While the continuation of the inner-city area as the main center of employment and shopping was regarded as highly desirable, it was recognized that not all new business and industrial growth could be contained there. The suburban localization of business and industry, it was thought, would help to rectify a shortcoming of the suburban housing areas of the 1930s, which were lacking in jobs and retail facilities along with other urban services.

The scheme which resulted from these decisions, as outlined in the General Plan for Stockholm published in 1952 (and developed between 1945 and 1952), called for suburban districts of from 10,000 to 15,000 inhabitants strung like beads along the subway line, each with a small commercial and cultural center of its own. Blocks of flats were proposed at distances of up to 550 yards from the subway stop, to permit easy access on foot and limit the use of feeder buses and automobiles; up to 1,000 yards away, but no further, would be single-family houses, amounting to no more than 10 to 15 percent of the total number of dwelling units in each district. The districts would be separated from each other by permanent open space, linked together to form fingers of green extending well into the city, and in some cases connected up with existing city parks. Contained within the open space would be the automobile access roads.

Further, it was intended that several of the suburban districts should be major outlying shopping and community centers serving populations of 50,000 to 100,000. These should contain virtually the full range of urban services, including theaters, restaurants, business offices, medical clinics, and libraries. At the other extreme, there was to be provision for small neighborhood-based shopping clusters scattered through the residential zones. Thus the 1952 master plan called for a hierarchical network of facilities and services arranged in terms of area centers (serving 50,000 to 100,000 persons), district centers (serving 8,000 to 15,000 persons), and neighborhood centers (serving 4,000 to 7,000 persons).

Such a hierarchical network automatically leads to the development of residential areas in the form of distinct neighborhoods—and the neighborhood concept was quite important in the minds of most of the Swedish planners of the time. The neighborhood pattern was strengthened by the decision to provide for nearly complete separation of pedestrian from motor vehicle traffic. One mechanism for doing this that figured prominently in the master plan was the Radburn planning scheme first tried out in the 40s: the "introversion" of housing areas around a central pedestrian-oriented area, with the automobile relegated to the periphery. The buildings themselves thus help to maintain pedestrian-vehicle separation, and at the same time are arranged in neighborhoodlike clusters, with their main entrances facing the common area—unlike the American suburban pattern where dwellings are strung out along an interconnecting street system.[33]

To a remarkable degree, the postwar suburbs of Stockholm were built in a way which realized the design goals of the 1952 master plan. By 1970, twenty-seven suburban units had been completed.[34] Perhaps the single most important fact which accounts for this success is municipal land-ownership. As early as 1904, when the self-help housing schemes were begun, the city of Stockholm began an active policy of buying up large amounts of land on its periphery and even in adjacent municipalities. The land which is now Farsta was purchased in 1912; most of the land which later became Vällingby was purchased in 1927 and 1931. Today, Stockholm owns more than 70 percent of the suburban land inside its own boundaries,[35] together with large tracts of land outside of its municipal jurisdiction on which it is building housing and ancillary facilities.

The public ownership of land removes impediments to planning in Stockholm which loom large in the cities of other nations. In addition, local planning powers are strong in Sweden, and much of the building of the new suburbs was done by municipally owned housing corporations, similar to public utilities.[36] These elements combine to make the public planning function in Stockholm remarkably comprehensive and effective, especially when compared to the weak, sometimes almost nonexistent, planning function in U.S. cities.

It was almost a decade after the end of World War II before much of the planners' grand design was to be seen in brick and concrete. During the years 1947–51, housing production was curtailed due to even higher-priority needs for scarce resources by other industries. The first part of the new subway system was not opened until 1950, and this was just a small link. In 1951, the occupation of the first suburban district took place—Blackeberg, in the Vällingby development area. Finally, in 1954, the first major suburban center was opened—Vällingby.

Stockholm Today

The mass building of apartments in planned suburban communities continued into the 1970s, spurred by a housing shortage in Stockholm. There were very low vacancy rates and lengthy waiting periods for a dwelling until about 1973. By the middle of the decade the population growth of greater Stockholm had started to level off, and for the first time very high vacancy rates began to occur, in some new developments as high as 25 to 30 percent. The rate of construction of apartment units has recently slowed down sharply, and Stockholm's planners are currently rethinking plans for the city during the last quarter of the twentieth century. The postwar development period in Stockholm has come to a close, and a new phase of development is beginning to emerge.

Since about 1940, the population of greater Stockholm has nearly doubled.

Unlike in most American cities, a very high percentage of greater Stockholm's residents live today in multifamily housing (76 percent in 1970), and they mostly rent rather than own.[37] The average size of each dwelling is quite small: 3.3 rooms per dwelling unit in 1965.[38] But household size is also very small, possibly the smallest in the world, with an average of 2.4 persons per household in 1970.[39] Sweden has the world's highest percentage of one- and two-person households: 60 percent of all households in the Stockholm region in 1970.[40]

In spatial distribution, 22 percent of the residents of greater Stockholm live in the inner-city area (the same area which constituted the entire city at the turn of the century), 37 percent live in the outer city (which includes Vällingby), and the remainder, 41 percent, live outside the Stockholm municipal boundaries in adjacent municipalities.[41] As in most cities, the location of work places in Stockholm is much more centralized than are residences: in 1965, 53 percent were in the inner city, 20 percent in the outer city, and 25 percent in the suburban municipalities.[42] The importance of the municipal boundaries was greatly diminished when, in 1971, the city and county of Stockholm merged to form one Greater Stockholm County. Many of the separate administrative agencies, including planning, are currently in the process of being merged in whole or in part.

Much of the planning effort of the sixties was focused on the downtown area. While the resident population of the area continues to drop, the city has made a serious and for the most part successful effort to maintain large sections for residential purposes. In addition, it has undertaken a massive renewal effort aimed at thoroughly modernizing the downtown shopping and business district and has initiated programs designed to remove industries from the center city to outlying districts. While these downtown renewal efforts have been the subject of great controversy—especially in their architectural design and in their attempts to deal with the automobile—it is generally agreed that Stockholm has one of the most livable inner-city environments among the world's major cities.[43] In many U.S. cities, by contrast, the middle and upper classes have abandoned the inner city for the suburbs, leaving behind mainly the poor.

Though the automobile density in Sweden is 3.1 persons per automobile (1971),[44] Stockholm relies very heavily on mass transportation, by comparison with the cities of North America. In greater Stockholm, 60 percent of all journeys to and from work are made by public transportation (70 percent within the city of Stockholm proper). The median commuting time by public transportation is between thirty-five and forty minutes (twenty-five to thirty minutes by automobiles, which are used for shorter trips).[45] One recent survey found that an estimated 20 percent of the population walks to work.[46]

Indeed, 45 percent of Stockholm's households in 1970 had *no* automobile; only 7 percent had two or more cars.[47]

Finally, a word should be said about the quality of the greater Stockholm environment, which is much higher than for most other cities of its size in the world. With some exceptions, the air and the streets are clean, the waters around Stockholm are relatively pure, even fishable and swimmable, the vegetation is luxuriant and well protected. There are many reasons for this fortunate state of affairs. Stockholm has little heavy industry—most of its industry is of the clean, service-type. The city is much more modern than it appears; it was built for the most part in this century, and has thus managed to avoid the massive obsolescence which is a residue of nineteenth-century industrial development in many countries, such as England. Moreover, cleanliness and environmental protection are strongly emphasized in Scandanavian culture. Other factors which help to account for Stockholm's high environmental quality are the centralized governmental control of land use, the relatively high suppression of automobile traffic, and the fact that Stockholm, off in the forests of the far north, is not surrounded by the landscape of urban industrialism.

There may be no other city in the world quite like Stockholm. It stands as a reminder that the excesses of urban industrialism can be checked, that it is not absolutely necessary for the modern urban citizen to live in an environment in which many conditions essential for a decent, humane, and tranquil life have been choked out.

The Decision to Build High-Density Suburbs

Sweden has been a rural and small-town society until quite recently. Much of its adult population either grew up in, or at least remembers, a family tradition which includes the small house with a yard, a garden, and woods nearby. Why is Sweden now a nation of apartment dwellers? Why does Europe's wealthiest nation, with the highest number of automobiles per capita, have also one of the highest percentages of apartment residents? Why did the city of Stockholm after World War II (in common with the other large cities in Sweden) decide to build suburbs around Stockholm which have some of the highest suburban densities in Europe—a course the opposite of that followed by the United States and even by England, and to a certain extent by France and Germany? In this section I shall review what seem to be the major factors which were involved in this key decision about the development of postwar Stockholm, including the views of the decision-makers who were involved. This decision, and the reasons behind it, take on added significance due to the fact that in the last year or two the policies of the Swedish government have changed. It is quite probable, as will be explored in the final chapter, that most future development in Swedish urban areas will be considerably lower in density than the urban growth of the postwar years.

First, it is important to mention factors in the general housing and building situation in Sweden which suggest that Stockholm's suburban development decision was not especially unique or pioneering. Apartment living has long been characteristic of European cities. At the end of the Second World War, only one-twelfth of the population of the city of Stockholm lived in single-family houses,[48] a figure far lower than for almost all U.S. cities. The reasons for this characteristic include, in many European cities (as compared to cities in the U.S.): shortage of land, low reliance on the automobile, greater desire of the population for proximity to urban services, lower personal incomes, centralized building-production systems, and the high density of the extensive pretwentieth-century districts to serve as a model. (In the U.S., apartment living became established in the Eastern big cities but virtually disappeared by the time urban development reached the West Coast.)

Stockholm shares some but not all of these European characteristics; in addition, it has some unique features of its own which militate in favor of high-density development. One is the climate. The long Swedish winters prevent the use of outside yard space for much of the year. In addition, single-family houses must be heavily insulated. They are therefore expensive to construct, costly to heat, and tend to be small. The apartment dwelling thus becomes a comparatively better buy.

Swedish families are smaller in size than U.S. families—a detached house typically has more space than a small family requires. In addition, many Swedish families have a tradition of owning a small summer cottage in the woods or by a lake or sea. In the 1940s, every seventh family in Stockholm had such a cottage,[49] and presently one-fourth of all Swedes either own or have access to one. The cost in time and money of maintaining two single-family homes can be high and sometimes is beyond the capacity of the average urban dweller.

Finally, in spite of the fact that Stockholm is surrounded by a great amount of open land, the terrain is rough and rocky, and automobile access is made difficult because of the great number of waterways which must be traversed. Single-family home building is a rather expensive activity under such conditions.

A number of factors in the Stockholm situation, on the other hand, suggest that a decision to develop low-density suburbs would at least not have been unreasonable. Unlike many European cities, Stockholm had plenty of land that could be used for extensive building. Sweden had, at that time, a high rate of automobile ownership by European standards (one car for twenty-three persons) and it was foreseen that the automobile would become a dominant means of transportation in the years to come. Like U.S. cities, Stockholm had had no housing destruction during the war; all the immediate postwar residential building was done on vacant land at the periphery of the city, not on redeveloped inner-city sites. Further, Sweden, along with the U.S., was one of the most prosperous nations in the world; it probably could have afforded single-family housing had the decision been made to develop in that way.

Stockholm also had the early twentieth-century experience, mentioned above, of low-density garden suburbs. While these areas were not large in number, they were generally thought to be quite successful and were highly desired as places to live. To this day, the prewar single-family housing in such Stockholm districts as Bromma and Enskede ranks very high in the residential desires of the middle class. It has greatly appreciated in value over the years, and also to some extent in class level, though to the eyes of an American observer it often has the appearance of small, look-alike, California working-class bungalow developments. Moreover, the new postwar suburbs of Stockholm were built just beyond, and often in full view of, these low-density developments. Stockholm's planners were faced with the necessity of consciously overriding the general urban development principle that density drops with distance from the central city. The city of Stockholm today follows this principle to the point of the garden suburbs—then the density suddenly leaps up again to resemble that of the inner-city areas.

The final factor which favored a low-density development decision is perhaps the most important and has recently figured quite prominently in the political debate which has called Stockholm's postwar development policy into serious question. There was at the end of the war (and still is) a strong and widespread consumer preference for single-family homes. A housing survey was undertaken before the war's end of a sample of about 1,200 young Stockholm families—the stratum of the population most in need of new dwelling units. This survey generated some quite unambiguous findings.[50] Forty-six percent of those questioned made the single-family detached house their first choice as a desired dwelling type (37 percent picked the garden apartment and 17 percent picked high-rise apartments). Of those presently living in the city, 35 percent chose detached houses; of those living in the outer areas, the figure was 68 percent. While only 58 percent picked the suburbs as the most desirable *place* to live, 88 percent of those wanted a detached house. Of those who expressed unhappiness with their present dwelling in the city (and who were thus the most likely families to actually move to the new suburbs), 90 percent preferred detached houses.

Some of the families questioned already lived in suburban apartments. Only 21 percent of them expressed satisfaction (nöjd) with their situation (partly due to the lack of transportation and other services), compared with 57 percent of those who lived in inner-city apartments and 95 percent of those who lived in suburban houses. In choosing a combination of dwelling type and place to live, only 7 percent picked as their first choice an apartment in the suburbs. Yet that is what the great majority ended up getting!

By adjusting the figures somewhat to compensate for the fact that the survey only questioned young families, who have traditionally desired small houses of their own, Stockholm's planners calculated that only about 20 percent of Stockholmers in need of a dwelling unit preferred a suburban apartment.[51] As Sven Markelius and Göran Sidenbladh (the Stockholm planning directors in the postwar years) later said, "if this consumer desire could be met, only one-fourth of the new suburban homes would take the form of flats."[52]

The housing reality turned out very differently from the consumer desire. In Vällingby and Farsta, the first two postwar suburban developments to be completed, the percentage of total dwelling units that are single-family houses is 8 and 13, respectively.[53] Throughout Sweden, about two-thirds of all postwar housing production consisted of apartment units[54] (compared with 35 percent for Denmark and 24 percent for Norway).[55] In Stockholm, the figure was even higher. In the municipally built Stockholm suburbs that have followed Vällingby and Farsta, the percentage of single-family dwellings has increased very little, and in some cases decreased. The figure for Skärholmen (opened in 1968) is 14 percent, and for Tensta (opened in 1970) it is 3.5 percent.[56] At the same time, overall densities for apartment construction have been considerably increased in those later developments, both in ground coverage and in the height and mass of individual buildings. These municipal developments have been somewhat counterbalanced by the building, partly through the private sector, of single-family houses on Stockholm's outskirts. Nevertheless, between 1940 and 1970, the percentage of single-family dwellings in the greater Stockholm area increased only from 17 to 24.[57]

So the postwar development policies, which ran against the desires of the people, and were almost precisely the opposite of the policies made in North America, have had long-range effects. Why were these policies established? As is true for almost all major policy decisions, they stemmed from a complex of interweaving factors and judgments.

The Transportation System

There is little doubt about the prime factor which shaped the development decision. As stated in the general plan of 1952, "The changes in Greater Stockholm's structure are primarily dependent on the build-up of the communications [transportation] system."[58] A suburban transit system for Stockholm was seriously thought of as early as the beginning of the century.[59] The Stockholm city council decided in 1941, in principle, to build such a public transit system although it was not entirely clear what form it would take.[60] The original intention was some kind of local railroad or streetcar line, but new information came to the transportation planners in the early 1940s that estimated a rather drastic increase in population and economic growth for the Stockholm region. This prompted the decision to make a heavy investment in a fullfledged subway system—two separate systems, in fact, which would link up the western and southern suburbs (a third system, providing service to the northern suburbs, was opened on August 31, 1975).[61] The subway decision was made, apparently without any serious prior investigation of the type of residential and urban development which was most desirable. The decision was questioned by some public officials on financial grounds, but its planning implications were not seriously challenged. On the contrary, the evidence suggests that Stockholm's planners were in general agreement about the need for such a transportation system, partly, as will be made clear below, because it fit in well with their own ideas about the future use of land in Stockholm.[62]

Economic Pressures

A subway system does not inevitably lead to high-density residential development, but it does virtually rule out most single-family housing in the vicinity of the subway line if the system is to be a financial success. Ideally, masses of people will be concentrated within walking distance around the subway stops, where the necessity for feeder bus systems and reliance on the automobile are minimized. In the 1940s, cost-saving considerations were given especially high priority because of wartime shortages and the competition for scarce resources which marked postwar development. Strong financial pressures showed up not only in the design of transport systems but also in the desire to make housing production as economically efficient as possible. Markelius and Sidenbladh stated in the 1940s, in response to the question of why so little single-family housing was built in the face of consumer demand, that "detached or terraced houses require more labor and material than flats, and that is why building production cannot be directed along those lines [of housing preference] in general, at the present time." Yet they also showed some concern for consumer choice when they continued, "It has not yet been decided just what proportion of the production plan could take the form of the much coveted house."[63]

Not only did fiscal necessity dictate the decision to build a high percentage of flats; once the flats were decided upon, economic considerations pushed up the densities at which flats were actually built. Each successive suburban development in Stockholm has been built at a higher density than the one previous—up to the present day. This phenomenon will be discussed in the final chapter; the economic factor is not the only one involved, but it seems the most important. The same economic effect can be seen clearly in the development of Vällingby, whose final density is significantly higher than that envisaged in the early plans.

A 1946 plan for the Vällingby area proposed just three districts, each with 13,000 population, for a total of 39,000 people (instead of the ultimate 55,000).[64] The idea of creating a major shopping center in Vällingby came later than 1946, but early plans called for a shopping area of 3,300 square meters. The center finally built contained about 24,000 square meters of shopping. (This was enlarged still further in a major expansion of the Vällingby Center completed in 1966.) In both of these changes, economic considerations were highly influential, especially pressures from the Stockholm Retail Trade Federation to establish a larger market for retail services.[65]

A similar escalation occurred in the percentage of dwelling units in multifamily buildings. While Stockholm's general plan called in principle for each suburban district to have only 62 percent apartments, Vällingby was constructed with 92 percent.[66] As David Pass concluded from his research into the development of Vällingby, "after the 1946 master plan proposal, the proportion of apartment units rose with each proposal."[67] He presents strong evidence that economic interests had a major hand in this escalation.[68] The situation was summed up in a report to the UN Conference on the Human Environment, prepared by the Swedish government in 1972: "The demand for a large enough population by the service producers has often been allowed to determine the size and design of areas, with the result that these interests indirectly promote a high density."[69]

The Ideology of the Planners

Yet it would be a mistake to assume that the effects of these economic pressures ran counter to the ideas of Stockholm planning experts. These experts, in fact, showed a striking unanimity in favor of the higher-density developments. This is not surprising; architecturally oriented planners the world over have favored higher-density residential development. Such developments give greater scope to the talents of architects than do single-house developments. They involve more organization, design, and building; they sometimes even lend themselves to the "grand design," a testimony to the vision of the architect.

Further, architects themselves are inclined to be rather urbane and cosmopolitan in character, a result of their long training, aesthetic sensitivity, high position, and sometimes high class-background. Thus they often show a preference for city as opposed to country or small-town life, for the built environment, for variety, "culture," and a high level of services. Few nationally or internationally famous and respected architects have become associated with low-density, suburban living patterns.

These ideologies and personal tastes seem to be as predominant among architects in Sweden as elsewhere. They take on a special significance in Sweden, however, because architects have relatively great power in affecting the course of urban development, in marked contrast, for example, to the powerlessness in this regard of architects in the U.S. Indeed, due to the fact that planning is such an important governmental function in Sweden, and because the practice of planning is dominated by architects, the architecture profession is more powerful and influential in Sweden than in almost any other Western nation.

Had there been a consensus among Stockholm's planners after the war in favor of a *low*-density pattern of development, it is reasonable to speculate that the economic and transportation pressures noted above might have been decisively muted, especially in view of the strong desires of Stockholm residents. There was, however, a consensus among the experts in quite the opposite direction. Moreover, due to the centralized nature of the sociopolitical system which exists in Sweden, there was relatively little need for the planners to pay much attention to public opinion except as it was expressed through organized political processes.[70]

The chief architect of Stockholm's postwar suburban development was Sven Markelius. It is significant that he was put into the position of head of Stockholm's planning (in 1944) by Yngve Larsson—the Swedish politician who was instrumental in the establishment of the subway system and who, in 1940, became the Stockholm planning commissioner. This helped to insure close coordination between transportation and general planning during this period.

Markelius summed up his planning philosophy in an article in *Byggmästaren,* the Swedish builders' journal, in 1956.[71] In many ways his real interests seem to have been focused on ways of protecting the inner-city area for residential use rather than on suburban development. One senses that if some reasonable way could have been found to do it, he would have been pleased to see all Stockholmers living in an inner-city situation. (As the general plan rightly pointed out, Stockholm was one of the most livable cities in Europe at that time, without many of the serious problems which plagued other cities of its size.)[72] His planning proceeded on two fronts: urban and suburban. Within

the city, he sought to preserve and even expand the existing residential areas
by:
—moving as many work places as possible to the suburbs;
—protecting the city as much as possible from intrusions of the automobile;
—rebuilding downtown commercial districts with high-rise buildings, so as
not to unnecessarily take space from existing residential areas.

The first two of these considerations had important ramifications for the
way he proceeded on the suburban front. His interest in the decentralization of
jobs led him to think of the suburban districts in these terms: "They must be
able to live their own lives,"[73] meaning that these districts had to be to some
extent balanced, self-contained communities. His interest in keeping automobiles as much as possible out of the downtown area reinforced his ideas
about the desirability of high-density, public-transportation-oriented suburbs.
He wanted to make it not only difficult but unnecessary to drive an automobile
into downtown Stockholm.

The central theme of his view of suburbs was that they should be quite
"urban" in character; he often referred to them as "outer town districts."

An important condition for the building of the new districts is that they
shall be big enough, both as to size and population. The fault of the older
suburbs has been, above all, that they were too small. The whole of the
inner suburban ring is, with few exceptions, split up into small units,
with between a couple of thousand and 10,000 inhabitants, with small
badly-equipped centres and, as a rule, no possibility for grouping around
a larger collective center. If such a centre is to be equipped with department stores, high-class shops of different kinds, premises for spare-time
activities, theatre and cinema, this planning must be carried out on an
entirely different basis.[74]

There was even serious consideration given at the time to eventually rede-
veloping the garden suburbs. "In my opinion, it is not absolutely certain that
the old villa and cottage areas of Äppleviken, Ålsten, and Enskede ought to
make way for areas of flatblocks when the leases run out. It could be that,
when that time comes, it will appear better to let them remain."[75] This
ambivalence toward low-density suburbs is expressed also when Markelius
gives his views on single-family house development—he feels that they must
always be offset with high-density housing:

It is, in my opinion, desirable to allow increased space for the one-
family houses, in the first place in the form of the terrace (row) house.
This can be realized in a manner acceptable from the financial point of
view also by giving final shape to the flat-block areas around the com-

mercial centre and tube station by means of distinctive multistorey building. . . .

Here one would first and foremost serve a clientele, small families and bachelor households, less interested in those installations requiring space in planning than in the advantages gained by building concentration—proximity to station, comfortable access to shops, restaurant, cinema, theatre and other spare-time activities and to various kinds of collective household services. Such things can obviously be better and more easily organized in a multistorey block than in a lower, widespread type of building.[76]

Markelius's views were shaped by the planning ideas which were current at the time, especially the British garden-city movement, the Radburn plan, and the neighborhood-unit theory. Each of these ideas was given special importance in Lewis Mumford's *Culture of Cities* (1938), which was widely read by Swedish planners after it first appeared in Swedish translation in 1942. Also influential was the expression of these ideas in Sir Patrick Abercrombie's plan for London, done in the early 1940s, which proposed the postwar building of satellite towns around London of 50,000 to 100,000 residents each. Markelius himself attempted to minimize the importance of the British new-towns idea on his own thinking: "I have no feeling that Vällingby is copied from the New Towns, even though they were planned about the same time and there are some general ideas they have in common."[77] "The fundamental reason is that the English New Towns were genuine satellite towns, but Vällingby and the other suburbs were to have a much less independent function."[78]

There is some doubt about the extent to which Markelius and his associates really did want to develop the new suburbs as independent satellite communities. Pass concludes from examining the early plans that the original intention for the Vällingby area was a much higher degree of self-sufficiency than actually materialized and that the reason it didn't materialize was mainly due to the lack of cooperation by Stockholm's business and industrial community, who preferred to stay downtown and were reluctant to take the risk of moving to the new, untested location.[79]

While this judgment is probably true, it also appears reasonable—in view of what else we know about Markelius's ideology—that his underlying preference was for suburban districts which were closely tied to the city and to an urban way of life. Markelius was quite clear on this, at least in his later writings: "These town sections cannot be expected to function as satellite towns in the proper sense. The distance to the towns' main working districts and to the great magnet, Stockholm City, is far too small."[80] (Vällingby is about eight miles from downtown Stockholm; the British new towns are twenty-five to forty miles from downtown London.)

The independence, the self-support, is a question of contentment, comfort and rational organization. But it does not mean near-isolation. The Stockholmer at Vällingby still remains a Stockholmer as much as the inhabitant of Östermalm, Södermalm or Kungsholmen [inner-city districts of Stockholm] and the quick and comfortable communications [transportation] make it just as easy for the one as for the other to move about within the big town. Nor does anyone anticipate that we shall wholly achieve the target whereby place of work lies at a pleasant walking or cycling distance from the home. The very fact that Stockholm—to the advantage of both employer and employee—constitutes, in a certain degree, an individual labour market, acts as an obstacle.[81]

Yet Vällingby was not to be "true city"; Markelius was realistic enough to know that he had to compromise with many of the forces which lead people to choose suburbs in the first place. In answer to critics who felt that Vällingby was too *low*-density, built at a scale in which "the sense of urbanity is lost,"[82] Markelius pointed out that such a criticism takes no regard for the great need for open space for public purposes, especially automobile access, and for social development—parks, playgrounds, and recreation. A consideration of these essential needs means that "only 50% of the ground can be utilized for the actual construction of buildings."[83] This great amount of open space had a problematic quality in his planner's eye, however: "Generally speaking, this openness in the modern townscape, the wide streets and distances between buildings entailed by the motor traffic, the large open spaces for play and sport, the enormous but frequently inadequate parking places, is one of the big environmental problems."[84] What he also had in mind in this regard was the years it would take for vegetation to mature in these areas and to improve their appearance aesthetically.

In summary, it is fair to say that Markelius envisioned Vällingby more as an "urban extension" than as a true suburb in the usual sense. He wanted people to maintain a strong tie to the inner city and indeed to live, as much as possible, by an urban life-style. He recognized, however, that the "outer town districts" would "work better" if they contained a rather high percentage of work places as well as local shopping, cultural, and social facilities—indeed that they would be more desirable places to live. Further, he felt it essential to decentralize work places if the liveability of downtown Stockholm was to be preserved. In order to provide the open space necessary for the new standards and styles of living, he realistically decided on densities for Vällingby which were much lower than those in existing urban districts; yet his partiality for high-density living led him to easily accept increases in density as these were suggested by economic forces and interests. Finally, he sought to greatly minimize the role of the automobile by providing excellent and easily accessible public transportation, by focusing Vällingby on a system of pedestrian walkways, and by providing a bare minimum of parking facilities.

There is no indication of serious disagreement with this vision on the part of Markelius's architectural co-workers and associates. Indeed, it is a vision which one feels a great many of the world's architects and planners could hold with great ease. Vällingby, in fact, has since become one of the world's leading attractions for members of the design professions. Yet the vision has been realized in very few countries. Either economic forces have been allowed to run roughshod over the amenities that are possible in this kind of environment (the case in Eastern Europe especially, but also in many Western European countries and even in the Eastern U.S.) or planning has given way to consumer demand (as in most of the U.S.), and all planning and architectural visions of the built-environment have gone by the board.

Not only was there general agreement among planners and architects about the conception for Vällingby, there seemed to have been general agreement among most of the other decision-makers who were involved. A major reason for this agreement was doubtless the happy concurrence between transportation requirements, the needs of business, and planning ideology. David Pass uncovered, in the city administration of the day, only one outspoken advocate for the low-density alternative. This was the city's real estate director, Axel Dahlberg, a man who was instrumental in initiating the earlier self-help housing program in the garden suburbs.

According to Bertil Hanson, in his book *Stockholm Municipal Politics,* Dahlberg "wanted to fill the urban landscape with cottages and gardens. . . . He thought high-rise apartment buildings abominable, and he had no use at all for parks."[85] As Göran Sidenbladh later recalled, Dahlberg "was against separating pedestrian and car traffic . . . as for greenbelts, Dahlberg believed they were just nonsense; he wanted to develop them into areas of one-family dwellings."[86] Dahlberg maintained (perhaps with good reason) that his views "represented what ordinary people wanted."[87] According to Markelius, Dahlberg's views did have some effect, such as in lowering densities in several cases. But his power gradually diminished, and he finally left office in the early 1950s.

Vällingby stands today as the first complete example of a historically unique kind of suburban residential environment, one that falls between the extremes of high and low density. This type of environment can be considered as one of two major urban development alternatives to the low-density suburb, the other being the British new town. But the real question is, especially in view of the fact that it is a "planners' alternative" and goes against some expressed wishes of the people, How does Vällingby work as a place to live?

Do people really like it? Would they rather live elsewhere? These questions will be answered in later chapters. In a final chapter, the fate of the Vällingby conception in Sweden in recent years will be explored.

Vällingby

Characteristics of
the Residential
Environment

Vällingby after Twenty Years:
First Impressions

The typical approach to Vällingby is by subway.
Shortly after leaving the downtown area of Stockholm, the train emerges from its tunnel, providing
the traveller with some spectacular views of the
city as it glides over several high bridges which
bind together Stockholm's islands. The city-
scape, dominated by six-, eight-, and ten-story
apartment blocks, has a sense of order; everything seems to be in its place. There is also a
feeling of openness which is uncharacteristic of
most cities, a feeling created by waterways,
interconnecting fingers of parkland, jagged hills,
and outcroppings left in their natural state. Yet
very little open space seems transitional or unused.

One passes from the inner city through the
prewar suburbs of small, single-family houses
(looking much like California bungalows) only to
abruptly encounter further high-density expres-
sions of city life. One does not meet the expected
uniform decline in building densities with distance
from the central business district that the real
estate market generates in most Western cities.
Stockholm's densities are very uneven; the high-
density developments may be followed by green
parkland or, in one instance, what looks like a
working farm with grazing sheep. The dark green
of the wooded areas, the shimmering blue of the
waterways, and the lovely pastels of the built-
environment, make the trip to Vällingby, espe-

cially on a sunny day, a memorable one. It is hard to believe that this is all part of a major city.

Just as one has begun to feel that the city may at last be ending, the Vällingby development area emerges in the distance. Each subway stop soon becomes encased by a sizable urban center, or centrum,* surrounded by apartment buildings—some as high as ten stories. The apartment buildings, in turn, are encompassed by heavily wooded parkland. Finally, the main Väl-lingby centrum comes into view, built on a hill which commands the surrounding area.

The subway tunnels through the hill under Vällingby centrum, the visitor disembarks from the train in partial darkness and heads up the escalator toward the light. A step outside and one is back in the city, which was supposed to have been left behind. Vällingby centrum is a large, pedestrian shopping mall. The scene is dominated in spring, summer, and fall by open-air stalls selling fruits, vegetables, and flowers; sparkling fountains; people walking to and fro and sitting on benches as they watch the urban milieu. The feeling is calm and peaceful, yet with a touch of gaiety, especially on a bright, sunny day. The environment is colorful, alive, and ever-changing, as new people continually enter the field of view.

One immediately recognizes that the centrum is not just a retail sales venture. Prominently in view are the modernistic church, the community and youth centers, and office buildings. Attached to the centrum on the periphery are high apartment buildings that overlook the urban scene like giant sentinels. The centrum is a place to walk through on the way home from work, also to linger for a while. It is more like a downtown district than a U.S. shopping center; that, of course, was the planner's intention.

The centrum, with its high buildings and urban ambience, is surrounded by a green belt, which sets it apart from the garden apartments and town houses which make up the bulk of the Vällingby area. Pedestrian walkways underpass the traffic arteries around the centrum and lead across the green belt to the housing beyond. The Vällingby residential areas are heavily wooded and quite hilly; one can follow the paths for hours, through parklike settings, seldom having to cross even a minor roadway. Lateral paths veer off from the main walkways, leading to the garden and high-rise apartment complexes. There is scant feeling of being in either a city or a traditional suburb; the overall impression is of being in a large park, within which apartment houses have been placed.

Much of the parklike area between the residential buildings is given over to children's activities. Conspicuous visual features are the day-care centers:

*The term used by the Swedes to designate the combined commercial, social, and cultural centers that form the core of Vällingby districts.

long, colorful, interconnecting buildings with attached playgrounds and play facilities. Tot lots, children's parks, wading pools, and sports grounds also are frequently in evidence. The apartments look out on these facilities the way houses overlook streets and back yards in the American suburb. The parklike character of the setting is further enhanced by strollers, park benches, cyclists, public gardens, and the absence of the automobile. Parking lots are placed on the traffic side of the buildings, where they are seldom the focus of any activity apart from the use of the car. The pedestrian pathways, which take on many of the functions of the street in the U.S. suburb, are clean and well lit.

At the outer edge of the residential zone, yet still within easy walking distance of the centrum, the town houses are encountered. They commonly front onto a traffic street and back onto a pedestrian-oriented, public park area. The small front and back yards are heavily planted with flowers and shrubs; the homes are charming and well cared for.

This kind of residential environment is visually very striking to most Americans because it is so attractive and at the same time so unlike anything found in the United States. Yet, after a moment's reflection, the American may begin to wonder how such an environment would work out in the United States. How can these people live their lives in such small apartments? How can they get along without a private yard? Wouldn't this park turn into a trash heap if it were located on the edge of any American city? Why do people walk so much when they could use their cars instead? How can the dwelling unit be used as a symbol of social status? How do the residents keep out of one another's hair? These are some of the questions I myself raised, and sought answers for.

The term "Vällingby" is used in Sweden, causing some confusion, to designate three different areas. Smallest in size is the "city district" in which the Vällingby centrum is located. The *Vällingby city district,* together with several other districts of about the same size but with different names, make up the *Vällingby development area,* the planned suburb whose development was discussed in the last chapter. It is this area to which "Vällingby" will be applied in this inquiry, unless otherwise specified. The main Vällingby centrum has a retail service area which includes a number of city districts in addition to those in the Vällingby development area. Consequently, "Vällingby" is sometimes used also to designate this third area, which can be called the *Vällingby service area.* Its boundary is indefinite but normally includes parts of the neighboring areas of Spånga and Bromma—the two best-known place names in the western suburbs aside from Vällingby. The city districts outside of, but adjacent to, the Vällingby development area are quite different in character from Vällingby; they contain mostly detached and newer housing, with very few apartment blocks.

The total population of Vällingby (the Vällingby development area) on December 31, 1972, was 43,189, housed in 18,889 dwelling units and distributed among six city districts. The breakdown of population and dwelling units by Vällingby's city districts, together with the years in which most of the development in each district took place, is as follows:[1]

	Period of Development	Population	Dwelling Units
Blackeberg	1951–55	7,229	3,370
Råcksta	1951–55	4,000	2,117
Vällingby	1951–55	8,344	3,618
Grimsta	1951–55	3,886	1,638
Hässelby Gård	1951–60	10,611	4,659
Hässelby Strand	1956–60	8,120	3,487
		43,189	18,889

The city district called Vällingby, which contains the principal centrum, is located roughly in the middle of the chain of six districts and is some eight miles (twenty-seven minutes by subway) west of downtown Stockholm. Each of the other districts is located less than two miles from the Vällingby centrum. The districts closer to Stockholm were built earlier and at somewhat lower densities than those further out.[2]

In the following pages, the residential environment of Vällingby is described and analyzed in terms of three major components whose conceptual derivation and importance were discussed in chapter 1. The first is the environment itself, the tangible and perceived world of things which surround the resident. In urban areas, of course, a large part of this environment is built, or man-made. The second component of the residential environment is its demographic structure, the kinds of people who live there. The major units of demographic structure have become well standardized in sociology, including age, sex, class, race, ethnicity, and stage of the life cycle. Third, is what I have labeled community system characteristics: those aspects of the community which give it structure as a social system, apart from the nature and behavior of particular residents who happen to live there.

The Elements of the Vällingby Environment

The major environmental elements in Vällingby are the apartment building, the individual dwelling unit, the pedestrian path, the street, the parking lot, play and sitting areas, service facilities (schools, day-care centers), neighbor-hood and town shopping centers, the automobile, other people in the process of utilizing the environment, vegetation and landscape (especially hills and rocks). These are the tangible things one sees, uses, or comes into contact with in the close vicinity of the dwelling unit, on a regular, usually daily, basis.

The most conspicuous element of the environment is the apartment building—typically three-story, often faced with stucco, and painted with the muted and earthy pastel colors which one associates with Europe. The build-ings can be quite long, often as much as a block without a break in the denser areas of Vällingby. But clusters of such buildings, sometimes forming superblocks, are separated from one another by seas of grass, bushes, and trees. This quickly distinguishes them from their counterparts in more urban settings. In the more recently built sections of Vällingby, and in the areas adjacent to the centrums, the low-rise buildings are interspersed with ten-story tower blocks.

The six-to-eight-story "slab" buildings which are characteristic of more recent Swedish suburbs can also be found in Vällingby. They are not as high as the tower blocks but are far more massive and obtrusive in appearance. They exist only in the last two districts to be built in Vällingby; for the most part, the Vällingby buildings show far more continuity with Swedish subur-ban architecture of the 1930s and 40s than they do with the architecture of the 1960s and 70s. A principal reason for this is that the use of industrial building techniques did not become widespread until Vällingby was nearing comple-tion; the introduction of these techniques into residential construction created a discontinuity in the type and appearance of multifamily buildings in Swe-den. The Vällingby buildings of the early and mid 1950s typically have brick siding, a construction material which has become almost extinct in recent years because of the high cost of labor and the virtual impossibility of adapt-ing brick to industrialized building processes.

The architecture of Vällingby is actually quite diverse. Many different architects were used, and different styles sometimes vie for one's atten-tion in a limited area. Some architects have denounced this as "eclecticism"; but it was instrumental in saving Vällingby from the often monolithic uniformity of the later suburbs.

The individual dwelling unit, unlike in the U.S. suburb, is probably the least prominent element of the Vällingby environment to the outside observer, although it may be the most important for the resident. The outsider encoun-ters only two aspects of the dwelling: the balcony (almost all Vällingby apartments have balconies) and the entrance door. The small balconies tend to

look alike, though the residents often dress them up with flowers. Many
Swedes take the same care in dressing up their balconies as they do in their
dwelling interiors; in spring, summer, and fall these efforts make a delightful
addition to the outdoor visual scene. The balconies are also used to a limited
extent for drying and airing clothes and rugs, and sometimes for the storage of
household accessories such as toys.

Entrances to the dwelling units are clustered typically in groups of six, two
to each floor, opening off an interior stairwell with one large door to the
outside. One must go into the building and up at least half a flight of stairs to
encounter the individual entrance, which invariably has a mail slot and a name
on the door. Beyond the door is what seems a totally private world.

Adjacent to almost every apartment building, but usually on one side only,
is an open parking lot which empties onto the area's traffic circulation system.
Because of the sharp physical separation between pedestrian and automobile,
together with the abundance of mature vegetation, the traffic system is not
always very obvious to the observer on foot. Yet the car is never more than a
stone's throw from the apartment unit. Almost no Vällingby households have
two cars, and a significant percentage (35–40)[3] have no car at all, so the small
parking lots and narrow streets (by U.S. standards) seem adequate. Driving a
car through Vällingby is a very different experience from walking. One sees a
contrary face of the same environment, a face which is more typical of the
U.S.

Most streets have sidewalks, and it is sometimes necessary for the pedestrian to use these sidewalks to get where he is going. Planners frequently
comment on how inadequate the separation of vehicular from pedestrian
traffic is in Vällingby compared to the separation in later Stockholm suburbs.
Yet to an American this distinction is lost. One can walk virtually the length
of the Vällingby area (except for one major gap in the middle) and never cross
a street. The pedestrian paths are for the most part paved, wide, and well
lighted; they often lead through heavily wooded areas where one is but dimly
aware of the presence of buildings. Sometimes the buildings themselves,
jutting up in a sudden and unexpected way from the crest of a hill, add to the
beauty of the scene. It is no wonder that many Vällingby residents, as I shall
discuss in the next chapter, take walks for pleasure; indeed this is their major
form of exercise and regular recreation.

Many persons, young and old, also ride bicycles. Cyclists share the paths
with pedestrians but are not allowed inside the centrums. Motorized bicycles
(Mopeds) are restricted to the street system, although they sometimes stray on
to the pedestrian paths. Cycling is mainly a recreational pursuit, yet the
bicycle is also a not unimportant vehicle for shopping, work trips, and visits

to friends. While bicycle riding is not uncommon in U.S. suburbs, it is mainly limited to the young. In Sweden, it is an activity of all stages of the life cycle except for the very young and the very old.

The pedestrian circulation system in Vällingby, together with the pedestrian-only character of the shopping centers and the diminution of the need for and visual presence of the automobile, gives Vällingby an environmental character that is relatively unknown in the U.S. There is an atmosphere of peace and quiet, fostered also by the tall trees and mature shrubbery, which normally is difficult to obtain in a residential environment of this density. The human scale that comes with an area designed mainly for pedestrians can be found in the U.S. only in those special environments, typically nonresidential, from which the car has been excluded: boardwalks at resorts, pedestrian malls in downtown areas and shopping centers, historical districts like Williamsburg, amusement parks like Disneyland. These environments give a unique kind of contentment and even exhilaration in the U.S.; they are much sought after. But one drives to get to them, and they are invariably surrounded by a sea of parked cars—the "real world" in an almost extreme form. In Vällingby the human scale is natural and spontaneous, built into daily living. It is not the destination for a special trip but the basic dimension of a way of life. As I shall discuss in chapter 4, Vällingby residents are well aware of, and greatly appreciate, this environmental quality. It is uppermost in the minds of a majority of Vällingby dwellers in their positive evaluation of the area.

The other elements that Vällingby residents rate very highly are the vegetation and landscape, and the proximity of the suburb to "the country." Vällingby lies on a very attractive site: hilly, heavily wooded terrain bordered on two sides by an arm of Lake Mälaren which marks the outer boundary of the city. The Vällingby area was originally the site of farms which supplied produce for the city of Stockholm. It is easy to forget that when Vällingby was first built it had the same raw look which is characteristic of new developments everywhere, and it came in for the share of criticism faced by all new developments because of this fact. Now, as is also true in Levittown, the vegetation has matured and become a focus of great pride and positive feeling.

It is significant that the residents often combine, in their positive assessment of Vällingby, the pedestrian orientation with the assets of nature. Thus Vällingby is often described as quiet and peaceful, with lovely walkways, and close to nature and beauty. The natural world would seem to be the world par excellence at the human scale. The pedestrian facilities provide access to Vällingby's natural assets, allowing these assets to be more than a mere backdrop.

Plantings and even woodland in a heavily populated area require a high
level of maintenance. In the American suburb, most maintenance rests in the
hands of the individual property owner, a situation that leads to a network of
social pressures and often sporadic deterioration in quality. In Vällingby,
"gardening" is done by trained employees—except in the cases of the balcony flower boxes and indoor plantings, and the small gardens connected with
single-family homes.* This gives an even level of maintenance throughout the
area, a level that in Vällingby seems quite high. The public spaces, the
equivalent of the private yards in the U.S., appear well cared for and indeed
are often planted with masses of flowers and shrubbery which are well beyond
the means of the average citizen.

As the American suburban dwelling is mainly oriented toward the rear yard
and the facilities it contains, the Vällingby multifamily dwelling is oriented to
public open spaces. These open spaces far exceed their U.S. counterparts in
variety and quality. The facilities range from small tot-lots with a sandbox,
through larger playground areas with play apparatus of some kind, to large,
supervised play parks which throughout the year (except during summer
vacation months) have planned programs of activities for children up to the
age of about twelve. Finally, clusters of low, colorful buildings surrounded by
fenced-in play areas signal the Swedish day-care centers with facilities for the
care of babies (over seven months old) and infants, toddlers, kindergartners,
and schoolchildren during after-school hours. There are also wading pools
(used for skating in the winter) and sports fields.

These facilities give the Vällingby environment a domestic quality which is
not characteristic of most public park areas; and the children generate in the
environment a liveliness which one does not always associate with apartment
living. Facilities for children and youth are generally within view of the
dwelling units; the squeals of the children can sometimes be heard through the
open windows. These facilities and spaces represent an extension of the living
environment of the apartment dwelling, just as a private yard is an extension
of the house in the United States. The Vällingby apartment dwellers have no
private yard space—all yard space is publicly owned. As in the American
suburban yard, however, the activities of children in the "public yard" tend
to prevail.

Schools in the Vällingby area do not visually stand out as much as in the
U.S. School buildings are often similar in size to the low-rise apartment
buildings and are interspersed within residential complexes in ways which
blend them naturally into the built-environment. They are in every sense

*Some Vällingby apartment residents do tend garden plots; these lie on the edge of Vällingby or
outside the area in adjacent districts.

neighborhood schools, near at hand and readily available to both child and parent; often they are close enough to be within the visual field of the dwelling units from which students are drawn. Indeed, the activities of the school—children on their free time, groups in supervised play, children and teachers going to and from classes—tend to spill over into adjacent residential areas.

The several churches in Vällingby, on the other hand, are not residentially based; they are located in the centrums and associated with the other social and cultural institutions which can be found there. Although they are typically dominant architectural features of the centrums, this dominance exceeds their functional importance, as will be discussed below.

The American suburb seldom has a true focal point; it typically consists of street after parallel street of detached houses. While one often encounters a school, a church, or a shopping center, it is rarely the case that the adjacent residential areas *focus* on these facilities. Rather, the facilities are distributed on pieces of land which happen to be available. The church seldom draws exclusively from its local area, and the automobile provides a freedom of movement which may well lead away from the nearest shopping center to a preferred one at greater distance. In Levittown, only the elementary school is designed to be a neighborhood focal point, but it is quite distant from the average home and is not perceived as a focal point by most residents.

In Vällingby, all paths lead to the town centers, or centrums. These hubs of activity represent concerted attempts by the planners to bring physical and functional focus to clusters of about 10,000 persons, and the planners have achieved a degree of success in their attempts, certainly in physical terms. The high-rise apartments around the centrums can be seen from great distances and provide a strong sense of orientation to persons walking the paths through the outlying residential districts. During the day, at least, the centrums, which are bustling with activity, provide a social counterpoint to the calm and quiet of these districts. In a sense, one can go from country to city in the distance of a few hundred yards. No apartment unit lies more than five or six hundred yards from a centrum, so residents are always within easy walking distance; the great majority of Vällingby residents do their regular shopping entirely on foot.

An additional element of the environment should be mentioned, though it is not commonly classified as environmental—the presence of strangers. The people who are visually encountered on the pedestrian path system are typically strangers, as on a city street. For the most part, however, these strangers are limited to fellow residents of the 4,000-to-10,000-person clusters of which Vällingby is composed. Over time, therefore, some of these strangers become familiar faces, as in a socially enclosed residential district of a city or in a small town of similar size. This element is seldom found in American suburbs, where streets are usually not throughways for pedestrians. When residents leave their homes in the U.S., they typically are enclosed in an automobile. It is the automobile, therefore, which takes on the quality of being unknown or partially known.

A final word about the Vällingby environment. One has there a pervasive sense of being linked to the city. The subway runs above ground the length of Vällingby, and a subway stop is never far away. The constant shuttling back and forth of trains, by day and well into the night, is a continuing reminder that Vällingby is a part of something else. There is an easily accessible world beyond, a world which is much larger and more interesting for those whose mood or necessity would carry them in that direction.

The Demographic Structure of Vällingby

Age, Sex, and Stage of the Life Cycle

The population of Vällingby is almost evenly split between men and women. The percentage in significant age groupings (compared with groupings in the city of Stockholm) is as follows:[4]

Age	Vällingby	Stockholm
0–6	6%	6.5%
7–20	24	16
21–44	30	31
45–64	33	30
65+	7	16

It can be seen that Vällingby differs from Stockholm as a whole in having fewer older persons and slightly more teenagers and their middle-aged parents; the community is typical of a twenty-year-old suburb in these respects. The fact that the percentage of young children is the same today as in the rest of Stockholm indicates that Vällingby has changed significantly from its early days as a suburb of young families.

The percentage of older persons (over sixty-five) is higher than in most American suburbs of a similar age, not because the typical person who moved to Vällingby was older than his U.S. counterpart, but because a number of dwelling units have been set aside for pensioners (a pensioner in Sweden is anyone over sixty-seven). The pensioners live both in special pensioners' apartment buildings and in small apartments which are scattered throughout the area, and their presence in Vällingby is quite obvious to the outside observer, as they are commonly seen on the pedestrian walkways and in the shops. In contrast to most suburbs around the world, Vällingby has a marked degree of age heterogeneity due to the elderly.

It is useful to discuss the population in families in terms of stages of the family life-cycle. Eight stages are commonly designated: the beginning family, childbearing family, family with preschool children, family with school-children, family with teenagers, family as a launching center, family in the middle years, and the aging family.[5] The typical Vällingby household consists of a family at the sixth, or launching center, stage of the cycle, at which time the children are leaving home. A significant portion of the Vällingby families, however, have reached the seventh stage—the family in the middle years, when the children have already left home (sometimes referred to as the postparental or empty nest stage).

Focusing on families masks a large amount of household heterogeneity in Vällingby, a heterogeneity one does not find in most U.S. suburbs. Sweden probably has the highest percentage of one- and two-person households of any society in the world, and Vällingby is no exception to this pattern. The average household size in Vällingby is 2.52 persons; but 26 percent of all Vällingby households are inhabited by only a single person.[6] Older persons make up only a very small part of these single-person households; the great bulk are young people newly on their own, and middle-aged singles, population components that are relatively unimportant in the single-family-house suburban areas of North America.

The percentage of one- *and* two-person households in Vällingby is 53, far higher than in any U.S. suburb or even in many American cities. Yet Vällingby is far more "familistic" in character than inner-city Stockholm, where the percentage of one- and two-person households is 84, and also is more than in Stockholm as a whole (68 percent).[7]

The picture of Vällingby, in sum, is of an aging, family-oriented suburb—but with growing age and household-type heterogeneity.

Social Class

Data on social class have become notoriously hard to obtain in Sweden in recent years because of the national concern for egalitarianism and perhaps, because of the actual diminution of class differences. In addition, there is the problem of finding data comparable to those available in the U.S.; for example, the Swedish census uses a different occupational classification than the U.S. census.[8] Prior to 1966, however, when the practice was ended, eligible voters throughout Sweden were classified into three social groups (based on occupational titles): I, II, and III, which correspond roughly to the upper-

middle, lower-middle, and working classes. Using this scheme, the social
class makeup of Vällingby in 1966 was 11 percent class I, 57 percent class II,
and 32 percent class III.[9] Thus, Vällingby is a predominately lower-middle-
class community with a fairly sizable working-class element and a not insignificant upper-middle-class population. In this distribution it is similar to
many older suburbs in the U.S.

Unlike in the U.S. situation, however, Vällingby had almost precisely the
same class distribution as the city of Stockholm as a whole:[10]

| | Distribution of Population by Social Class | | |
	I	II	III
Vällingby	11%	57%	32%
Stockholm	13	51	35
Sweden	8	35	57

The amount of residential differentiation by social class is much less in
Stockholm than in U.S. cities, due to such factors as the absence of slums, the
placement of public housing in the suburbs (like Vällingby), and the continued liveability of the inner-city areas.[11] Indeed, the inner city was somewhat *higher* class than the outer city in 1966 (16.2 percent I vs. 9.9 percent
I).[12] It is also worth noting that Sweden as a whole ranked lower in class level
than Stockholm.

Ethnicity (Race, Religion, National Origin)

There is a very high degree of ethnic homogeneity in Vällingby. The number
of persons of other races is negligible, and the overwhelming majority of
residents are of the Swedish Lutheran religious faith (a state church) with a
mere handful, probably not more than 1 or 2 percent, belonging to the so-
called Free Churches (all Protestant churches outside the state church).[13]
While accurate figures for national origin are not available for the Vällingby
area, the percentage of foreign-born is certainly below that in the newer
Stockholm suburbs (where it may be as high as 15–20 percent). I would
estimate the figure for Vällingby to be below 5 percent, consisting mostly of
Finnish people. Two Finnish households emerged in my household sample.

Residential Mobility

The amount of residential mobility, or change in place of residence, is one of
any community's most significant demographic facts. In the U.S., rates of
residential mobility are especially high, averaging about 18 percent per year.

Comparisons with Sweden are very difficult because statistics are not collected to determine the number of Swedes who lived in a different house one year earlier, a question which is asked in the U.S. census. The best guess of various experts with whom I spoke was that Swedish rates of residential mobility are in general significantly below those of the U.S., perhaps by as much as one-half. In the Vällingby area in 1971, in-migrants accounted for 7.1 percent of the population, and out-migration amounted to 11.4 percent—a net loss of 4.3 percent. The city of Stockholm as a whole had a net loss of 1.7 percent during the same year.[14] These figures do not include residential mobility within each area, which can be substantial. The loss of population in Vällingby, explained more fully below, stems mainly from shrinking family size, as families reach later stages of the life cycle. In my household sample, the average length of residence in a flat was nine years, and 16 percent of the families were the original renters of the flat, that is, they had lived in the flat since it was first built eighteen to twenty years ago.

Other Characteristics

Two other social characteristics of households are especially important in considering the question of environmental adaptation: employment of women and automobile ownership. In one selected area of Vällingby, Grimsta, the percentage of women sixteen years of age and over who were gainfully employed outside the home (including part-time) was 57.[15] In my household sample, 88 percent of the adult women worked—somewhat higher than the average because the sample was weighted in favor of the working class.

National automobile ownership per capita in Sweden is fifth in the world, (3.6) behind the U.S. (2.3), New Zealand (3.0), Canada (3.2), and Australia (3.4).[16] It is first among the European countries in this respect. The per capita auto ownership in Stockholm is very close to that of the nation as a whole. In a sample area of Vällingby (Grimsta), the figure is 5.11.[17] Thus the planners, in conjunction with other influences, have been successful in holding down the rate of automobile ownership in Vällingby and, even more, the *use* of automobiles. In my sample, 40 percent of the households interviewed had no car (compared to 45 percent for Stockholm as a whole).[18] Only one household in my sample had more than one car; this was a second car owned by a teenage son.

The Maturation of Vällingby: Demographic Changes

Each type of community has a characteristic maturational profile or life cycle.

This feature of a community has an important impact on the long-term residents as well as on such matters as employment, services, taxation, and real estate values. It is an aspect of communities which has been the subject of very little serious research. Data were not available to develop a time series over the twenty-year life of Vällingby, but accurate data do exist for the ten years from 1960 to 1970, data that seem indicative of the longer-term trend.

The peak in Vällingby's total population was reached about 1960, when there were 58,701 residents. By 1970 this number had dropped to 47,606, a decline of almost 19 percent, or about 2 percent a year, and this rate of decline is continuing to the present time.[19] Since the number and size of dwelling units in Vällingby has remained almost constant, the population loss indicates a drop in the number of persons in each household, which has declined from 3.08 to 2.50 in the ten-year period. The number of four-person households declined from 28.9 to 17.2 percent of total households. At the same time, the number of two-person households increased from 15.9 to 26.7 percent and the number of single-person households increased from 17.3 to 26.8 percent.[20] While this reflects to some extent the movement of larger families out of Vällingby (into the newer suburbs, for example, which have larger dwelling units) and their replacement by smaller families, it is also indicative of families which are shrinking in size through advancement in stages of the life cycle.

The advancing life-cycle stage is also reflected in the changing age distribution of the population. The percentage of the population six years of age and under declined from 17 to 6 in the ten-year period, and the percentage of young adults aged twenty-one to forty-four declined from 44 to 30. At the same time the percentage of persons forty-five and over shot up from 15 to 40. The period from 1965 to 1968 was the time in which the youth population in the central areas of Vällingby reached maximum size (in Råcksta, Vällingby, and Grimsta, built between 1952 and 1958).[21] The nineteen-to-twenty-year-old age group reached its peak in the early 1970s; this is the age at which most Swedish youth leave their family of orientation. Thus the continuing population decline of Vällingby seems assured.

By and large, this kind of population decline is beneficial. The moderate overcrowding which characterized Vällingby at its inception is now gone, as the number of persons per room has decreased from 0.94 to 0.77. Gross residential densities have dropped from 32.6 persons per acre to 26.4 persons per acre, giving everyone a little more open space. Vällingby has also become significantly more age-heterogeneous. In 1960, the area was characterized by the typical suburban pattern of "young familism"—young couples with young children. Thirty-five percent of the population was under sixteen, and another 44 percent was between twenty-one and forty-four—a total of 79 percent. By 1970, this total had shrunk to 50 percent—half the population was entirely outside the ages of young familism.

The social-class level of Vällingby residents appears to be dropping over time, a pattern which is quite common in older suburban areas. The drop in class level seems to have occurred mainly from the out-migration of upper-middle-class households and their replacement by households of a lower class level. In one sample area (Grimsta), the percentage of class I persons declined from 19 to 11 between 1960 and 1966.[22] The Stockholm housing market was very tight in the 1950s, and many class I families were forced to take apartments in the newly built suburbs. In the 1960s, when the amount of private housing increased substantially, especially single-family houses, these class I families were among the first to leave places like Vällingby in an effort to upgrade their housing standard. Some class I families have remained in Vällingby; many of them live in the few single-family houses which are there.

Comparable data are not available on the decline of class level in Vällingby since 1966. But it is the opinion of many outside observers that the area is becoming progressively more working class, as the middle class continues to leave for larger dwelling units in the more distant suburbs and is replaced by the working class moving out from older dwelling units closer to the city center. This process is apparently characteristic of most of the suburbs of the Western world.

The government of Stockholm has recently been introducing into the Vällingby area a number of welfare cases—such as alcoholics—in an effort to upgrade their living conditions; this move is part of a general attempt to more widely distribute the welfare load throughout the districts of Stockholm. The policy has become a source of concern to some Vällingby residents, as much as they may sympathize with its goal, and it will doubtless have the effect over time of a further lowering of Vällingby's class level.

In regard to other variables, little information is available on ethnicity and residential mobility, but there is no indication that there have been significant changes over time. There has been a substantial change in the percentage of working women, which increased from 44 in 1960 to 57 in 1970 (Grimsta).[23] Automobile ownership has also increased significantly from 7.22 persons per car to 5.11 (for the Grimsta area).[24] In 1960, almost every other household was without a car; by 1970, the figure had dropped to about 40 percent. The actual *number* of cars increased by only about 14 percent in Grimsta (736 cars in 1960, 841 cars in 1970).

The moderate downgrading in social class has not yet had much impact on the character of Vällingby, which is still considered to be a very desirable place to live within the Stockholm region. Indeed, it is reasonable to conclude that Vällingby has "mellowed" and improved over the years. This is certainly the way the residents with whom I had contact view their community. In addition to such obvious changes as more mature landscaping and improved services and facilities, the area is now less crowded. It has also become more diversified in character, in terms of age and household type. In this sense, it has become more urban, and this was a goal of Vällingby's planners, if not necessarily the desire of all its residents.

The Vällingby Area: Community System Characteristics

Employment Structure

The Stockholm suburbs built prior to Vällingby, especially those of the 30s and 40s, were dormitory communities. It was expected that residents would commute to work elsewhere, mostly to downtown Stockholm. This situation was singled out as especially undesirable by Stockholm's postwar planners, who were quite strongly influenced by the satellite new-towns ideas coming at the time from Great Britain. While the planners apparently never intended to make self-sufficient satellite communities out of the postwar suburbs, they did strive for a relatively high percentage of local employment and were greatly enamored of the "walk to work" principle. It is not clear just what percentage of local employment they were seeking, but it certainly was something over 50 (the number of jobs available in Vällingby as a percent of the number of employed residents).

Industry was reluctant to move out to Vällingby in the early years. There was fear of the unknown; Vällingby was a new concept, and industries did not want to undergo the risk of the possible failure of the housing development. Consequently, industrial development lagged behind housing development, and new residents in Vällingby had to work elsewhere. When the jobs finally came, the new employees found the local housing fully rented. In 1960, there were locally available jobs for 36 percent of the employed residents but, due to the development lag, only 20 percent of Vällingby's residents actually worked locally.[25] The job picture improved somewhat by 1965, when jobs within the community were available for 54 percent of Vällingby's employed residents. The early pattern of working outside of Vällingby continued, however, and only 24 percent of employed Vällingby residents worked locally, taking up 45 percent of the local jobs.[26] The number of local jobs has increased further in recent years, while population size has dropped, making a still more favorable local employment situation. Of those who both live and work within the Vällingby area, a surprisingly large percentage—a majority in several districts—work in the same neighborhood in which they live.[27]

There is no heavy industry in Vällingby, but there is a diversity of light industry and services, restricted to a number of specific areas within Vällingby which are separated from residential zones and well serviced by public transit. The largest industrial district—Johannelund—has its own stop on the subway. A sizable number of government, institutional, and commercial concerns are located in Vällingby, the largest of which is the National Power Board (in Råcksta), with 1,900 employees (1966 data). The centrums are major employment areas; Vällingby centrum alone employed 2,200 persons in 1966 in its shops, commercial offices, and government institutions. At the present time, the largest job categories found in Vällingby are residential services and office work.

The range of jobs in Vällingby, together with their ready accessibility to local residents, makes the Vällingby economic situation especially attractive for part-time workers. Working women in Vällingby, for example, have an enviable situation, especially in view of the fact that they have in addition easy accessibility to the job market of downtown Stockholm.

Means of Transportation to Work. Based on information from one subarea (Grimsta), the largest percentage of Vällingby workers (40) get to their jobs by subway. Second in importance is the automobile (29 percent). The remainder get to work by foot (15 percent), by bus (9 percent), and by bicycle or moped (6 percent). Thus over 47 percent use collective means of transportation, and a relatively small percentage (by U.S. standards) rely on the automobile.[28]

Governmental Structure

Vällingby is not a separate political entity; it is a part of the city of Stockholm. The suburb has neither its own local government nor special representatives to the government of Stockholm, where the major political decisions about the area are made. (Since 1971, the city and county of Stockholm have been combined into a single political jurisdiction, under the administration of what is called the Greater Stockholm Council.)

The hold of the city on Vällingby is even stronger than in many other Stockholm districts because the land on which Vällingby was built is municipally owned and because most of the housing and shopping centers of Vällingby were built and are managed by one municipally owned corporation: A.B. Svenska Bostäder. Thus the government of Stockholm is, at least indirectly, the landlord and caretaker of buildings and grounds in Vällingby, as well as regulator of social order and distributor of resources.

Although the absence of a separate governmental structure in Vällingby is in contrast to many U.S. suburbs, the structure of local government in Sweden has many similarities with U.S. local government. Political scientist Tom Anton notes: "Local governments have been the front line of public response to urban pressures in both countries, popular support for local government is strong in both, and the higher authority of the state intrudes into, and frequently controls, local actions in both." [29]

Residential Facilities and Services

In marked contrast to most American cities and suburban areas, the city of Stockholm has provided what appears to an American as an abundance of facilities and services of all types for Vällingby's residents. Indeed, a major part of the Vällingby idea was that high-density living was necessary so that residential services could be provided in greater amounts, with greater efficiency, and with higher accessibility. The relative lack of private space and private facilities (such as recreation rooms) within the Vällingby dwelling unit is compensated for by the intensive development of public services and facilities, for example, recreational facilities and meeting rooms. In comparison with the services provided in Stockholm's newer suburbs, however, Vällingby may appear deficient in some areas.

The residential services of Vällingby have been the subject since about 1968 of a very intensive investigation by the Master Planning Commission of Stockholm in an effort to gather information useful in future planning. This investigation, which is still going on, has closely examined the allocation and utilization of Vällingby's residential services and has found that in many cases these services fall considerably short of the norms and standards as set forth in the 1952 master plan for Stockholm. The results of the investigation to date have been set forth in a series of six monographs under the heading *Boendeservice i Vällingby* (Resident service in Vällingby), from which this section draws heavily. [30]

The Organization of Residential Facilities & Services. Stockholm is divided into about seventeen historical, functional, and administrative districts, many of which overlap one another. The most important of these are the parishes. Originally organized as church districts, they keep that function today but serve also as districts for census and other statistical data-keeping purposes. A citizen who changes residence in Sweden must immediately report the change of address to his local parish office. This policy has been in effect for many generations and has given Sweden some of the world's best statistics on intercommunity mobility. Vällingby lies in three different parishes: Hässelby,

Spånga, and Bromma. Some governmental services are organized along parish lines but most are not. For example, there are separate administrative districts for health, welfare, education, police, and recreation. It is typical for a resident of Vällingby to have to go to one district for welfare benefits, a second for medical care, and a third for education.

In spite of this seeming confusion of parishes and districts, the city of Stockholm has one of the most rationalized and efficient administrative structures in the world. Many major services have branch offices in the Vällingby neighborhood centrums. Further, there is in the hands of each resident a guide, updated annually, which gives complete information on precisely where a resident of a particular area should go for each service that is needed. The residents of Vällingby have little difficulty in knowing where to go for services, even if those services are in another part of town.

A major attempt was made in Vällingby to distribute geographically facilities used on a regular basis, such as libraries, schools, retail services, and day-care centers, according to "the neighborhood principle." Where possible, these facilities and services were to be clustered together to form a nucleus for neighborhoods for about 10,000 persons, leading to the establishment of the neighborhood or district centrums. Because Vällingby does not rely on the automobile as the main means of transportation, however, it was necessary to still further decentralize many services to the local areas to get the services within easy walking distance of the residents. Thus, the neighborhood centrums do not play as large a role as one might expect. Almost all educational facilities are located outside of them, as is about half of all indoor space for recreation and community activities and 43 percent of the floor space devoted to retail and related services.[31]

It was not economically feasible to provide each of the six Vällingby neighborhoods with the full range of services. The concomitant "hierarchical principle" led to the formation of Vällingby centrum as the largest and most dominant of the five district centrums (Grimsta does not have its own centrum because of its close proximity to the Vällingby district). The Vällingby centrum, in principle, contains those facilities and services which require a clientele of more than 10,000 persons for their efficient functioning.

In spite of this decentralization, a major conclusion of the master-plan investigation is that the facilities and services of Vällingby are not decentralized enough. A strong relationship was discovered between distance from a service and the amount that service is used—the closer one lives to a service, the more he will use it. This is especially true for such free-time services as libraries, youth centers, and recreational facilities, but it also holds for medical care and social welfare. At a distance of over five to six hundred yards, the use of many services drops off precipitously. This is especially true in the case of young people and for working-class households, two groups whose needs for residential services are relatively great. Swedish investigators have been led by this finding to the conclusion that centralization of services is a form of deprivation for some people; it deprives them of the use of the service in a way not dissimilar to the absence of that service entirely.

Retail Establishments. There are in the Vällingby area 374 commercial establishments of one kind or another. Thirty-seven percent of the retail facilities are in the Vällingby city district, and the bulk of those are in Vällingby centrum.[32] While the five neighborhood centrums clearly dominate the field of retail trade (and are themselves dominated by this function), a sizable minority of retail facilities exist outside the center, as was noted above. These include such establishments as small grocery stores, barber shops and beauty parlors, small dress shops, newspaper and tobacco stands, television repair shops, and laundries; they may be either clustered together into small shopping complexes or located apart from other facilities, usually on the ground floor of apartment buildings. All are primarily pedestrian-oriented, with some provision for automobile access. Many of these outlying shops have become increasingly unprofitable because of declining populations and the growing strength of the larger centers; some have gone out of business entirely.

The neighborhood centrums themselves typically contain, in addition to a relatively complete set of retail services, a post office, banks, a liquor store (state-run), and a café. They include also a variety of social, cultural, and governmental services. The smallest of the five neighborhood centers, Råcksta, is the closest to the dominating Vällingby centrum, and because of this fact it has not been as successful economically as the others.

Vällingby centrum, which is built on a 100-by-300-yard concrete platform over the subway, has about seventy retail facilities and 225,000 square feet of selling space. It was originally smaller in size, but a major addition was completed in 1966, after the success of the center became clear. The total cost of the centrum, including the addition, was about $15–20 million.

As part of the addition, the number of spaces for automobile parking was more than doubled—from 600 to 1,250—by adding Europe's first suburban parking building. The planners of Vällingby had underestimated the importance of the automobile in the centrum's future. In the early 1960s, one-third of the people came to the centrum by car, one-third by subway, and one-third on foot.[33] In recent years, the number of automobile trips has, of course, grown (figures are not available), but the percentage is doubtless lower than in any shopping center in the U.S.

Schools. The schools of Vällingby are part of the Stockholm school system. In the Vällingby area there are thirteen primary schools, ten middle schools, six high schools, and two gymnasia (upper-level high schools). There is also one high-school-level trade or technical school. The schools are distributed by neighborhoods with each neighborhood having several primary and middle schools and one high school. The two gymnasia are located in Vällingby and Blackeberg. A significant number of Vällingby youth go to gymnasia in other parts of Stockholm, usually in the inner city.

Almost all education in Sweden is public. A very few private primary or secondary schools remain, mostly for foreign children, but even these are gradually disappearing, often for economic reasons. Public education starts in Sweden at age seven, one year later than in the U.S. A large portion of the five- and six-year-olds go to play schools, the equivalent of our nursery schools and kindergartens. These will be described below under children's day-care services; they are not formally connected with the public education system. Education is mandatory in Sweden to age sixteen, but the majority of Swedish youth continue on after that to the gymnasia or trade schools.

"Going to college" as a goal of youth does not have the same prominence in Sweden that it does in America. The percentage of college-age youth in Sweden who go to the university is only about half that of the U.S. Further, there are not the range and diversity of forms of higher education found in America (small, large, public, private, community, state). Normally, the college-bound Swedish student goes to the university nearest his home; in the case of Vällingby, this would be Stockholm University or the Royal Technical University. (There are also separate schools for medicine, dentistry, forestry and agriculture, and various vocational fields.) University students in Sweden tend to be studying for a particular job or purpose. The idea of a liberal arts education—higher education for the sake of being better educated—is not pervasive in Sweden the way it is in America. On the other hand, Swedish high schools and gymnasia seem educationally superior to those in the U.S., and Sweden has a strong tradition of adult education, so that "lifelong learning" replaces the pressure-cooker atmosphere of higher education in the U.S.[34]

The primary schools in Vällingby are so localized with reference to the housing areas that it is common for a child's school to be within sight of his dwelling unit. Almost all trips to school are by foot or bicycle—a person can not drive a car in Sweden until age eighteen. Thus home and school are geographically much more closely related than in the American suburb. The Swedish school does not play as prominent a nonacademic role in the life of the child, however, and parents and teachers may not be in as close touch with one another as in the American system.

Schools in the U.S. have long been multipurpose facilities, providing more
than just academic instruction. The best example is sports, where almost all
competitive and most noncompetitive sports during the teenage years are
under the control of the high schools. In addition, schools commonly provide a
range of after-school activities in such areas as arts and crafts, orchestra,
journalism, and drama. In many American communities, indeed, the schools
are the only public agencies which regularly sponsor these youth activities.

In Sweden, all competitive sports are removed from auspices of the
schools. Competitive sports are handled by local sports clubs which are usually organized on the basis of neighborhoods or other geographic areas. Clubs
are established for many different age and ability levels, and for both boys and
girls. Noncompetitive sports are actively fostered through a variety of city
recreation programs. Two effects of this organizational arrangement are that
the number of youth who actually participate in sports in Sweden is probably
higher than in the U.S., and there is less conflict during the school day
between academic and nonacademic pursuits.

Other after-school activities are sponsored by youth centers and recreational programs and will be discussed below. There is a growing movement
within Sweden, however, to open up the schools for afternoon and evening
youth activities, so as to more efficiently utilize the school space. There is a
related trend toward the utilization of school space for general community and
adult activities, especially in the evenings. In these ways, the Swedish public
school may gradually become more like the U.S. school in its pivotal community role.[35]

At the present time, however, the Swedish public school does not com-
mand the same community attention as its U.S. counterpart. For youth, its
function is almost exclusively academic. The tradition of public (parent)
involvement in the running of the school is not strong in Sweden, so fewer
adults are involved. There is a Swedish equivalent to the parent-teacher association, but it seems not to have the same force as in the U.S. By and large,
the running of the schools is entirely left up to "the experts." Moreover,
public education is not a major topic of local political activity in Sweden;
community fights over school budgets are rare. Education is more interwoven
into the processes of government than in most U.S. communities; there are no
separate, "nonpolitical" school boards, and within local government education is regarded as a more technical, nonpolitical function.

Swedish public education has been changing rapidly in recent years, both in
structure and in content. This has been stimulated at the national rather than
the community level and has been accompanied by a lively national debate on
the subject. It is too soon to tell precisely where these educational changes
will lead.

Outdoor Recreation. The main recreation facility in Vällingby is the Grimsta woods, 450 acres of unspoiled woodland that lies between Vällingby and Lake Mälaren. It was the original intention of some of Vällingby's planners to use much of this forest preserve for single-family housing, but the idea was dropped in the later planning stages. The woods stand today as Vällingby's most used and appreciated outdoor facility. Dwelling units proximate to it are the most desired, and it is the one recreation facility, in addition to the bathing beaches of Lake Mälaren, which is regularly used by a majority of Vällingby residents. The main uses are "taking a walk" and "getting some exercise."[36]

The woods and connected recreational area serve a population which extends well beyond Vällingby, though the local residents are by far its most frequent users. In addition to the woods and an adjoining bathing beach on Lake Mälaren, the area contains two marinas for pleasure boats, tennis courts, a riding stable and academy (which during an active week is used or visited by almost one thousand persons), a pistol range, an ice rink, and a major sports field.

Major facilities in other parts of Vällingby include a second swimming beach on Lake Mälaren, two more boat marinas (which together with the Grimsta docks contain spaces for 368 boats), and ten large sports fields, a number of which are adjacent to schools. These facilities are all administered by Stockholm city government agencies.

For younger children, the outdoor recreational facilities are much more decentralized and even more numerous. At the lowest level in the hierarchy there are throughout the Vällingby area numerous small play and sitting areas, often with sandboxes, for the youngest children. At the next level, for younger children there are nineteen block playgrounds which contain playground equipment and places for parents and other child attendants to sit. Next are eleven play parks, fully equipped play areas which have professional leaders and a wide variety of organized activities in sports, arts, and crafts for older children. One of the larger play parks in Vällingby employs three full-time professionals and one part-time, plus additional personnel for special services such as skating instruction. Seven of these play parks are open all year; four in summer only. Six of the parks have a provision for baby-sitting during certain hours of the day, usually in the morning (for about three hours). This time is often used by mothers to do their local shopping. Most of the parks have indoor shelters so that they can continue to operate in all kinds of weather.

Ball-playing fields (eleven in all) are used by young teens and preteens and are often located adjacent to the play parks. The activities on these fields can be supervised by the play-park personnel.

Indoor Recreational Facilities and Community Meeting Rooms. Besides not
having private yards, the residents of Vällingby have little space within their
dwellings which can be used for meetings or for leisure-time activities. This is
compensated for by the provision of a relatively large amount of public space
(much of which can be reserved by groups for semiprivate purposes), which is
administered by many different city agencies. There are sixty-four indoor
facilities for organization, hobby, or study use (twelve of which do double
duty as school facilities).[37] Most of these have one room only; some have
several rooms. About half of the meeting rooms are situated in residential
buildings, usually on the ground floor or basement levels.

For gymnastics and sports there are fourteen special-purpose indoor
facilities the largest and most important of which is the major new Vällingby
swim and sports hall, completed in 1972, which contains an Olympic-sized
swimming pool. It is located adjacent to the Vällingby centrum. For large
private parties, there is a party hall (in Blackeberg) which can be rented out.
Finally, there is a major community-center building in Vällingby centrum
which is used for a variety of educational, entertainment, political, recreational, and other purposes. This listing of recreational facilities does not
include those in libraries, churches, and youth centers, which are discussed
below.

Youth Centers. Starting in the early 1940s, Stockholm began to establish a
network of leisure-time centers to serve youth between the ages of thirteen or
fourteen to twenty. The original impetus for the establishment of these centers
was the many children, often from poor and large families, who were moving
into Stockholm during the war years. Now the centers are recognized as a
basic facility for all neighborhoods, and there were in the entire city in the
early 1970s some eighty complete youth centers and eighty more annexes or
specialized centers. These centers employ 1,400 full- and part-time youth
leaders.[38]

Vällingby has five complete youth centers—one in each neighborhood
except Grimsta—and four other special centers, for example, a facility in the
Vällingby centrum where youth can build boats. These centers are open from
about September 1 to June 15. The most complete information about the
Vällingby youth centers comes from the year 1968–69. During that year,
three full-time and 111 part-time personnel were employed. The youth center
in Vällingby centrum, the largest of the group, was paid forty thousand visits
by youth over the nine-and-a-half-month period.

The minimum age for admittance to the centers is fourteen, though
thirteen-year-olds often can go for special group functions. Visitors must have

a membership card, which is purchased annually for a nominal fee (about fifty cents). Fifty-eight percent of the card-holders are boys and 42 percent are girls; however, the sex ratio varies by age. Up to age fifteen there are an equal number of boys and girls; thereafter the boys begin heavily to predominate.

About a third of the Vällingby youth of the appropriate ages were youth center card-holders (1968–69), but this too is affected by age. In the fourteen- to fifteen-year-old group—the most active—the percentage of card-holders varies from 31 in Vällingby to 67 in Hässelby Strand. In the sixteen- to seventeen-year-old group, the percentages drop to 24 and 29; in older ages they are lower still. By no means are all card-holders regular users of the centers, however. On a typical weekday in 1968–69, 160 youth used the Vällingby center, for example, out of 771 Vällingby card-holders. Most of the actual visitors to the youth centers are concentrated in a very small age group. This is especially true for girls, with a median age for youth center visitors of 14.9, and a standard deviation of 1.1 years. For boy visitors, the average age was 15.5 (with a standard deviation of 1.5 years). Probably about 20–25 percent of the most active age group, fourteen- to fifteen-year-olds, are regular users of the youth center facilities and services.

What do youths do at the centers? The most desired activities are the evening discotheques, usually held on two evenings a week with a nominal entrance fee (twenty-five cents). During 1968–69, there were discotheques on eighty-seven evenings at the Vällingby center. Other activities for which a small extra fee is charged are films, shown on sixty-five evenings, casual dances on twenty, and other entertainment on sixteen. In the youth centers of the Vällingby area there were 120 named clubs in 1968–69; some were simply social clubs, others were for such purposes as weightlifting, stamp collecting, photography, and travel. In addition, there are the many unorganized, drop-in activities—Ping-Pong, chess, talks over coffee, hobbies, arts and crafts. Finally, the centers sponsor a great many lectures and discussions on such topics as sex, narcotics, the police, and alcohol.

Since 1968–69, when the survey of youth centers was made, there have been a number of changes which, though hard data about them do not exist, are significant enough to mention. The number of youth coming to the centers has been declining precipitously in the 1970s. It is estimated that a Wednesday or Saturday discotheque which would draw three to four hundred youths in the late 1960s, would have an attendance today of about a hundred or a hundred and fifty.[39] Further, the number of active clubs in the centers has diminished. This is reflected in a sharp decrease in the number of part-time leaders, one of whose major functions is to lead club activities. At the Vällingby centrum youth center, the number of part-time leaders has declined from a high of about fifty-five in the late 1960s to about thirty today.[40]

Several reasons for this decline in activity have been suggested. First, there
has been a marked drop in the youth population of Vällingby, as has already
been noted. Second, the teenagers have more money today, and they are able
to utilize more fully the range of commercial leisure-time facilities which
exist in center-city Stockholm. Further, these facilities have become more
adept over time in attracting young people. Third, and the reason which is
most discussed, drugs have entered the Swedish scene in recent years, as they
have in every other advanced society. It is estimated that 10–15 percent of the
youth who come to the Vällingby centers have drug problems of one kind or
another, including alcohol (about 30 percent of the problem cases are girls).[41]
These cases have the effect of keeping other youth away and of lowering the
reputation of the youth center in the eyes of the community (this problem
turned up strongly in my family interviews). While the drug users may well
profit from their contact with the youth center, as compared with being forced
onto the street, the unintended consequence is a diminution in the number of
youth that the centers are able to serve.

Libraries. There are two main branches in Vällingby of the Stockholm city
library, one in Vällingby centrum and the other in Hässelby Strand. In addition, there are three neighborhood branch libraries for children and youth—all
three connected with schools.[42]

The Vällingby centrum branch (opened in 1956) had 41,000 books in 1970,
and 150 magazines and journals to which it subscribed. Other materials could
be ordered from the main library. The library employed five full-time and two
part-time persons. The smaller Hässelby Strand branch, opened in 1964,
contains 7,000 volumes and 25 magazines and journals. It employs the equivalent of one full-time person. The major class of users in the Vällingby branch
are young people between the ages of sixteen and twenty (perhaps because of
the proximity of a gymnasium); the major users of the Hässelby Strand branch
are pensioners. Between 2 and 5 percent of the residents of Vällingby, depending on such factors as location and social class, are regular users of the
libraries.

The three libraries for children and youth—each housing between 4,000
and 5,000 volumes—are only open seven to twelve hours per week (weekdays
only) during the school year, and each is staffed with a part-time library
assistant. They sponsor a variety of youth activities which are held on their
premises.

Two neighborhoods in Vällingby—Grimsta and Blackeberg—have neither
an adult nor a children's library. Blackeberg is serviced by a library bus which
comes around twice a week, staying for approximately one hour in the early

evening. The Grimsta neighborhood is felt to be close enough to the Väl-lingby branch library so as not to require this special bus service.

Religious Institutions. Vällingby has three churches: two state churches (Lutheran) and one free or nonstate church. In marked contrast to churches in the U.S., these churches play a very small role in the life of the community, both religiously and as centers for social organization and contact. Only four adults in my sample of Vällingby residents were churchgoers. One couple was very active in a Baptist church in downtown Stockholm; one was a middle-aged woman who said she was "not very active," and the fourth was a woman pensioner who was a regular churchgoer at the Vällingby church. I encountered no youth who were active church members. In Sweden as a whole, only 6 percent of the population regularly attends church services.[43] The figure for Vällingby, though not precisely known, is almost certainly below that.

The Swedes have a large amount of respect for the church, however, especially as a part of the Swedish tradition. An overwhelming percentage of Swedes are still baptized, confirmed, and married in the church, though these practices seem to be declining among the young. In 1973, 109 children were born in Vällingby parish, but only 70 baptisms were held.[44] Although they may still hold allegiance to the church as an institution, Swedes show a strong disinterest in religion as ideology or faith. For example, religion is seldom invoked by Vällingby residents in public or private conversation as a "live" aspect of society or of one's personal fortunes or misfortunes.

The churches in Vällingby have a religious function but it is over-shadowed—as is often the case in the U.S.—by social functions. The sponsorship of adult social activities and youth activities, such as scouting, remains important though relatively insignificant when compared to govern-ment-sponsored activities of a similar nature. The largest church func-tion of all is probably the census-taking, which was mentioned above.

Day-care Centers for Children. As was emphasized in the discussion of the built-environment, day-care centers in Vällingby are important visual focal points of the residential areas. They are even more important in the lives of those Vällingby parents who are fortunate enough to have their children enrolled in them.

When Vällingby was first built, the concerns of the working mother were not as much in the forefront of thinking as they are today, and there were fewer working mothers. Vällingby has always been underserviced with day-care facilities relative to the demand, although the situation has improved

somewhat over the years as additional facilities have been built and as the
child population in Vällingby has decreased. Each day-care center in Vällingby has a waiting list, and the actual percentage of children in each age
group who receive day-care services is quite low. But the situation in Vällingby is better than in many other areas of Stockholm.[45] In the more recently
developed suburbs, the lack of day-care facilities has been one of the leading
causes of complaint.[46]

Public day-care facilities in Sweden are of three main types (data used in
the following discussion are from a survey conducted in 1968).[47]

1. Day homes. For children from six months to six years, whose parents
are away from home for purposes of work or study. The homes take care of
the child for the entire day. In Vällingby there were sixteen day homes, with a
total of 611 places.

2. Play schools. For children ages four to six. These take the child for only
part of the day, usually three hours. They have the same functions as the
American nursery school. (There is no Swedish equivalent of the U.S. kindergarten; students do not start school until age seven.) There were in Vällingby twenty-two play schools, with 275 places.

3. Leisure-time homes. For younger school children (up to age eleven) in
their out-of-school daytime hours (including school holidays not matched by
parents' work holidays). Children can go directly to the leisure-time home
after school and sometimes are dropped off before school starts if the parents'
work hours require it. Thus, in conjunction with the school, full day-care is
provided for the school-age child of working parents. Vällingby had eleven
such homes, with 275 places.

The typical child in the Vällingby day home had a mother who must work
because of low income, or a mother who was living alone (46 percent).
Four-year-olds were the predominant group; about 19 percent of all four-
year-olds in the Vällingby area had a place in the day homes. There were
day-home places in Vällingby for 15 percent of the children in all qualifying
age groups. These percentages have probably increased somewhat in the last
few years.

The day homes of Vällingby had on the waiting lists about the same
number of children as were enrolled. The largest group on the waiting list
were the very young infants, for whom there were few places because of high
personnel costs. Waiting time for a place in a day home averaged about one
year.

In addition to the day home, the Swedish parent has the option of a "family
day-home"—the child is left in a private household which must meet stringent, government-established standards and be officially licensed for that
purpose; or the parent can use a variety of private, informal arrangements—

grandparents, teenage sitters, neighbors, and so on. Such informal arrangements are not as common in Sweden as in the U.S. because of the availability of the established public institutions, plus the licensed family day-homes.

A much higher percentage of Vällingby's children went to the play schools than to the day homes. Among six-year-olds, the figure was 77 percent; among five-year-olds it was 40 percent. There is still a waiting list today, especially of four- and five-year-olds, but the supply may soon catch up with demand. In a recent public policy change, the Swedish government has stated that each Swedish community should strive as soon as possible to have a place in the play school for every four- and five-year-old child. In this respect, the Swedish play school will become more comparable to the American kindergarten.

The leisure-time homes mainly drew on seven-year-olds (grade one), who made up a third of the enrolled children, and eight-year-olds, who made up another fourth. The parents of leisure-time-home children are very similar to those of day-home children; indeed, the leisure-time home is a kind of postgraduate institution for children of the day centers.

Conclusions

While the services and facilities provided to the residents of Vällingby fall short of the Swedish planners' ideal, there can be found nothing comparable in U.S. communities, especially the postwar suburbs. The more recent suburbs of Swedish cities sometimes surpass Vällingby in the quantity and quality of services, but many housing areas in Sweden, especially areas of single-family houses, are not as well supplied. Swedish housing officials place a high priority on the provision of local services in residential areas, almost as high as the priority on housing production itself. As the following chapter will make clear, the social importance of these services and facilities to the residents is considerable.

4

The People of Vällingby Patterns of Environmental Fit

Social-scientific views of the relationship between man and the environment have in the past been heavily influenced by the doctrine of environmental determinism, which, in its pure form, holds that there is an identifiable cause-and-effect relationship between environment and human behavior so that, when certain antecedent environmental conditions occur, specified behavioral effects will inevitably follow. Most contemporary perspectives do not see the relationship in this way, with man the passive product of his environment; they emphasize instead man as a goal-directed being who, in the words of a recent environmental textbook, "is in dialectical tension with his milieu, interacting with it, shaping it, and being shaped by it."[1] The large majority of environmental social scientists today would probably agree with Louis Wirth's early formulation: "[Characteristics of the environment] . . . are at best conditioning factors, offering the possibilities and setting the limits for social and psychological existence and development."[2] This formulation holds to the notion that the environment has determinate "effects" on human affairs, for a "conditioning" factor is a kind of "causal" factor, but it rejects the inevitability of environmental consequences and the passivity of man's environmental role.

One contemporary perspective on the relationship between the environment and social behavior (the special concern of this book) stays away entirely from the use of such deterministic terminology as "effect," "consequence," or "influence," and speaks instead of the "fit," "match," or "congruence" (these terms are typically used interchangeably) between environments and patterns of behavior. Thus, in a particular environmental setting, some patterns of behavior and social structure are viewed as easier to develop and maintain, others as more difficult or even impossible. This is the perspective—environmental fit—that is used in the following discussion of the people of Vällingby. From this perspective, residents are held to be well matched or congruent with an environment when the environment readily accommodates their needs, goals, and patterns of social behavior without undue limitations and constraints, especially those which generate social and psychological stress. Congruence is a matter of degree, and at one end of the scale the term "incongruence" may be used. A very large family in a small dwelling unit might be considered poorly matched or incongruent, or so might a cosmopolitan person in a small, rural town, or a single "swinger" in a community of families; in such cases the social and psychological characteristics of the individuals or groups do not mesh well with the characteristics of the environment; the environment is not appropriate to their needs, desires, and behavior patterns.

At heart, the concept of environmental fit or congruence is normative because it involves evaluations of the social and psychological characteristics of people and groups of people; especially sensitive is the judgment about *which* social and psychological characteristics are most salient in making the evaluation of fit or unfit, congruent or incongruent. Yet the concept of environmental fit is no more or less normative than many other concepts that have importance in the social sciences, such as mental health, social deviance, or even family functioning. While the normative character of the concept may have retarded its use in research, it has not affected its position as a central concept in the fields of environmental sociology and psychology, where it frequently is a major component of the theories and perspectives which focus on the social and behavioral aspects of environmental quality.

The term "congruence" has been used by environmental sociologist William Michelson in his discussion of the relationship between cultural, social, and personal systems on the one hand, and environmental systems on the other. He states: "The model I suggest is not of determinism or the dominance of one system over another, but rather one of congruence—of states of variables of one system coexisting better with states of variables in another system than with other alternative states. It is an intersystem congruence model."[3] The concept is also central in the work of ecological psychologists such as Roger Barker and Paul Gump, who speak of the good fit between behavior and milieu as being "synomorphic," meaning similar in shape.[4]

The goodness of fit is a term also frequently invoked by architects and designers in their discussions of the relationship between design and behavior.[5]

The concept of environmental fit is not only normative but temporal; needs and patterns of social interaction change, as do environments, and a person may be well matched at one point in his life, but mismatched at another. On the other hand, many mismatches between social behavior and environmental elements are maintained over time because, in a single environment, elements that match behavior outweigh those elements that do not match. For example, the large family in the small dwelling may continue to reside there because it is in a good neighborhood, rather than move to a larger and more appropriate dwelling in a poor neighborhood.

The concept of environmental fit is also subject to varying bases and standards of evaluation, especially the distinction between a person's environmental preferences and the reality of his behavior. If a person states that he loves his present environment and has no desire to move, yet the evidence indicates that he would be much better off if he did move, is that person incongruent? William Michelson has labeled this a distinction between mental congruence and experiential congruence. "Mental congruence exists if an individual *thinks* that particular [environments] will successfully accommodate his personal characteristics, values, and styles of life"; "Experiential congruence, on the other hand, deals with how well the environment *actually* accommodates the characteristics and behavior of people" (emphases mine).[6]

Mental congruence is often the standard used by survey researchers in determining how well an environment works for its residents: What percentage say they like it "very much"? How many plan to move? The use of this standard alone can be misleading, although it is often the only one available; Michelson places it in the proper perspective:[7]

> People cannot be expected to be consistently rational in their preferences. Even though their feelings about environment are usually based to some degree on observation and experience, most people haven't seen or lived in various types of physical environments. Therefore, what is involved in mental congruence is in the nature of hearsay evidence. Yet it is important evidence, since people's beliefs about these relationships affect the objectives they demand.

A contradiction between mental congruence and experiential congruence arises not only where people state a preference for the environment when the experiential evidence indicates incongruence, but also where a dislike of the environment is verbalized when the evidence indicates congruence or where realistic alternatives are unavailable.

Despite the complexity of the concept of environmental fit and the difficulties involved in its empirical use, the frequent discussion and seeming theoretical importance of this concept in the environmental fields dictate a much wider research application. In this chapter, drawing on cases from the household interview sample, patterns of environmental fit in Vällingby are explored. The life-styles of representative Vällingby residents are described and compared with the characteristics of the residential environment discussed in chapter 3; judgments are made in each case about the degree of fit or congruence between the resident and the environment. The study of environmental fit is in its infancy, and no claims are made that the judgments about fit or congruence in Vällingby are more than rather impressionistic assessments based on limited evidence. I hope, however, that my impressions will be of value to the reader in the same way that the informal observations of many other social scientists have been of worth. In each example, much of the evidence used has been included in the case description, and the considerations that went into making the judgments have been noted. The astuteness of the judgments must rest on the fortunate opportunity I was afforded in having access to extensive materials and observations on Swedish life and culture, and on my dual background in both sociology and urban planning, which in the present circumstance seems peculiarly suited to the task.

The household interview survey was designed to collect information on the life-styles of a sample of Vällingby residents, emphasizing those aspects of life-style that involve the use of the local environment. Max Weber, in his early twentieth-century analysis of the German social system, devised the term "life-style" to signify the behavioral style common to social classes or "status groups." [8] The term has come to have a general meaning in contemporary sociology similar to the meaning which the term now has in popular use—the pattern of values, roles, and social behaviors characteristic of a person, family, or other grouping—and its sources are held to include many phenomena in addition to social class, particularly stage of the life cycle and ethnicity.

In recent empirical research within sociology, the concept of life-style has been given a more operational definition—the allocation of time, energy, and money to selected roles, activities, and patterns of living. [9] This definition informed the semistructured questionnaire used in the interviews, designed to elicit information about the respondents' major allocations of time during the day, week, and year, the principal activities engaged in, the location and distance from the dwelling unit of these activities, the environmental facilities used, and social interaction with significant others. Questions also were included concerning environmental attitudes and preferences and socioeconomic background characteristics. In addition to the use of a questionnaire, I queried respondents about their general feelings toward alternative environments, their specific likes and dislikes about the Vällingby environment, their attitudes about moving, and the ways in which, in their view, the environment both limited and facilitated their desired patterns of behavior.

The adult cases which have been picked for discussion (teenagers are considered in a following section) are divided into two groups: those illustrating a high degree of congruence and those illustrating a low degree. A situation of high congruence between a resident and his or her environment would show all or most of the following characteristics.

1. Few social or personal problems manifest which are environmentally related; that is, which would be affected if the environment alone were to change. This judgment requires an assessment of the degree to which particular problems are environmentally sensitive, a question of the greatest importance in the environmental field and about which there is as yet scant information.

2. A feeling of contentment on the part of the resident with the environment as it is, with few environmental limitations or constraints on behavior noted by the resident (or indicated by other evidence), few environmental problems cited, and few desired environmental changes suggested.

3. A high evaluation of the environment by the resident, in comparison with alternatives to it, and no desire to move.

In the determination of a low degree of congruence it is suggested that two considerations rank highest in importance. First is the presence of environmentally related problems or environmental constraints on desired behavior. Many problems and behavioral constraints are only weakly related to environmental characteristics, if at all. Second is the knowledge that an alternative environment exists which presumably would be more appropriate or congruent. If the concept of congruence is to be meaningful, it must be regarded as relative to realistic alternatives, and these alternatives should be stated.

Households Illustrating a High Degree of Congruence with the Environment

The Characteristic Vällingby Household

Despite growing demographic diversity in Vällingby, one household and family type emerged from the demographic analysis as most characteristic of the community today, in the sense of occurring more frequently than any other single type: the family of middle-aged adults whose teenagers are leaving home. This is the type into which the original Vällingby settlers, who came as young families with children, now fall. Within this category, nine of the twenty-five households in the interview sample were remarkably similar in life-style and attitudes toward Vällingby, as well as in age, family size, and class level. The common elements shared by most of these nine cases have been put together into the following composite case, a descriptive sketch of the characteristic Vällingby household. In many respects, such as age, income level, family size, and residential accommodation, this composite household is similar to the typical or statistically average household in Sweden as a whole.

The characteristic Vällingby household consists of two working or lower-middle-class adults in their forties or fifties, with one teenager still living at home. Both adults work, the man going into downtown Stockholm on the subway and the woman working locally. They have lived in their present one- or two-bedroom apartment seven or eight years and own one car, which is used mainly on weekends and for summer vacations.

Almost every day, on the way home from work, food shopping is done by the wife at a small grocery store which is no more than a few hundred yards away; other purchases, such as household supplies, are made several times a week at the neighborhood centrum. Aside from work trips, she and her husband go into downtown Stockholm no more than once or twice a month, often on Saturdays, for shopping or occasionally for entertainment.

In the evening, after supper, the adults take care of household chores, read the Stockholm newspaper, take a walk around the Vällingby area in nice weather, watch about one hour of television, and go to bed by eleven o'clock. On weekends, they visit friends or relatives in the Stockholm area by car, take a long walk, or in spring, summer, and fall, drive to their summer "stuga," or cottage.

The family's summer cottage typically is located by a lake or the sea, several hours drive from Stockholm. It is grouped with perhaps five or six others, forming a small neighborhood; sometimes the parents' cottage is nearby. Trips to the cottage are made as often as possible. The husband may drive to the cottage every nice weekend in the spring, for a change of scene and to do maintenance and repair work on either the cottage or the boat that the couple also own, and the family spends most of its summer vacation there, about three or four weeks. One week of the vacation is spent visiting one set of parents in their home county. Often the teenager past the age of thirteen or fourteen stays in Stockholm for the summer or takes a vacation apart from his family; usually he or she holds a summer job. Every few years the family will take a trip to southern Europe or North Africa, commonly for a week during the colder months.

At least one of the spouses was raised in the Stockholm area and has parents who still live there. Visiting with relatives is common; major holidays such as

Christmas and Easter are almost always spent with close relatives. Apart from relatives, the couple have only a few friends, usually met through work, and the entertaining of friends at home is not common, taking place about once a month or less.

In their three-story, walk-up, garden apartment building none of the neighbors are seen socially, but most of the neighbors on their stairwell— about six households—are known by name and sight. The adults nod or say hello to their neighbors when they happen to pass on the stairs, entry way, or on the street; they feel that the people in the building are "friendly enough."

Neither spouse is a member of any community organization apart from work, neither reads more than a daily newspaper and sometimes a magazine, and regular exercise is limited to occasional walking, bicycle riding (they own several bicycles), and activities having to do with the summer house and boat. Regular participation in cultural or educational activities is rare, and they seldom eat out in restaurants.

The characteristic family likes Vällingby very much, pointing out that it is quiet and near woods and lake, has all the services that are needed, is "settled," and is close to the city. They can think of few problems in Vällingby, except perhaps for some rowdy youths or the growing visibility of alcoholics in the centrums; these phenomena are regarded as problems in the abstract, not as serious social problems which directly affect their lives.

Though they have no plans to move, they would like to have a larger apartment. There is nowhere else they realistically would rather live than in the Stockholm area: "Of course, it would be nice to live in a small town or farm, but we wouldn't be able to find work there." It might also be desirable to live in a single-family detached house, they feel, but it would be much more work, and they might have to give up their summer cottage. They talk of living during their retirement years at the summer cottage, keeping a small apartment in town so they can be near their children.

In summary, the characteristic Vällingby household is quite home- and family-centered. Outside activities for the adults revolve mainly around work and summer cottage. Their life is not culturally or intellectually rich by upper-middle-class standards, and their social life is focused on extended-family members and a few friends from work and perhaps childhood.

The spheres of work, home, and leisure seem well integrated and balanced. Both adults work, yet not excessively; each holds only one job, they are not driving to "get ahead" in a career, and they appear to have, and themselves believe they have, adequate time off from work during the week and in the course of a year for home and recreational pursuits. It is relatively easy for them to get to and from work each day. Moreover, the relatively small amount of time spent on home upkeep, because the apartment is rented and limited in size, does not unduly conflict with work hours, or with leisure and recreational pursuits. Indeed, the family is able to focus a rather high proportion of its time and energies on the summer cottage; it provides a complete change of life-setting for about 8 to 10 percent of the year, with such recreational activities as fishing, boating, swimming, hiking, and wild-food gathering. The family appears relaxed and contented with life, and there seems adequate time for parent-child contact.

By all accounts, Vällingby works very well for this family. It is near the city, which offers abundant work opportunities, but not really of it; the family values highly the natural, nonurban qualities of the Vällingby environment. Apartment living combined with easily accessible services—the most important of which is public transportation—give the family a relatively large amount of time which can be disposed of as it desires. While the upper-middle-class family might use this time for cultural or intellectual pursuits, for which there are many opportunities in Stockholm, the working-class family chooses a different pattern: relaxation, informal socializing with family and friends, and outdoor recreational activities.

The characteristic family thus seems highly congruent with the Vällingby environment. Though such families are enamored of the idea of a small town, the city is willingly chosen because it provides a higher standard of living; they do not, realistically, want to live anywhere else. There is little or no clash between the residential environment in which they live and their own interests, attitudes, and desires.

The great majority (twenty-one out of twenty-five) of the respondent households seemed to be as congruent with Vällingby as the composite case just described. Within this majority, however, there was widespread variation in life-style and stage of the life cycle, as the following six examples illustrate.

The Working Mother of Young Children. While the working mother of older children has become a common figure in all advanced societies, what is not yet so common is the working mother of very young children. Swedish women differ in their views on this, many feeling that the mother should be with her children full time until they at least reach school age. A growing number of younger Swedish women, however, either out of desire or necessity, return to work when their children are still infants. Swedish day-care centers will take children after the age of seven months; ordinarily, in addition, a woman's job is held for her until the child reaches that age. It is typical for her then to return to work, although only to part-time work until the child is older. Many other concessions also are made to the working mother in

Sweden, such as time off to care for sick children and the unlimited paid sick leave granted to all Swedes.

Although the government has increased its subsidies to day-care centers in recent years, spaces in the centers are still in short supply and are assigned on the basis of priority, with the highest priority going to the mother who has to work, either because she has no husband to support her or because the family is poor. The middle-class working woman, who wants to work but does not have to, is given the lowest priority. One such woman in a sample household, for example, had been unable to get a space for her child, and both she and her husband switched to part-time work (two and one-half days a week) so that they could share equally in childrearing. But they were having difficulty holding their jobs; both employers were putting pressure on them to return to full-time status. The man finally had to change jobs; the woman was on the verge of changing. For them it was a fortunate circumstance to be living in a metropolitan area with a large labor market; their chances of finding suitable employment were not hopeless.

A large number, perhaps a majority, of the mothers in Vällingby hold full-time or part-time jobs. In the following example the working mother is unmarried but has been living with the same man for about five years. The unmarried couple has become a common and accepted feature of Swedish life in the last few decades; it is not regarded as unusual or generally frowned upon, as it is still in the U.S., though typically the couple marry with the birth of a child. In this case major reasons in their remaining unwed may have been their desire to be assured space in a day-care center, as well as to enjoy housing and other benefits that come to unwed mothers in Sweden. Information was not available on the prevalence in Sweden of situations like this or on the degree to which it is regarded as a problem by Swedish authorities.

Miss M. and Mr. J., a very attractive couple in their twenties, live with their two-and-one-half-year-old daughter in a tastefully decorated second-floor apartment near Vällingby centrum; only Miss M.'s name appears on the door and in the landlord's records. Born and raised in Stockholm, she has worked part-time as a clerk in an electrical equipment factory in Vällingby since her daughter was six months old; unless the weather is terrible, she rides her bicycle to work. On the way to work she drops off her daughter at the day-care center, located just a few hundred yards from her apartment, and picks the child up again on her return from work about 1:00 in the afternoon. The child is given lunch at the center. Except during nap-time, Miss M. devotes the rest of the afternoon to the child.

Mr. J. grew up in a small town in the center of Sweden; he also is employed in Vällingby, as a skilled factory worker, and rides his bike to the job in all but the worst weather. Arriving home from work about 4:30 in the afternoon, he devotes an hour or more each day to playing with his daughter. The child is in bed by about 6:30 P.M. or 7:00 P.M., and the couple then are able to spend the evening in adult pursuits.

Miss M. and Mr. J. are a very active and social couple; they entertain once or twice a week friends or relatives, some of whom live nearby. Several times a week they go into Stockholm to see her mother, to shop, or for recreational purposes, sometimes leaving their daughter with her mother while they spend an evening on the town.

In a neighboring district, Mr. J. tends a small garden plot during the warmer months; on the plot is a little garden hut where it is possible for them to sleep over for a night or two. He also goes fishing often, in a small boat which is kept at a dock in Lake Mälaren. They have no summer cottage; their vacations are usually taken in the spring or fall, often consisting of a trip to southern Europe, always with their daughter. His parents in central Sweden are visited once or twice a year.

The couple have a car, not used much in Vällingby. Mr. J. would just as soon not have it; Miss M. finds it a big help, however, in transporting her daughter, together with the baby equipment, to such places as her mother's and their friends' homes in other parts of Stockholm. The car is used regularly for shopping—a weekly trip to a supermarket in a neighboring district.

In good weather, they often ride their bicycles around Vällingby for pleasure, and they also take long walks. Every few weeks during the winter months they go swimming in the Vällingby pool. Neither partner belongs to any club or organization; they read little more than the daily newspaper.

The neighbors do not figure at all in their lives. The couple say hello to perhaps four of the neighbors who live in their stairwell; they don't even know who lives in two of the dwellings. "We just want to see people we like, not those one happens to live next to."

Miss M. and Mr. J. like Vällingby very much, and feel that Vällingby is an especially good place to bring up children. "Everything is here: the centrum, the subway, swimming at the lake, the sports hall, doctors' offices." They can think of no facilities which should be added.

A single-family house is not a dream of theirs. "Things are always breaking down." "You have to be social with your neighbors." "My sister, who has a single-family house, is having a fight with her neighbors over putting up a fence."

This unmarried couple seem very well matched with the Vällingby environment. Miss M. is able to hold a part-time job yet still devote a large amount of uninterrupted time to her daughter; Mr. J.'s short commute allows him a relatively large block of free time. Vällingby's recreational facilities enable them to keep physically active, while Stockholm is near enough for regular diversions from their normal milieu. Friends and relatives are within easy access. They have the money to travel to foreign countries. And they obviously value highly the anonymity of apartment living, with its relative lack of neighboring.

By all appearances, Miss M. and Mr. J. make good parents, and they express deep satisfaction with life. It is doubtful if they would find their situation improved in almost any other type of residential environment.

The Nonworking Mother of Young Children. While apartment living is felt to be desirable for many working mothers, because of low maintenance and the accessibility of services, this way of life is commonly thought, especially in the U.S., not to be as satisfactory for the nonworking mother as living in a single-family house in a low-density suburb, owing to the latter's larger dwelling- and private-yard spaces. But the residential services and facilities provided in Vällingby are as beneficial to the housewife-mother as they are to the working mother and help to compensate for the lack of private space. The full-time housewife-mother in Vällingby is often a little defensive about her roles in life, however, feeling that some look down on her for not going out to work; the social pressure for women to hold jobs outside the home has become strong in Sweden within the last few decades.

Mr. and Mrs. D., a personable couple in their thirties, have lived in their apartment since 1966. With two children, ages six and two, they were fortunate in that, as their family size increased, it was possible to enlarge their apartment by breaking out a wall into an adjoining unit. Mr. D. has a low-skilled office job in the Vällingby area; he walks to work.

The older boy goes to play school during winter mornings; it is a stone's throw from the apartment. He spends much of his time outdoors. Since the age of four he has been allowed out on his own but only within the confines of the large, pedestrian-only superblock which the apartment buildings surround. This is his ''yard'' and contains playfields and play equipment, supervised play programs, and guided activities in sports, crafts, and hobbies of various kinds. There are many others in his age group within the superblock neighborhood.

The younger boy goes outside with his mother almost every day to play in the special ''under six'' playground. The mothers are friendly outside and chat on the park benches while they are watching their children at play, though they seldom get together socially in each other's apartments. When Mrs. D. has to go shopping, she uses the baby-sitting service in the park for up to three hours each morning. She visits her mother in inner

Stockholm almost every week; her mother also helps with the baby-sitting.

After the children go to bed at 8:30 P.M., the couple read newspapers, talk, and watch more television than most Vällingby families. While they seldom entertain at home in the evenings, they do entertain during the day on weekends, or visit other families, taking along their children. Their friends, mostly former work associates, live in other parts of Stockholm. Most of the people in their building are known and liked but none are seen socially. Mr. and Mrs. D. go into downtown Stockholm only for an occasional errand. Before the children were born, Mrs. D. was in a gymnastics club and Mr. D. in a running club; he still runs several times a week, but they no longer belong to any clubs or organizations. On weekends they take walks, swim in the Vällingby pool, perhaps go to one of the centrums to look around.

The one car in the household is used on weekends and for the summer holiday. Summer vacation is spent either at the summer cottage of Mrs. D.'s family in Dalarna or at the family place of Mr. D. in Värmland, both in the central part of Sweden.

Mr. and Mrs. D. like Vällingby very much: "It is near nature, yet also close to the city, to work, and to schools. And it is a very fine place to raise children." They are well satisfied with the facilities in Vällingby and can think of little else they could use. "One thing that would help is a teenage girl to babysit in the evening." Mrs. D. knows no teenage girls in her neighborhood. Other teenagers, however, are all too obvious: "The only problems in Vällingby are the youth who hang around, break things, write on the walls." Mrs. D. finds riding the subway from Stockholm in the late evenings unpleasant because of the teenagers hanging around in the cars and at the stations.

The apartment, the outside services, and the Vällingby milieu enable this couple to have a relaxed, informal, familistic life-style involving a large amount of parent-child interaction. While they profit from the standard of living which a metropolitan area can provide, they express no need for downtown cultural facilities or any desire for an urbane way of life. They are close to their own families, seem to have as many friends as they want, and say they are very content with their lives in Vällingby. The children are growing up in an extremely safe environment, with adequate playmates and constant adult supervision. By all accounts, Vällingby works as well for this nonworking mother as it does for her working counterpart.

The Young Childless Couple. What about the young couple without children? They are thought to face a bleak existence in the family-oriented U.S. suburb; increasingly in North America such couples have become relegated to singles' or childless communities where their nonfamilistic life-style has a greater chance to thrive. In Vällingby, however, childless couples are integrated into the same environment that families with children share.

Miss B., a tall, attractive blond, is in her late twenties and, like a growing number of Swedes, has chosen not to marry. She has lived with her "man"* (he was not present for the interview) for several years in an apartment next to Vällingby centrum near her middle-class office job. It takes her less than ten minutes to walk to work.

After growing up in a medium-sized town in the northern part of Sweden, Miss B. came to Stockholm in her late teens. The first few years were lonely ones, but she does not regret having moved to the city. Before moving to Vällingby, she lived in many different places in the inner city and the western suburbs.

Miss B. has a socially active, cosmopolitan life-style, in common with many other childless Stockholm women at her age-level. At least every two weeks Miss B. goes into downtown Stockholm for shopping, movies, and restaurants. She and her man have a very large circle of friends, both separately and together. They do a great amount of visiting and entertaining, often giving small dinner parties, though they are not at all neighborly and indeed do not even know any of their neighbors' names. Through her place of work she is a member of a number of hobby clubs, and she regularly plays squash and tennis, goes swimming in the swim hall, and takes pleasure walks around the Vällingby area.

Miss B. and her man jointly own a car, which is used mainly on weekends. But her pride and joy is their sailboat, which is docked in the Vällingby area. She beams when discussing it and the long weekends and summer holidays when she and her man tour the islands of the Stockholm archipelago, often with another couple. Another facet of their social life is connected with the boat club, which sponsors various social events.

Miss B. comes from a family of five children. Most years she visits her family four times, at holidays and for one or two weeks each summer. (She usually takes an added vacation week to southern Europe each winter or spring.) Though Miss B. was raised in a familistic environment, to which she maintains strong ties, she does not plan in the near future to have children. "When you are able to choose whether or not to have children, it is not easy to have them." Children would mean a loss of freedom for her; her life-style would suddenly change. She is well aware of this through many friends who do have children.

Miss B. considers her life idyllic at the moment. She loves Vällingby, and can think of no place she would rather live. Vällingby is beautiful; it is near the city, yet it is a little like a small town: "You come to recognize many people, here, even though you don't actually know them. This

*The word "man" is used in Swedish to refer to both a husband and a steady male companion.

isn't the case in the city, where everyone is a stranger. It was also dark and dirty living in the city, and too far from the woods."

In advanced societies Miss B's life-style has become the dream of many modern young people: socially active, combining city life with vigorous outdoor activities, reasonably affluent, relaxed and informal, and free of major responsibilities. As fertility rates drop well below the replacement level, her disinterest in children may present a long-run problem for Swedish society, and her own future may not be as rosy as her life at present: middle-aged and retirement years without offspring and perhaps without a husband. But for now her life is full, and it appears that Vällingby is the ideal environment for her; it is hard to think of ways it could be improved upon.

The Single Pensioner. The old person living alone has become a common phenomenon around the world; often she or he is living in a situation in which the quality of life is pathetically low and in environments where other life stages are not common. At first, elderly persons were rare in Vällingby; the community was designed mainly for young families. Over the years pensioners have moved into the smaller apartments, especially in the high-rise buildings next to the centrums. Vällingby also has a significant number of "service houses," apartment hotels especially designated for old people which contain provisions for, among other things, nursing care and short-term convalescence. This enables the elderly, when they become sick and handicapped, to remain near their friends. If elderly persons are able to take care of themselves, however, it is still most common for them to have their own apartments. Here, too, many outside services are provided to elderly apartment dwellers in Sweden which permit them to better manage this desired way of living. These services include home visitors to help with cleaning and shopping, taxi service, and hot meals brought to the dwelling unit.

Miss V., in her seventies, lives alone in a cheerful and airy one-room apartment on the seventh floor of a high-rise building facing one of the larger district centrums; she has lived there seven years. Born and raised in Finland, she lost her parents when she was very young and was brought up by relatives. After coming to Sweden in 1949, already in her fifties, she worked as a housekeeper for a doctor and his family with five children in downtown Stockholm before she became handicapped (bad leg) and was forced to retire. Miss V. never married, but the five children she worked with treat her as a "second mother"; she has no known relatives living in Sweden.

Because of the elevator in her apartment building, Miss V. is able to go out to the centrum each day for shopping; she used to go farther before her legs got worse, including into downtown Stockholm. She now has a taxi card which entitles her (because of her age and handicap) to one round-trip taxi ride each week within the Stockholm area for only fifty cents each way. The taxi is used to visit friends as well as to run errands. Another card enables her to use a taxi (for fifty cents) at any time for the purpose of visiting a doctor.

Miss V. cooks her own meals, but once each week a city employee comes in for two hours to clean her apartment. The city service-worker also helps with the wash, though the laundry is done mainly by another Finnish family that lives in the building. She is friendly but not social with the neighbors on either side of her and knows few others in the building ("It is so large, and people move a lot"). Evenings are spent reading newspapers, books, and magazines, and listening to the radio; she does handwork of various kinds, such as sewing or knitting, while radio-listening. She has no TV and doesn't want one: "a person can go kind of crazy if she sits alone and watches it for a long time. . . . if something special is on, I can always go to my friends to watch it."

Every two weeks a bus picks her up and takes her for the day to a leisure center in Stockholm for handicapped persons. She has lunch at the center, watches an entertainment program, has her feet and hair taken care of by trained service people, and sometimes participates in a market for the sale and exchange of crafts and other handmade goods. Several times a month Miss V. attends the meeting of the pensioners' association in the Vällingby area, where the elderly talk, dance, and drink coffee. The association used to meet at the youth center; this was outgrown, however, and the group now meets in one of the pensioners' service houses.

Miss V. likes Vällingby very much and prefers it to the city. "Everything is nice here," especially the pedestrian walkways (she used to walk a lot), the many services which she uses, fresh air, and being close to the water. She is concerned about the youth in Vällingby and about the growing number of alcoholics, but they haven't bothered her directly. "It is much better since they put on the extra block patrolmen, especially around the subways."

It is hard to find defects in Miss V's living situation. When she no longer is able to take care of herself, she will have to move but probably will be able to stay within the Vällingby area. Until that time, she can continue to take pride in her relative self-sufficiency. She says she seldom feels lonely, which is quite remarkable for an old lady with no relatives, who lives alone in a high-rise apartment building in a foreign country to which she immigrated in late middle-age. Much of her sense of contentment is due to the services she receives, which are available in most urban areas in Sweden, but the special characteristics of the Vällingby environment seem also to play an important role.

The Divorcée and The Bachelor. The flexibility of Vällingby as an environment suitable for a wide range of life-styles, life stages, and family structures becomes even more evident in the final two congruent examples to be considered: a divorcée and a bachelor. They differ from the previous subjects in that they would prefer to live in a residential environment other than Vällingby, yet they say they are reasonably content with the community and seem to have few problems living there.

Mrs. F. has lived in her first-floor apartment since 1967. A gracious, soft-spoken woman in her late thirties, she lives with her twelve-year-old daughter and works as a secretary for a large firm in downtown Stockholm. Her former husband lives in the Stockholm area, and their daughter sees him often (at the time of the interview, the daughter was with her father on a trip to England).

Though born on a farm, Mrs. F. has no desire to return to one, much preferring the culture and amenities of an urban milieu. She has lived in Stockholm for the past fifteen years and would not want to live anywhere else.

She has no car and feels no strong need for one, preferring instead to go by subway, bus, and taxi; she also walks and rides her bike on weekends for recreation and pleasure. Shopping is done at the local neighborhood store and is organized so Mrs. F. ordinarily does it only once a week.

Mrs. F. has an active life after work. She takes language courses several nights a week, visits friends who live in other parts of Stockholm, sometimes stays in town to go to the theater or restaurant, reads quite a bit (getting books from the main library in downtown Stockholm), and is a member of an art appreciation club at her work place. Sometimes her daughter joins her in town for an evening out. Mrs. F. frequently comes to town on weekends and sometimes visits her family in nearby Uppsala.

The neighbors are seldom seen and then only to say hello to; there is one neighbor that she can use for such neighborly purposes as keeping a key to let in a delivery man. Mrs. F. expresses some concern about the lack of neighboring in Vällingby. "It would be nice if people here were more friendly" she says, "but they work long hours."

With her daughter, Mrs. F. spends summer vacations in a small apartment which is rented at a well-known Swedish resort town on an island in the Baltic Sea.

Mrs. F. likes Vällingby very much, especially the natural setting in which it is located. Yet she says she is so involved in downtown activities that she would prefer to live in the inner city. "There are more shops

there, and I could walk to work—spend less time on transportation."
Moreover, there is very little to hold her in Vällingby—"the only thing
I would miss is the nature, and I could always come out here from time to
time to see that." Mrs. F. had recently had a chance to get an apartment
in the city and wanted to move, but her daughter was opposed. "My
daughter loves it in Vällingby and has all her friends here." Her daughter
is involved in many Vällingby activities and, in common with most
others in her age group, finds the environment well suited to her own
needs and interests.

Mrs. F. has little interest in a single-family house. "It would be nice,
but not in my present situation; it would be too much work to take care of
it." She feels much safer in an apartment, preferring, in fact, to live on a
higher floor than her present one. In a single-family house she would
feel compelled to lock up tightly each night because of a generalized fear
of darkness (*mörkrädd*—a fear, not uncommon in Sweden, which seems
more related to the long winter nights than to the crime rate, which is
relatively low).

The Vällingby environment has presented Mrs. F. with few difficulties in
holding a job, leading an active social and cultural life, and raising her
daughter alone; indeed the environment appears to have been beneficial in
easing the transition from married to single life. Nevertheless, Mrs. F's
downtown cultural and activity orientation pulls her toward central Stockholm; when her daughter leaves home, she will probably make the move. At
the present time, in view of the daughter's needs and interests, one could
reasonably conclude that Vällingby is a workable compromise which best fits
the differing situations of the two family members.

Mr. U., a slight and diffident middle-aged bachelor, was also raised in
nearby Uppsala but has lived for ten years in his present sparsely furnished and meagerly decorated apartment on the fourth floor of a high-
rise building. Having previously worked as a baker, he now holds a low-
skilled job in an electrical equipment company, to which he commutes in
about fifteen minutes by car. He drives to shopping two or three times a
week; local shopping is of limited value for him because he is a health-
food devotee and must use the larger shops and health-food stores in the
main centrums.

After work Mr. U. comes home, runs a little in the woods or takes a
bike ride in nice weather for exercise, reads the newspapers and an occasional book, and watches TV on the average of one hour per evening.
About once a week he goes into Stockholm, perhaps to a restaurant and
the movies. Twice a month he visits a friend in another part of Stockholm
or has a friend over to his flat.

Though friendly, Mr. U. is not an outgoing person, nor is he a member
of any club or organization; he never has parties or other group social

activities in his dwelling unit. No one in his apartment building is known to him except for the neighbors on either side, whom he knows only by sight. While he feels it would be nice if people in the building were more social, he seldom feels lonely and never feels bored.

Mr. U.'s main interest is his summer cottage, about one-half hour's drive away, and he goes there as often as he can. He is proud of the flowers, potatoes, and vegetables he grows there. While there, he socializes some with the six neighbors who live in the vicinity, especially over work projects, in contrast to his social life in the apartment building. Part of his summer vacation is spent at the cottage; the other part is spent visiting his parents in Sweden's far north. Christmas is spent with his sister in Uppsala, and Mr. U. is able to take a short vacation abroad every few years.

Mr. U. likes Vällingby very much; he feels it is well planned, and especially likes the swimming nearby. He can't think of any problems in Vällingby. Living in the city would be undesirable because he doesn't like crowds and traffic. He would prefer to live in a smaller town, however, perhaps a town of about 30,000 population in Dalarna (a beautiful folk culture and resort county northwest of Stockholm), and in a detached house with a beautiful garden. With such a house he would sell his present summer house, no longer having a need for it. He has no plans to leave Stockholm, however, because it would be difficult for him to get a job elsewhere.

Mr. U. is a "loner"; his life seems relatively limited, yet his summer place gives him a quality of living which few members of the urban working class possess in other countries. He has few ties to Vällingby; his apartment appears mainly to be a place to "sleep over" in connection with his job. Yet by all accounts Vällingby works well for him, and he has no complaints. Mr. U. might be happier in a smaller town; but it is doubtful if his situation there would be any richer, for he would be giving up the combined variety and diversity of city, suburb, and country which now shape his life.

Households Illustrating a Low Degree of Congruence with the Environment

The Ruralists

Many of the residents of Vällingby grew up in small towns and rural areas, locales which have a revered place in Swedish culture and tradition. These residents still hold strong attachments to their places of origin and visit them often; it is common for their parents or other relatives still to be living there. But most of these urban migrants have made their peace with the city and with an urban way of life. Some have rejected the parochialism of small-town life, in addition to the lack of opportunity there. They enjoy visiting "back home," but they would never consider living there again. Others have made an ideological compromise; they would rather live "in the country" but only if they could have their highly valued "good job" and present standard of living. Jobs in small towns are a special problem for women, particularly those who wish to work only part-time.

Both the rejectors and the compromisers have typically embraced an urban way of life without any difficulties, even if, perhaps, without much enthusiasm. They have become adapted to living among strangers, to having little neighborhood life, to maintaining a network of friends spread over a large geographic area. They have developed a taste for urban public services and for the more rapid pace of life; a tolerance for the higher levels of noise and dirt in the air and for the occasional groups of rowdy youths. While they do not want to live "in the city," where it is too crowded, noisy, and dirty, they don't mind living near the city. Only a handful of Swedes truly desire inner-city, urban living; indeed the percentage of such people may be smaller than in most other advanced societies. Vällingby, along with many other outer areas and suburbs of Stockholm, is the kind of "near city" environment they find desirable, though many would prefer a medium-sized town of perhaps 50,000 to 100,000 population, an environment which is much like that of the outer city but without the proximity of the inner city.

Even the people who grew up in the city tend to hold views of the city similar to the small-town emigrant; they don't like the "real" city and they have a "strong positive feeling" about small-town and rural life in Sweden, a feeling which is deeply imbedded in Swedish cultural tradition. Yet they generally are well adapted to the metropolitan area and have no particular desire to move.

Some of the emigrants from rural areas and small towns remain unadjusted to the urban way of life, as the following case illustrates. Such people feel uncomfortable in the city; their hearts lie in the countryside. For reasons of employment, they feel forced to stay. Give them any kind of a decent job in the country, and they will leave tomorrow—so they say, at least.

Family H. has lived for the past two and one-half years in a three-room (plus kitchen) apartment in a three-story garden apartment building near Vällingby centrum; they have one remaining child at home, a teenager. Three other children have left home, but all still live in the Vällingby area and frequently drop in on their parents. When all the children were at home, the family lived in a four room apartment in a neighboring district, moving to their present lower rent dwelling when the family size dropped; they much preferred their previous location because it was closer to the Grimsta woods. They have no car, and keep several large dogs.

Both adults are in their forties. Mr. H. works as a printer in downtown Stockholm; he takes the subway to work. Mrs. H. is employed by the government as a home visitor in Vällingby with old people. They are very eager to return to Norrland, where they grew up, but it would be very hard for Mrs. H. to get a job there. Having been in Stockholm since 1949, they still visit Norrland "every chance we can get" (once or twice a year).

When their children were growing up, their parents had almost no leisure or recreational life. They never "went out or did anything for fun," just stayed home and raised the children. Life was very hard. Now that the children have grown up, it is much more fun. They are members of a folk (*gammal*) dancing group and go dancing several times a week; through this group they have met friends (also from Norrland) who live in the Vällingby area. "Perhaps we can begin to drop in on them, just like in a small town." They almost never entertain friends at home, although the boys had parties when they were younger.

The three sons (the fourth child is a daughter) all play musical instruments. When they were growing up, they had many parties. The neighbors would complain about the noise, "But what can you do?"—the walls are thin. They see very little of the neighbors socially and have only been in the apartment of one who keeps big dogs, as they themselves do.

Mr. and Mrs. H. dislike Stockholm and apartment living. "What kind of place is it where everybody has extra locks and security chains on their doors?" "People aren't friendly, here." "They'll come up and sit right next to you on the subway, even though there are plenty of other empty seats—they want to be near you, but not get to know you. The same thing happens at the beach." "A young person can sit alone all night in a pub, here, and no one will speak to him. That never happens in Norrland—everyone is milling around, very friendly. . . . People aren't kind to children here, either."

"Apartment living is not good, especially for kids. Kids who live in high houses seem to want to destroy things—they have no sense of ownership." The man used to pass through a middle-class, detached-house area on the way from work; it was very clean, but when he got to the Vällingby line, he noticed a difference: "People don't seem to care when they have an apartment."

The woman adds: "It takes a special kind of person to live like this"—not the kind she's used to. "The women here clean their apartments over and over again, they seem to have nothing better to do."

Neither parent has much good to say about Vällingby. "People have no concern for others here, they throw stuff around, destroy things." "Everything must be locked up; if not, someone is sure to steal it."

"There are many fine flats here, but they are too small. You can't have friends in; the children can't play at home or have their friends over—they are forced to play outside too much. Nobody goes in much for activities or social life here; people are too tired from work. Also they have their TV, and a car so they can go other places. Gangs of boys hang around the fields and the center. They scare the old people. The community tries to do a lot for teenagers, setting up activities and all, but the kids don't care. It is lucky our boys had their music; otherwise they probably would have gotten into trouble." "And the schools are much too big; the classes are too large."

"It is not like this at all in Norrland. There are all kinds of things to do there. Nature, the woods provide all the activities that a young person could desire. When we were growing up, we didn't have these problems. Even in Sundsvall [a large town in Norrland] you still walk to see your friends and walk to nature—it is very close by."

This is an excellent example of an unreconstructed rural-based family. With their love of the outdoors, their strong extended family ties, and their preference for an easy, informal kind of socializing, they would probably be happier in a small-town or rural atmosphere. One can picture them in a rather isolated old house where they would have adequate space for the large family, the relatives, the dogs, and the music. They appreciate virtually none of the advantages of city living except the higher material standard of living—which is enough, however, to have kept them for the last twenty-five years from actually returning to the small town. At the same time, many aspects of city living—such as anonymity—are special targets of antipathy for them.

On the other hand, these antiurban views were less strong in the wife than in the husband, and they were very weak among the children. Mrs. H. was reluctant to share all of her husband's antiurban diatribe; she realized, I think, that her situation in Norrland would not be as good as his might be. She especially appreciated the services that were available to her in Vällingby. The children showed little enthusiasm to go to Norrland, although they "wouldn't mind going there if. . . ." In fact, they were quite favorable toward Vällingby; the two older boys and the girl had chosen to take apartments in the Vällingby area when they left home (the girl was living in an apartment hotel for single people at the time of the interview).

None of the other respondents whom I interviewed, or any of the informants with whom I spoke, shared the very negative views of Vällingby held by this couple.

The Lonely

It is often said that an apartment house is a lonely place; people live so close to one another, yet there can be such great social distance. Though only three respondents admitted to being lonely, loneliness was thought by many respondents and informants to be quite common in Vällingby. Loneliness appears mainly to be a problem, naturally, for those who live alone, such as pensioners, and for those who are alone much of the day, such as housewives. In addition, it is a problem for those who have difficulty, for one reason or another, in making friends. In the city one must actively make friends; primary relationships are not naturally a part of the fabric of society through familiarity and tradition, as has been the case in most communities in history.

Family L. consists of four persons living in a sunny and attractive two-bedroom corner apartment on the second floor of a garden apartment building. Two children, a boy of nineteen and a girl of twenty-one, still lived at home; they had been given the two bedrooms, and the parents slept on a daybed in the living room. Mrs. L. was very apologetic about how crowded things were. They have lived in this area for about twenty years.

Both parents were born and raised in Finland, although the woman has been in Sweden since she was twenty-two years of age. She holds two jobs—as a home helper for the old and the sick, and as a cleaning woman in a nearby office building (several hours each evening). They have no car, and she often walks to work in nice weather instead of using public transportation; her husband rides his bike.

Her parents died years ago and she has no relatives in Sweden; her husband has some relatives but they don't see them very often. They used to have more friends than they do now; "It is hard to make new friends here." On the Finnish island of Åland they have a summer cottage, where they take their vacations. The husband cultivates a small garden plot in the Vällingby area during the warmer months they are in Stockholm.

Mrs. L's major concern is loneliness. She would like to go out in the evenings, but her husband isn't interested. "He has his people at work to talk to; often he is working on his other job in the evenings and on weekends." "I would go out alone, but I don't know where to go.... the only thing a woman can do here alone is play Bingo.... No one ever talks to you.... Swedes are so silent... they only talk to each other when they go abroad.... Vällingby needs places where people can go and meet one another.... I wish people were more friendly here. It would be much more fun if people could just drop in; several weeks ago one of my husband's work friends dropped over. We had such a good time."

Mrs. L. is not a member of any club or organization ("no time for activities like that"). She goes into Stockholm once every few months at the most. She feels it is very limiting not to have a car—hard to get to see

friends and to get into Stockholm. To make matters worse, Mrs. L. encounters many lonely people on her job helping old, sick people in their
homes; and her cleaning job is at night, when the office workers have all
left.

The family's cottage offers little relief. It is far from Vällingby and
isolated, with little chance for neighborly contacts. "We used to go many
different places in Sweden for our vacation; now we go only to our summer cottage because there is so much work to do there."

Her son and daughter suffer the same problems that Mrs. L. does. The
daughter has few friends. "There is no place here for her to go and meet
people." She typically stays at home in the evenings and watches television. "She should get away more from her parents," her mother says.
She works in downtown Stockholm at a low-paying clerical job but hates
to ride the subway; it makes her nervous—she feels everybody is looking
at her. The son also hangs around home a lot; he is in no clubs or organizations. At the moment, he has no job, but soon he expects to enter his
required period of military service; he has very few friends.

In spite of her troubles, Mrs. L. likes Vällingby very much. There is
no other place she would rather live; she and her husband have never
talked about any other place. She likes the woods nearby, the services
provided in Vällingby, and she feels that her apartment is nice.

At the root of Mrs. L's problem is probably her inability to make and keep
friends, or the inability of the couple to make friends, a difficulty aggravated
by their immigrant status and disadvantaged background in comparison with
the Swedish neighbors. Her loneliness is compounded by a rather cool relationship with her husband, by her lack of relatives, by her work situation, and
by the problems of her children. Her situation is certainly not enviable. It
might be improved by an environmental setting in which neighboring was a
more important element in the social structure, but it is easy to misinterpret
the social consequences of such a change. One would think that the inner city
would be worse for her; so, probably, would a farm. A low-density suburb
might provide some relief, if she had the right neighbors, because neighboring
is more common in such settings. She also would be better-off in a small
town, surrounded by relatives and lifelong friends, but now that is obviously
not a realistic alternative for her.

Apart from living in overcrowded quarters, Mrs. L. may be as well-off in
Vällingby as she realistically could be. The ease of home care and proximity
of services remove many burdens from her daily routine. There is variety
in her life—within Vällingby, Stockholm, her work, the summer place—
in marked distinction, for example, to the life of the working-class woman
in the low-density U.S. suburb. At the same time, the environment is
quiet and peaceful; environmental stress is minimal. Mrs. L. indicates, in

her generally favorable evaluation of Vällingby, that she is aware of these comparative advantages; she senses that there are few other places where she would be better-off.

There may well be many lonely people in Vällingby who *would* be much better-off moving to a different environment. The old and the sick may be better-off in pensioners' homes; those who have been uprooted from family and relatives and forced to live in the city may be better-off going back home; some young, single people may be better-off out of city and suburb entirely. The problem of loneliness is a pervasive one in most modern environmental settings, where close friendships are based more on achievement than ascription. Many people are not able to achieve the kind of social network which is necessary to their psychological well-being.

The Upwardly Mobile

Concern about one's status or position in society is a universal phenomenon and often a major component of general feelings of dissatisfaction and discontentment with life. In working- and lower-middle-class residential environments, status concerns seem most strongly associated with persons who feel that they are wrongly placed; they have a firm sense that they really belong in a higher-class environment. If this concern is deep enough, it can color many of their evaluations of environmental quality. Though the persons may be experientially as well adapted to the environment as could reasonably be expected at their income level, they are not mentally and attitudinally adapted and indicate strong negative opinions about their place of residence.

Mrs. B., a well-dressed woman in her thirties, lives on the third floor of a garden apartment building with her husband, one teenager, and two younger children who are six and nine; her husband works as a service maintenance man for an equipment company. She works part-time as a "day mother," taking in about five young children each day during the week.

Having moved from another section of Vällingby to get a larger dwelling unit, she has lived in her present apartment for two years. It was very friendly where she used to live. In her new apartment she has made few friends and feels lonely; there are few other mothers with young children in the area. She wishes the neighbors here were more social. Mrs. B. has many friends outside of her local neighborhood, however, and the family has an active social life; also, her parents live nearby, and she sees or phones them several times a week. The family has one car, which the husband drives to work. She has little need for a car during the week.

In the evenings Mrs. B. takes an English course (she has a strong interest in languages), listens to semiclassical music on her new hi-fi, and spends a great deal of time with handwork—sewing and making dresses.

She does not have strong cosmopolitan interests, such as the theater or downtown restaurants, and goes into center-city Stockholm about once a month. Along with *Dagens Nyheter*, one of Stockholm's more intellectually oriented newspapers, she reads about four magazines a week.

A few hours' drive away, the family has a cottage by a lake where she spends the entire summer, plus weekends in spring and fall. The cottage is in a community of twenty-five families, most of whom are middle-class; the families have an active neighborhood life. She loves it at the summer place, enjoying the nature, peace and quiet, and informal socializing, and would like to live there all year.

Mrs. B. doesn't especially like either Vällingby or apartment living and her great desire is to move to a detached house. She wants the freedom to fix her house the way she wants, to have a yard, to not have to be concerned about bothering people in the next apartment. And she wants to own it. In her own mind she often compares the summer place with her apartment, much to the latter's disadvantage. She speaks of the opportunity to fix house and yard, of freedom and privacy, and of the values which come with home ownership. If the family ever did get a detached house, she says she would sell the summer place (feeling that the detached house would serve many of the needs now filled by the summer cottage) and that she would have to get a second car.

Her criticisms of Vällingby stem from the same set of values that prompt her desire for a detached house. People in Vällingby in general, she feels, are not much concerned about taking care of things in the residential environment because they don't own them. This leads to graffiti, trampling the vegetation, litter, etc. Vällingby is not a very good place to raise children, she maintains, because they learn bad things from other kids; in a detached house you can better control the child's play environment and social contacts. Mrs. B. doesn't like to walk around Vällingby at night because of her fears about "gangs of youths"; she does walk around if she has to, however.

In summary, Mrs. B. is living at a working-class standard of living, in a partly working-class environment, but she has middle-class interests and values. While it is clear that she could use more space for her relatively large family and for her work as a day mother, and that her neighboring situation is not satisfactory, the roots of her discontent may also rest in her status concerns and aspirations for upward mobility. Mrs. B.'s negative views about Vällingby find scant support in actual conditions or events or in the views of most other residents. She indicated that in her negative opinions she was referring more to apartment areas in general, especially to some of the more recent suburbs, and indicated that she had read in newspapers and magazines the extensive criticisms of these suburbs and that these criticisms affected, and also corresponded with, her own views.

It is probable that her general discontentment would decrease if she had the extra space and "freedom" provided by a single- family house, especially if it were located in a middle-class neighborhood where she had many friends, including other mothers of young children; and if the family could afford the higher standard of living. But it may be that Vällingby is the environment which best fits the family at its present working-class income level. A move now to a single-family house might entail the sale of her summer cottage, the necessary second car could be financially prohibitive, and the costs of adequately furnishing a new and much larger home would probably be out of the couple's financial reach. In such circumstances, located far from public services, Mrs. B. could end up more lonely and discontented than she is now, and in a milieu of single-family houses even her job as a day mother might no longer be possible.

Many families who could afford it have left Vällingby for a single-family home of their own and have never regretted it. One of the first purchases is a second car, which the husband drives to work. Such families take great pride in their homes and gardens; their children have more internal space; and they have a better situation for formal entertaining. Higher-income families will often own a summer cottage in addition. Suburban, middle-class wives in single-family houses are the least likely to work outside the home in Stockholm and the most likely to hold part-time jobs if they do work. This is because they don't have to work for extra income to the same extent as working-class wives; because they have larger families (the opposite of the situation in many other countries, where larger families are found in the working class); and because access to work is poorer and it is more difficult for them to get child-care services (which are typically less plentiful than in the apartment suburbs).

Families I have talked to that have made such a move clearly prefer their single-family-home situation. Though they look back on Vällingby with some nostalgia ("It was a nice place to start a family"), they feel it is not for their type of person.

A variation within the upwardly mobile category is the family that moves from a Vällingby apartment to a larger and more expensive apartment in the inner city of Stockholm. Such families are usually upper-middle-class cosmopolites, with few children and a working, often career-oriented, wife. Though their destination is different, they hold views of Vällingby which are very similar to those of the suburban-bound families.

Because of the severe housing shortage after the war, it was sometimes the case that higher-class families found themselves housed in Vällingby apartments simply because they were the only dwelling units available. The status discrepancy they faced there sometimes engendered a bad taste about Vällingby which has lasted long after the move away. Vällingby was, after all, a mostly "public housing" suburb. These families didn't "belong" there; their stay was temporary, and they left as soon as they could. Many other higher-class families have stayed in Vällingby, however, and among the postwar Stockholm apartment suburbs it ranks highest in class status, though the majority of residents are working- and lower-middle-class.

The Teenager in Vällingby

The teenagers in the household sample expressed a higher level of content-ment than their parents. Only one of the teenagers whom I interviewed stated that he was bored in Vällingby, and the great majority indicated that they would be happy to live in Vällingby as adults, although they felt that at their age it was rather unrealistic of them to state a preference of this kind. A few preferred to live "in the city," others on a farm or in a small town; in these cases, however, negative reaction against Vällingby was surprisingly weak.

What did they like about Vällingby? It is near nature, quiet and peaceful, yet also near the city—these were common answers. They also liked the ser-vices and facilities which Vällingby provides, such as public transportation and recreation; very few could think of any services or facilities for young people which might usefully be added to the community. Similarly, few could think of any "problems" in Vällingby.

In marked contrast to the American suburban situation, teenagers in Väl-lingby have almost no transportation problems; there is no dependence on parents to drive them places within the community or even within the met-ropolitan area. Public transportation is well suited to their needs, and its cost is low. As an indication of their geographic mobility, many youth from the age of about ten or eleven are allowed to make trips by themselves into downtown Stockholm for specific purposes. In addition, teenagers in Väl-lingby can walk to school, bike riding is common, and many boys get motor bikes at age fifteen. Because the minimum legal age for driving a car in. Sweden in eighteen, the automobile plays a relatively insignificant role in their lives. Some teenagers are even antiautomobile; they plan never to own a car or to get a driver's license when they become of age.

One concern which was expressed by both teenagers and their parents was that the individual apartments are too small. Some families are overcrowded, so that a young person does not have his own room. I encountered families that placed strong restrictions on the activities of their children; the young people were not allowed to invite their friends over because of the noise, confusion, and dirt which might be created in so small a space.

The teenage life-styles in Vällingby seemed less school-related than those in the U.S., having more to do with activities undertaken during nonschool hours and outside of school auspices. The school plays a smaller nonacademic role in the lives of Swedish teenagers than its American counterpart, and a larger academic role. Swedish teenagers are given an equal or larger amount of homework, but the absence of interscholastic competitive sports in Sweden removes a nonacademic school attraction which is quite powerful in the lives of American teenagers. The nonacademic functions of the school in the U.S., such as competitive sports, social and hobby clubs, and other recreational services, have traditionally been performed in Sweden by other institutions in the community.

It is useful to describe the teen life-styles in Vällingby in terms of the two "polar-extremes"—what might be called the "youth center" group and the "culturally active" group. The first of these was more common among working-class youth, and the second among middle-class youth. Together, these two groups probably include much less than half of Vällingby's teenagers, most of whom would range in the middle, sharing some of the attributes of both. Indeed, Vällingby's teenagers are less easily pigeonholed than American teenagers. This is probably because there is less peer pressure and therefore peer conformity in Sweden; teenagers have somewhat more "freedom of maneuver" in selecting their life-styles.

The most visible and widely discussed of Vällingby's teenage life-styles is that of the youth-center group. While only about 25 percent of the qualified age groups had membership cards to the youth center, and an even smaller number than that actually participated, for a small segment of Vällingby teenagers the youth center was a major focus of their lives. Two or three evenings a week, plus several afternoons, would be spent at the center by these teenagers; their friends were mostly youth-center friends; and many of their main experiences were in youth-center activities. The big attraction of the youth center is that it is a good place to meet members of the opposite sex. The unofficial qualifications for being oriented toward the youth center, therefore, are being sexually mature, being a "social" type, and having a working-class background (this qualification was not as strong as the others).

There seemed to be a strong overlap between those who go to the youth center and those who "hang out," that is, stand around in small groups in public places and informally socialize. The major hang-out places were the sports fields, the subway stations and centrums, the local neighborhood shopping centers, and building entrances—in roughly that order of importance. The youth centers are closed during the summer months, "forcing the kids to hang out," as one person put it.

As the Vällingby youth matures, interest in youth centers gradually gives way to the lure of downtown Stockholm. Trips to the commercial discotheques in the city become more frequent, until the youth center is left behind entirely. Since the discotheques are not cheap, however, they are only available to those who have a source of income; the youth centers charge merely a token fee for membership and for the major activities that they sponsor.

A sizable portion of Vällingby youth want no part of the youth-center life. Many have never set foot in a center and have no desire to. The youth center has an image to them of being rowdy, working-class, and a waste of time, or worse, for those who have better things to do. A small portion of this group might be called the "culturally active." Their lives are actively taken up with a variety of cultural pursuits—music lessons, theater in downtown Stockholm, arts and crafts. The resources for such activities in Vällingby, because of the proximity to downtown Stockholm, are great. Though they have a few good friends, these youth tend to be less social and to be at home more often than their youth-center counterparts.

Most Vällingby youth fall between these extremes. They lead quiet lives—listening to music in their rooms, talking with friends, taking an occasional trip into town, and perhaps participating in one cultural pursuit. A popular recreational activity is swimming, outdoors in the summer, indoors in the winter. Some youth are very active in sports clubs, where they participate in competitive sports.

An orientation toward college is considerably less among Swedish than among U.S. teenagers. Only about half the number of students actually go to college than is the case in the U.S. (between 20 and 25 percent of the college-age group, vs. 40–45 percent in the U.S.). Further, the college years are more extended in Sweden. Rather than the concentrated four years full-time, the college student is likely to go part-time for a longer period. Almost none of the teenagers with whom I spoke mentioned college plans. Instead, they were concerned about getting a job that was secure and that paid reasonably well.

Though finding the right job was thought to be problematic, few teenagers seemed worried about being squeezed out of the job market entirely. Because of the excellent labor market in the Stockholm area, most teenagers in Vällingby who want them can get summer and part-time jobs after the age of about sixteen. The jobs typically are easily accessible by public transportation. The same situation prevails for those older teenagers who are seeking full-time, year-round work.

In summary, the youth of Vällingby, with but few exceptions, seemed highly congruent with their environment and remarkably content with life and with themselves. The antisocial bitterness and cynicism which one encounters in American youth were absent. I did detect a certain goallessness, however.

Many had no idea what they wanted to do in life; they apparently had given little thought to the question. Interest in going to college was, as indicated above, virtually absent. Even marriage was not a goal, since many and perhaps most will live for years as unmarried couples. Most were concerned merely to get a job which would provide them a reasonably comfortable life.

But as the American "achievement orientation" was weak among these Swedish teenagers, so was the American acquisitive drive for material gain and "success." The youth of Vällingby do not aspire for wealth, prestige, or power. Their aspirations are for a productive job and, through that, a comfortable, happy life. These are more expectations than aspirations; perhaps that is why they seemed "goalless."

Patterns of Environmental Fit in Vällingby: Some Conclusions

No single residential environment can work well for all types of people; the range of human needs and interests is far too great. Yet Vällingby provides a close environmental fit for a surprisingly wide range of individuals and families. In this respect it must be ranked at the top of urban settlement types. It works well for the young family, especially if the family is not too large or too desirous of personal, private space. It works even better for older families, because it is especially well suited to the needs of teenagers and working women. For parents whose children have left home, it provides a maintenance-free dwelling close to desired services and facilities and often close to the children themselves. It seems to work just as well for singles and young couples with no children, and for many pensioners.

Neither urban nor suburban in the U.S. sense, Vällingby combines some of the advantages as well as the disadvantages of both settings. In the process of attracting persons with such diverse needs and interests, it has become a very heterogeneous settlement, quite unlike most in the U.S. This demographic balance gives it an urban flavor which most suburbs lack. Yet with its natural environment and its air of peace and contentment, Vällingby is very un-urban; indeed, it is almost rural in character.

Which households are not congruent with Vällingby? The large family finds apartment living of any kind difficult; the need for a sizable amount of living space becomes paramount. Since they can afford it, the middle- and upper-middle-class families often find the lure of the single-family house irresistible. They are willing to give up the benefits of a Vällingby for the space, the status, and the privacy of a separate dwelling unit. Those whose roots or preferences lie in rural or small-town living find any form of urban settlement an uncomfortable place to be, and Vällingby is no exception in this regard. At the opposite extreme, every society has a small handful of people whose tastes and interests run to urbanity and cosmopolitanism—Vällingby can be a dull place to them. Finally, the lonely of the world find an urban way of living difficult, whether in city or suburb. Vällingby does not offer much help for their problem, although the best environmental alternatives are by no means clear.

Yet the range of persons Vällingby serves, and serves well, remains perhaps its most unique and positive characteristic. In the U.S., new residential environments are becoming more highly specialized: for families, rich or poor; for singles; for senior citizens; and so on. The specialized environments have many social drawbacks, such as the loss of diversity and the fostering of needless residential mobility. Moreover, these environments become fragile commodities in the buffeting of the urban real-estate market. As neighborhoods change, what works today may not work tomorrow; the environment can quickly head down the path of premature obsolescence.

If anything, Vällingby has improved over the years as a stable, desirable, and efficient residential environment. One can reasonably conclude that it works even better for its present population than it did for its original settlers.

Photos and Maps

Top: aerial photo of a
Levittown neighborhood.

Bottom: aerial photo of the
Vällingby centrum area.

Neighborhood layout and
location of major facilities.

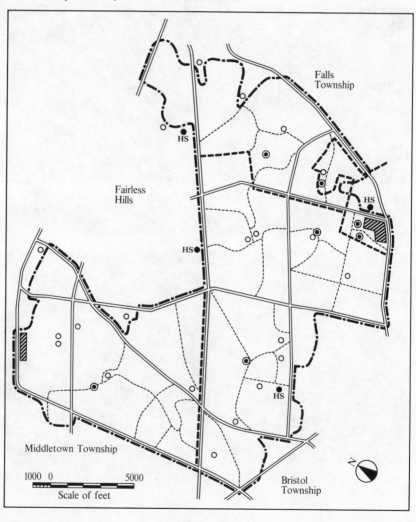

- ·- Levittown boundary

= Major thoroughfares

----- Neighborhood boundaries

- - - Municipal boundary

▨ Main shopping centers

◉ Recreation areas

HS● High School

○ Primary and
Middle Schools

Falls
Township

Fairless
Hills

HS

HS

HS

HS

Middletown Township

Bristol
Township

1000 0   5000

Scale of feet

N

The total land area purchased by the Levitt organization was approximately 5,750 acres, and the number of Levitt-built houses was 17,311, designed for 70,000 persons, which gives a gross residential density of 3.0 dwelling units (twelve persons) per acre.

All of the dwelling units built by Levitt were single-family detached houses. In 1960, the average size of these houses (median rooms per dwelling unit) was 5.5 rooms, including kitchen, with a variation ranging from 4.8 rooms per dwelling unit in the working-class areas to 6.6 rooms in the middle-class areas. While large by international standards, the Levittown households were also quite large—about 4.2 persons per dwelling unit—giving a persons-per-room ratio of 0.76 (almost identical to the current figure for Vällingby!).

Comparable data for 1970 are not available because of the intrusion of new, non-Levitt dwelling units into the Levittown area during the decade. Data were obtained, however, from two Levittown tracts in which almost no new development occurred in the 1960–70 decade. These data showed a 5 to 6 percent decrease in the median number of persons per dwelling unit and a 15 percent increase in the number of rooms per dwelling unit, due mainly to alterations and additions. Generalizing from these data, the 1970 ratio of persons per room unit in the Levittown houses is approximately 0.60.

Source: *1960 and 1970 U.S. Censuses of Population and Housing: Census Tracts, Philadelphia, Pa.-N.J. Standard Metropolitan Statistical Area* (Washington, D.C.: U.S. Bureau of the Census, 1962 and 1972). The two census tracts specially examined are: Bristol Tract 0004E (1960), changed to 1004.05 (1970); Tullytown Tract B-0059A (1960), changed to 1059.01 (1970).

The Vällingby development
area and land use in the
Vällingby city district.

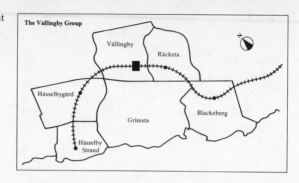

The Vällingby Group

Community center
Public use
Industrial use
Multi-family housing

Single story housing
Parks
----- Pedestrian and cycle paths
＋ Underground railway

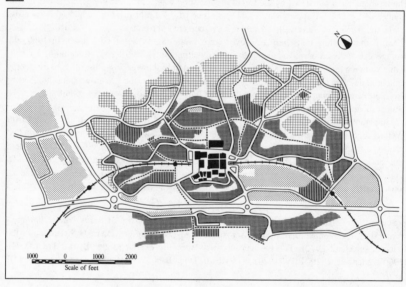

The total land area of Vällingby is 2,251 acres, which includes the sizeable Grimsta Woods (about 450 acres). Excluding these woods, gross residential densities range from 24.25 persons per acre (8.48 dwelling units per acre) in the Blackeberg district to 44.31 persons per acre in Hässelby Strand (14.96 dwelling units per acre).[a] Overall density for the Vällingby area (1970) is 26.43 persons per acre (10.5 dwelling units per acre). If Grimsta Woods is included, the density drops to 21.14 persons per acre (8.4 dwelling units per acre).

Of 19,050 dwelling units in 1971, 92 percent were in multifamily buildings and 8 percent in single-family units. By number of rooms per dwelling unit, the percentage distribution of total dwelling units was as follows:[b]

57%	2 rooms and kitchen and smaller
28	3 rooms and kitchen
10	4 rooms and kitchen
5	5 rooms and kitchen and larger

The average Vällingby unit is slightly more than three rooms (3.27) in size, including kitchen. This is smaller by about one room than the average in the more recent suburban apartment developments of Stockholm and is similar to the average in the "outer city" of Stockholm (3.44)[c] but substantially larger than the inner-city dwelling unit (2.65).

By U.S. standards, the Vällingby apartment is quite small, but it is important to take into consideration the average number of persons per household, which is also very low in Sweden. For Vällingby, there are 2.52 persons per dwelling unit, or 0.77 persons per room unit, including kitchen. Thus, the Swedish housing goal of one person per room (*not* including kitchen) is quite close to being achieved in Vällingby. Comparative figures are 2.44 persons per dwelling unit (0.72 persons per room) in outer-city Stockholm and 1.62 persons per dwelling unit (0.61 persons per room) in inner-city Stockholm.

Figures are not available for all of Vällingby concerning the distribution of multifamily dwellings by type. In the Vällingby "core area," however (Vällingby, Råcksta, and Grimsta) the figures are 68 percent in three-story garden apartments and 21 percent in high-rise buildings, with the remaining 11 percent in single-family houses (mostly attached town houses).[d]

[a]The data in this section are from the *Statistical Yearbook of Stockholm,* 1971, unless otherwise noted.

[b]*Stockholm—Urban Environment,* p. 52.

[c]The outer city includes Vällingby but not the more outlying, single-family-home suburbs of greater Stockholm.

[d]"Vällingby," A. B. Svenska Bostader, 1966, p. 28.

Levittown

Location in the United States and in the Philadelphia metropolitan area.

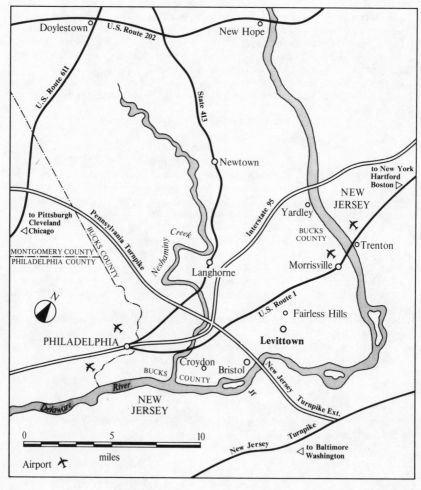

Vällingby
Location in Sweden and in the
Stockholm metropolitan area.

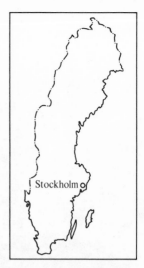

Stockholm

|—+—+—+—| Rapid transit
·—·—·— City limits

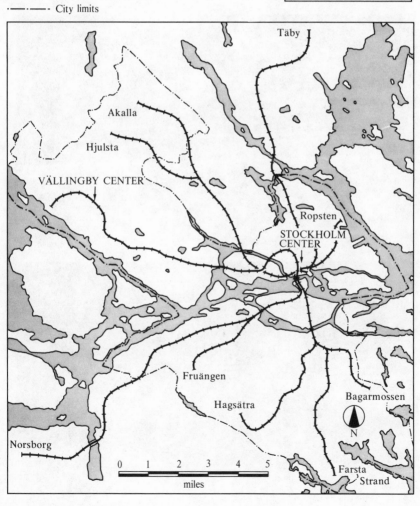

Täby

Akalla

Hjulsta

VÄLLINGBY CENTER

Ropsten

STOCKHOLM
CENTER

Fruängen

Hagsätra

Bagarmossen

N

Norsborg

0   1   2   3   4   5
miles

Farsta
Strand

Levittown   *Top:* crossing guard at a
                                 pedestrian crosswalk.

Bottom: mother supervising
child at play on sidewalk.

Vällingby

Top: separation of pedestrian and vehicular traffic.

Bottom: play park with trained attendants where parents may leave children on weekday mornings.

Levittown

Top: children playing in the street.

Bottom: lawn mowing—a common activity in Levittown.

Vällingby

Top: going on a shopping trip by bicycle.   *Bottom:* using the balcony of an apartment.

Levittown   *Top:* the main shopping center.   *Bottom:* entrance to one of the neighborhoods.

Vällingby   *Top:* the Vällingby centrum.   *Bottom:* a pedestrian path in one of the higher-density sections.

Levittown   Characteristics of
the Residential
Environment

*November 8, 1951, is a day to be remembered through-
out America. It was a day the largest residential
home builder in the world changed the life style of
thousands of American citizens. It was the day that
people of low and moderate income became a partner
and sharer of the opportunities in the free enterprise system. It was the day a $100 deposit bought
you a ranch type home, on a minimum lot of 70'
x 100' in a proposed planned, fully landscaped open-
spaced, garden community with paved roads and all
utilities. It was the day, which five years later, would
produce 17,311 homes and involve a population of over
67,000 residents. It was the day Levitt & Sons opened
their sales office at the intersection of Route 13 and
Levittown Parkway.*

So reads the introduction to the brochure prepared for the twentieth-anniversary celebration
of Levittown, Pennsylvania, June 23, 1972, a
celebration which took place twenty years to the
day after the first family moved into Levittown.[1]
In the intervening years, the housing development
has become established as one of the best-known
suburbs in America.

Levittown, Pennsylvania, located in south-
eastern Pennsylvania about twenty-two miles
northeast of Philadelphia, was the second of
the major housing developments built after the
war by the Levitt Organization. The first, built
in Long Island in 1946–47,[2] was a tremendous
commercial success, and Levitt and Sons soon
had visions of a second major enterprise. They
settled on land in Lower Bucks County near
Philadelphia because, as Levitt later said, the

area was next to the new Fairless plant of U.S. Steel Corporation, and there
were plans to build good road connections to Philadelphia (plans which
weren't carried out until some years later).[3] Levitt anticipated that most of the
family heads would work in either Philadelphia or nearby Trenton, N.J.

The Levitt Organization quietly purchased 5,750 acres of land, mostly
farmland, from between 150 and 175 different owners. In addition to housing,
Levitt built over ninety-seven miles of roadways; donated ground sites for
churches, schools, and recreation areas; helped to establish a private sewer
and water authority; built five Olympic-size swimming pools and a community center (donated to the community under the auspices of a nonprofit Levittown Public Recreation Association); and constructed what for a time was the
largest shopping center with a pedestrian mall east of the Mississippi (sixty
stores at a cost of $20 million dollars).

While Levittown, New York, may never have been thought of by the
builder as much more than a massive housing development (that is how it is
regarded by most planners—thousands of look-alike houses on a bewildering
array of 1,300 streets), Levitt had a grander vision in mind for his Pennsylvania project. He stated that it would be "the least monotonous mass-housing
group ever planned in America."[4] Early articles about Levittown, Pennsylvania, referred to it as the first large city in the U.S. to be preplanned since
L'Enfant laid out Washington, D.C.[5]

As a building and development process, Levittown was a good example of
planning, American-style: the comprehensive development of a large land
area by a private builder, as distinct from unplanned, piecemeal development
by a multiplicity of small builders and individual owners. Yet it was "planning" with little public or community input, representing mainly the views
and efforts of Levitt organization officials. As an environmental form, the
plan for Levittown, Pennsylvania, was unique for its time, at least in the
U.S.[6]

The approximately 17,300 single-family homes are grouped into seven or
eight superblocks, each of which is bounded by the major arterial roadways
and contains, at its center, the public schools. The housing along the major
roadways faces inward, and access to the superblocks is made possible at only
a few points via collector streets. It was the original intention to give each
superblock its own swimming pool and recreational center, but only five such
centers were built, and the areas they serve are not entirely contiguous with
the superblocks.

The superblocks, in turn, are divided into forty named neighborhoods
ranging in size from 51 to 990 homes, with an average size of 430 homes.
These were intended to be the main "social" units of Levittown. Each
neighborhood (with names like Stonybrook, Crabtree, North Park, and

Junewood) is bounded by a circumferential collector street which inhibits, to a large extent, through traffic. The neighborhood street plan was designed so that there are few four-way intersections, and almost all the interior streets are curved rather than straight, providing an additional impediment to through traffic. The collector street carries the same name as the neighborhood, and all of its interior streets have names which start with the same first letter. Thus Stonybrook harbors Starlight Lane, Sweetbriar Lane, Strawberry Lane, and Swan Lane.

Though every house in a single neighborhood is the same type and on a lot of about the same size (the houses range from the two- or three-bedroom "Rancher"—really a Cape Cod—in the least expensive neighborhoods to the very large "Country Clubbers" in the most expensive areas), the exact design and external color of the houses were varied so that a house of the same shape and color occurs only once in every twenty-eight houses (there are four different exteriors and eight different colors). Levitt was later to say that he made a mistake in not mixing up the house types, as indeed he has done in his later developments.[7]

There is no indication that Levitt ever thought he was building a "new town"—that label was tagged on by journalists. He made no attempt to develop an employment base for the community, and Levittown is situated within four different local government jurisdictions. Thus the suburb lacks two essential ingredients which are included in most definitions of a "new town"—substantial amounts of economic and political autonomy. Levittown is basically a large, preplanned housing development on the edge of a metropolitan area: what is often called a "packaged" suburb. In population size, however, it quickly became the tenth largest "city" in the state of Pennsylvania.

Levittown was an instant and continuing market success. The Levitt houses were relatively inexpensive ("a very good buy for the money"), they had the latest household equipment (which was included in the price), and there was still a shortage of new, single-family houses in the U.S. The "economic secrets" of Levitt and Sons were economies of scale, standardization of construction items, and the preconstruction of many house components off the site.[8]

Levittown after Twenty Years: First Impressions

One normally approaches Levittown by car; most of the major approach roads are clogged with automobile traffic and with facilities and services which are ancillary to that traffic: new- and used-car lots, gas stations, drive-ins of all kinds. Even by American standards the approach is neither a pleasant sight nor a pleasant experience; at rush hour it is a headache.

In its early years, Levittown was visually a very distinct development—a vast sea of raw houses and streets in the middle of open fields. Its boundaries were unmistakable. Today, the area around Levittown is mostly built-up, and within Levittown twenty years' growth of heavy vegetation softens the view. It is now sometimes difficult to pick out Levittown from its surroundings. Yet the interior of Levittown still remains a world apart from its outside environment. When one leaves the major access roads which traverse the area, separating the superblocks, an environment is entered which is unique in the history of the world, however common it may have become on the recent American scene. The interior of Levittown is nothing but house after house after house—all much the same, though the differences have become emphasized over time.

The main impression is not one of mass-produced "little boxes," however; Levitt invested heavily in landscaping, and the aesthetic legacy of this investment has been enormous. What was once a raw housing development, a visual blight on the landscape, is now virtually a parklike setting, especially in spring, summer, and fall. Most vegetation matures handsomely in twenty years; many of the Levitt streets, with their overhanging trees and abundant front-yard shrubbery, have a luxuriant facade, obscuring the fact that the homes basically look alike. and are for families with modest incomes.

Other features of the environment which delight the eye are the gently curving streets, the generally well-maintained houses and front yards, and the wooded and grassy areas which have been left as buffer zones between neighborhoods. The visual quality of the street is further enhanced by the fact that Levitt chose to run the utility lines behind the houses rather than along the street frontage. Levittown has unquestionably grown more aesthetically pleasant over the years; in no sense has it become the suburban slum that some predicted.[9] From a market point of view, Levitt houses have in fact appreciated more than those in surrounding areas.[10]

Yet the eye is jarred here and there in the working-class districts by a house that has been allowed to run down, often with a junk-filled front yard (the estimate of one housing inspector was that there is "one slob on every third block"), by sidewalks in which the concrete has rotted away, by broken street lamps, and by litter in the buffer zones. On several days a week the visual impression of Levittown is further worsened by the practice of putting the garbage and trash out by the roadway for pick-up. From an aesthetic point of view, this practice is gross indeed but nonetheless common in American cities and towns.

By far the most significant element of visual blight in the typical Levittown neighborhood, however, is the automobile. During the day the situation is tolerable; many of the cars are at their owner's place of work, study, or shopping. After the workday ends, however, the streets of Levittown change their character. With an average of two cars per family, and very few garages or even car ports (most of the Levitt houses were constructed with car ports in place of garages, yet the car ports have often been converted to living space), the presence of the automobile in some neighborhoods becomes almost overwhelming. Not only are curb spaces on both sides of the street often filled, but the front yards of many homes are given over as parking lots. The environmental predominance of the automobile is not as characteristic of the middle- and upper-middle-class areas, where houses and lots are larger and screening vegetation more abundant.

The worst instance of automobile blight is the abandoned vehicle; cars are left to "rot," commonly in the street or the front or side yard. This has become a serious problem in some sections of Levittown. A housing inspector's recent tour of three neighborhoods in a working-class district turned up twenty-four properties which had from one to five abandoned cars, all either on or visible from the street.[11]

Levitt did virtually nothing to limit the number of automobiles in his development, but he did seek to maintain a high degree of environmental control in other ways. The most noteworthy of these ways was his inclusion, in the homeowner's manual which each Levitt home purchaser received, of a number of "do's and don'ts," "which will be strictly enforced."[12] These regulations appear anachronistic today, but they were apparently followed in the early years, until it became clear that Levitt had no way of enforcing them. Among the restrictions were the following: (1) no homeowner could put up a fence (he was instead supposed to use shrubbery, and even that could be no more than three feet high); (2) he could not change the color of his house without the approval of the Levitt Organization; (3) no wash could be hung outside on Sundays and holidays (and only umbrella-type clotheslines could be used); (4) the grass was to be cut and the weeds removed at least once a week from April to November; and, (5) no home was to have more than two cat or dog pets. Regulations such as these are regarded by many Americans as a grave restriction of their personal freedom, but they are commonly found in residential communities that have a unique character to preserve.

To what extent do residents abide by these rules today? In one block picked randomly in a working-class district, 75 percent of the houses had backyard fences, though very few had front-yard fencing. In the upper-middle-class districts the use of fencing was significantly less, due mainly to the larger yard sizes, which give more privacy and increase the cost of fencing, and to the use of more "natural fences" such as tall and often well-manicured hedges. The

main reasons Levittowners give for needing fencing are to keep dogs and
children in (and out), to safeguard swimming pools, and to provide
privacy.

The exterior house colors have remained, by and large, aesthetically pleasing, and they generally do not clash with one another; but it is not uncommon
in Levittown today to encounter the house which stands out on the block like a
sore thumb, the result of a color selection that undoubtedly would have been
disapproved by the Levitt Organization. Levittown residents do hang wash
outside occasionally on Sundays and holidays, but it is in the backyards and
mostly out of sight; the overall level of lawn and garden maintenance has
remained high.

Next to the fence restriction, the pet restriction may be, at least in its intent,
the most frequently abrogated in today's Levittown. Many households keep
two or more dogs, often for safety purposes, and there is general agreement
that the Levittown canine population is very large, although the exact size is
unknown. While dogs are not allowed to run loose, their presence is made
unmistakable to the stranger walking down a Levittown street.

Apart from canine activity, Levittown has a lifeless quality during the day
which is characteristic of all low-density suburbs. On a half-hour walk
through one Levittown neighborhood on a warm sunny mid-day in March, the
streets, sidewalks, and front yards were deserted of people; not a single
home-dweller or pedestrian was seen or heard, and only an occasional delivery truck or car, plus the barking of dogs, broke the silence. This experience
is not unusual.

While the neighborhoods of Levittown are lifeless, however, the spaces
between the Levittown superblocks and on the periphery of Levittown are
alive with the activity of the vast number of automobiles spawned by the
Levittown milieu. The predominant position of the automobile in the Levittown environs is signified by the location immediately adjacent to the community of the world's largest car dealer—Reedman Motors—which normally
has on its 150-acre lot a car and truck inventory of over 5,000 vehicles.[13]
Next to the large volume of traffic, the most apparent environmental component is the number of gas stations; it is estimated that there are over one
hundred gas stations in the Levittown area.[14] At the once quaint village of
Emilie, now called Five Points because of the intersection of major traffic-
ways, there are six gas stations, one on each point and one in addition; a
single block along Route 13, bordering Levittown on the east, offers nine gas
stations.

Side by side with gas stations, small stores and shopping centers dot the
roadsides of the major traffic arteries. They are not a pretty sight; many are
old and run down, bordered by heavily littered vacant lots and always sur-

rounded by parking lots and a sea of cars. The commercial blight outside of the neighborhoods stands in great contrast to the order and neatness found within the residential zones. Most of the commercial establishments are built on pieces of land that were not included in the original plan for Levittown because they were not owned by the Levitt Organization. Alfred Levitt is said to have remarked, after seeing the commercial blight in the area, that it was a serious mistake not to have purchased the main road-frontages and the many scattered parcels of land where the owners balked at the sale.[15]

The Elements of the Levittown Residential Environment

There are five major elements, about half the number found in Vällingby, in the residential areas of Levittown; the single-family detached house, the yard, the street, the automobile, and the vegetation or landscape. The spatial relationships between these elements are repeated throughout the environment: the house fronts on a street and uniformly is sited in approximately the center of its yard; resting to the front or side of the house, or in the street, is the automobile.

The dominant visual element in the neighborhood environment is the individual dwelling unit. Not only does the house visually dominate; it virtually *is* the environment for many Levittowners who, when they go out of the house, get into their automobile and leave the remainder of the local environment behind. Thus, what lies outside the house is, with the exception of the backyard, not a very significant part of their behavioral space.

By the standards of most of the rest of the world, the Levitt house is almost palatial—private housing space for the average citizen at a very high amenity level. But it is not large by U.S. standards. The smallest of the Levitt houses has only 1,000 square feet of floor space, with a very small kitchen, a dining el, and two or three bedrooms. Many of the houses have been altered and expanded over the years, however. It is estimated that 25 percent of the houses have major exterior additions or alterations, and 50 percent have remodeled interiors.[16] The later-built Levitt houses are much more spacious, with recreation or family rooms and two-car garages.

The private living space of the dwelling is extended during the warmer months by the backyard, which may contain a patio or deck connected to the house. In most cases the rear yard is fenced in, or surrounded by border plantings, and often has recreational and play equipment such as a small swimming pool. The front yard, on the other hand, has much less behavioral significance. Its three main functions are: to permit the house to be placed away from the street, to provide a place for the storage of automobiles (which are almost never in the rear), and to serve sometimes as a show place for attractive flowers and plantings. The front yard is also used occasionally for young children's play and, near the house, as a place for adults to sit and talk.

There is a much greater privatization of life in suburbs like Levittown than has been characteristic of most communities throughout world history. With the exception of work activities outside the home, most of the daily life of Levittown adults is lived in house and yard, an almost completely private world. The house and its care and maintenance become a principal focus of life, even more important, often, than the job. For the stay-at-home housewife, it becomes virtually her whole world. Attitudes toward the adequacy of housing space are highly relative, and many Levittowners find their houses too small. But the combination of house and yard is large enough to enable the family to include within their private space many facilities, such as backyard play equipment, swimming pools, and recreation rooms; these facilities permit the private pursuit of recreational and entertainment activities which traditionally have been public or communal.

The automobile is the Levittowner's one means of transportation within the community and his main link to the outside world. Services and facilities are too dispersed to get to them on foot. There is almost no public transportation (small areas of Levittown have an infrequent bus service to out-of-town areas), and only teenagers in certain age groups ride bicycles. Levittown is in many ways well suited to the bicycle, but there is little interest in this form of transportation among adults, for reasons of distance, safety, and the habit of bulk purchasing. Typically, each adult member of the family has a car; without a car, Levittown becomes a place of great inconvenience and isolation. The main use of the automobile is not to move around the neighborhood but to leave the neighborhood. Work and shopping generate most automobile trips, and both activities usually take place outside the local area; there is little neighborhood shopping in Levittown.

Care of the automobile comes second only to care of the home. A common sight on weekends and evenings is the person looking under the hood of a car or lying on his back under one. Most car care is not a luxury but a necessity.

The fourth environmental element is the street, a hard surface which functions mainly to provide ease of movement for automobiles and as a parking lot. There is no "street life" in Levittown, and it is not uncommon for an adult walking to be offered a ride, with the question: "What's the matter, did your car break down?" The street has one other function, as a place for children's play. The private yards, Levitt's intended play areas, lack the hard surface which is necessary for many activities and games. Among the parked cars and with the constant threat of automobile injuries, children can frequently be found at play, moving to one side when a car comes along.

Sidewalks were not added to the list of major environmental elements because they do not exist in the newer and wealthier sections of Levittown. Levitt has stated that he left out sidewalks because he felt the streets would be more beautiful without them and also safer for children, who would have to play away from the street rather than at the street's edge.[17] Both alleged benefits are dubious. A sidewalk generally enhances the beauty of a street, and children are probably more liable to play in the street if there is no sidewalk than if there is one, for then they can use the sidewalk and not the street. It is likely that finances was the main reason behind the no-sidewalk decision—sidewalks are very expensive to construct. Whatever the reason, the decision virtually precluded pedestrian activity in the newer neighborhoods. A person seen walking in these neighborhoods is a rarity.

In the older neighborhoods, which have sidewalks, pedestrian activity is limited to children and teenagers and an occasional mother with baby carriage. The most common use is by children, in the immediate vicinity of the house, where the sidewalk becomes an extension of the front yard or perhaps an extension of the street.

Because it is a major part of one's first impression of Levittown, the final environmental element, vegetation and landscaping, was discussed in the last section. Levitt claims to have spent $500 per house on landscaping.[18] The residents are very proud of the result, and it is one of the positive attributes of Levittown most commonly mentioned.

The Demographic Structure of Levittown

The population in 1970 of the nine census tracts* which roughly correspond to the original Levittown area[19] was 75,071,[20] almost evenly divided between the sexes. This represents an increase of about 9 percent from 1960, most of which is accounted for by the addition of new, non-Levitt housing units within the Levittown tracts. Much of this new growth has been in the form of garden apartments, a negligible percentage in 1960 but in 1970 10 percent of the housing units.[21] The persons living in these units are different in age and household type from the Levittowners, and there is little social interaction between the two groups. Because the concern of this section is the population in the Levittown houses alone, 1960 census data are sometimes used in preference to the 1970 data to describe the community, where the earlier data are felt to be, in spite of their age, more accurate. In addition, one of the Levittown census tracts, reasonably representative of the others, has had

*A census tract is a subdivision of a city or urban region created by the U.S. Census Bureau for the collection and tabulation of detailed information.

almost no new development since 1960.[22] Many of the following generalizations about Levittown are based on 1970 data from this one tract, referred to as the sample census tract.

Age and Stage of the Life-Cycle

The Levittown population is relatively homogeneous in age and stage of the life-cycle. There are very few elderly people and few persons not living in families. The middle-aged family predominates, although there is a sizable number of younger families who have moved to the community in recent years, replacing older families who have left.

The 1970 age distribution in the sample census tract was:[23]

0–4	11%
5–19	37
20–44	33
45–64	17
65+	2

The modal age of children then was between ten and fourteen; in 1975 it is therefore in the late teen years. For adults, the modal age in 1975 is in the early to late forties.[24] These modal ages are strong demographic indicators of the middle-aged stages of the family life-cycle: families consisting of middle-aged parents and older teenagers.

Levittown is the habitat of the intact nuclear family. Of all households in the sample census tract in 1970, 97 percent were families; 75 percent of these contained children under the age of eighteen, and many of the remainder were probably families whose children had left home.[25] Almost all of these families were intact, rather than broken by divorce, separation, or death. Ninety-three percent of all the families were husband-wife families; of the remainder, 5 percent were headed by a woman and 2 percent by a male other than husband. Looked at from another perspective, 92 percent of all Levittown children lived in families where both parents were present. Divorce and widowhood are not common; only 3 percent of the females and 2 percent of the males fourteen years of age and older were divorced or separated, while 5 percent of the females were widowed and less than 1 percent of the males were widowers.

Social Class

Levittown is not as class-homogeneous as it is age- and family-homogeneous, nor as class-homogeneous as suburbs are commonly thought to be. The population is widely distributed among occupational levels, with an almost even split among employed males between middle- and working-class occupations. Because of the inclusion of non-Levitt homes in the 1970 census tracts, 1960 data on the social-class level of Levittowners was felt to be a more accurate source, though there may have been a slight drop in the community's average class level over the ten-year period, as discussed below. For all nine Levittown census tracts in 1960, the occupations of gainfully employed males were distributed as follows (based on the occupational categories used by the U.S. Census):[26] 20 percent upper middle class (professional, technical, and kindred); 30 percent middle class (managers, officers, and proprietors, 12 percent; clerical and kindred, 8 percent; sales, 10 percent) and 49 percent working class (craftsmen, foremen, and kindred, 24 percent; operatives and kindred, 18 percent; service workers, 3 percent; and laborers, 4 percent). The true occupational level of the Levittowners is understated by these figures, however, because gainfully employed females are not included. In the sample tract in 1970 (this tract includes some of the more heavily working-class neighborhoods in Levittown), the division of male occupations was 68 percent working-class and 32 middle-class, whereas for female occupations the division was just the reverse—68 percent middle-class and 32 percent working-class. Forty-three percent of the employed women worked in the clerical category, for example, a lower-middle-class occupation. Since females make up about 35 percent of the labor force in this tract, the inclusion of gainfully employed females in the determination of Levittown's occupational level would shift that level upward.[27]

The different occupational levels and income groups are by no means evenly distributed throughout Levittown. One Levittown tract had 34 percent upper-middle-class and 48 percent middle-class occupations in 1960, whereas another had only 14 percent upper-middle-class and 25 percent middle-class.[28] Similarly, median incomes (1970) range from $11,247 in the poorest district to $19,045 in the wealthiest.[29] Because income level determines the house price which a family can afford, the geographic distribution of income levels is strongly influenced by the grouping together, in Levittown, of similarly priced housing. The house prices (1973) range from $21,500 in the lowest-priced neighborhoods to $37,000 in the most expensive (houses which originally sold for $8,990 and $16,900).[30] For the Levittown area as a whole, 9 percent of the population aged twenty-five and over in 1970 has completed college, with a median school year completed of 12.4.[31] The percentage of college graduates varied from 4 in the tract with the lowest educational level (median school year completed, 12.2) to 35 in the tract with the highest level (median school year completed, 13.4).[32]

Race, Ethnicity, and Region of Origin

In the New York Levittown, a clause was included in each homeowners contract which stated that: "no dwelling shall be used or occupied by members of other than the Caucasian race, but the employment and maintenance of other than Caucasian domestic servants shall be permitted."[33] That community, today, has only about a 1 percent black population.[34] The clause did not appear in the Pennsylvania Levittown contracts, but informal methods seem to have been just as successful in keeping blacks from purchasing homes. Though Levittown, Pennsylvania, is more heterogeneous in social class than the suburban stereotype would lead one to expect, it matches the stereotype precisely in racial composition, which remains virtually all white.

The first blacks, the William Meyers family, moved into the Dogwood neighborhood of Bristol Township in 1957. The move caused a near riot, as irate neighbors milled about in the streets in front of the house for several evenings, hurling stones and shouting epithets. Levittown became nationally infamous over the incident, which was widely publicized by the media.[35] The Meyers family still lives in Levittown, and the overt hostility toward them has long since vanished, but very few other black families have joined them. It was estimated in the early 1970s that about one hundred black families were living in Levittown, spread out among a number of different neighborhoods.[36] The 1970 census revealed black populations in the Levittown census tracts ranging from 0 percent to 1.9 percent—the latter a tract in which a number of blacks lived outside the Levitt area.[37]

The reasons for this continued overwhelmingly white predominance are not entirely clear. (The Philadelphia SMSA as a whole is 17.5 percent black.)[38] Probably it stems in part from the great hostility shown to the first blacks in Levittown. Blacks now have other alternatives and can purchase single-family housing in areas where they know their reception will be more positive. The nearby New Jersey Levittown, for example, built several years later and containing slightly more expensive homes, did not have the same history of hostility and violence. A 1972 survey indicated a black population there of 17 percent.[39] Segregation in Levittown, Pennsylvania, has surely been assisted, also, by practices of the real estate dealers and private-home sellers, at least in the earlier years of the community.

There seem to be few racial tensions today within or among the neighborhoods. However, one of the main Levittown school systems includes within its jurisdiction a large black population from a neighboring town, Bristol, and this has been a source of school-connected racial conflict in recent years. A Levitt house in this school district sells for about $1,000 less than the identical house in another district,[40] a difference that real estate dealers attribute mainly to the racial tensions in the schools.

In respect to other aspects of ethnicity—religion and national origin—the situation is very different. Levittown is one of the more ethnically heterogeneous communities in the nation. The chances are very great of finding, side by side, families with different religious or nationality backgrounds, both because the population is ethnically diverse and because ethnicity is almost randomly distributed among the neighborhoods. Because the houses were sold on the open market over a short period of time to a wide spectrum of the population, there was little chance for the development of ethnic clustering.

Shortly after Levittown was built in 1953, a survey showed a religious distribution in the population of 41 percent Protestant (vs. 62 percent for the U.S. as a whole in 1955), 39 percent Roman Catholic (33 for the U.S. as a whole), 15 percent Jewish (5 percent for the U.S. as a whole), and for the remaining 5 percent no denomination.[41] Though more recent data are not available, it is estimated that the Jewish population has dropped to perhaps 10 percent and that the Roman Catholic population has increased to over 40 percent.[42]

The 1960 census revealed that 20 percent of the Levittowners were of foreign stock: 15 percent of these were foreign-born and 85 percent native-born but of foreign or mixed parentage.[43] Italians were the predominant foreign nationality (16 percent), followed closely by British (15 percent) and Russian (14 percent). Smaller in number were Polish (9 percent), German (8 percent), and a variety of other nationalities, including Swedish (1 percent). Persons of foreign stock are distributed throughout Levittown; none of the nine census tracts had less than 17 percent foreign stock or more than 27 percent.[44]

The Levittowners are also diverse in their origins within the U.S. Of those living in the sample census tract in Levittown in 1960 who had moved to their house within the previous five years, 46 percent came from outside of the Philadelphia metropolitan area. Most of these, 79 percent, came from the North and West, but 21 percent came from the South.[45] A sizable block came from upstate Pennsylvania—small-town Protestants, many from coal and steel towns. The exact size of this group is unknown but may make up 20 or 25 percent of the Levittown population in some working-class areas. Another large group was the urban Catholics who moved out from inner-city Philadelphia, making up perhaps 15 percent of the Levittown population.

Most new Levittown residents come today from other suburbs of metropolitan areas.[46] The idea that all suburbanites move out from the big city has never been true; today the great majority do not.

Residential Mobility

The suburbs, especially young-family suburbs, have become notorious as places of high residential mobility. In the United States, where about 18 percent of households change their place of residence each year, young-family suburbs and inner-city slums, both areas of "young familism," have the highest rates of residential mobility. The figures for Levittown indicate that residential mobility in suburbs with mature families may be below the national average, however; approximately 1,200 Levitt houses, about 7 percent of the total housing stock, are sold each year.[47] This percentage would be slightly higher if home rentals, a growing phenomenon in the community, were included.

Other data corroborate Levittown's position as a relatively stable environment in terms of residential mobility. Over 70 percent of the households reported in 1970 that they had lived in the same house five years earlier.[48] Indeed, it has been estimated that one-third of the original Levittowners still live there;[49] in my household sample, 25 percent of the households were original owners. In the 1970 census, between 45 and 50 percent of Levittowners said that they had moved into their homes prior to 1960.[50] Thus, Levittown is at least as much an "end of the line" suburb as it is a "stepping stone" suburb.[51]

The Maturation of Levittown: Demographic Changes

Data for the study of demographic change in Levittown have been drawn from the sample census tract, in which there was almost no new development since 1960. In the ten year period 1960–70, the total population of this tract remained approximately the same, a little more than 11,500 persons,[52] but the age distribution changed considerably.[53] In 1960, 37 percent of the population was under the age of ten; by 1970, this figure had dropped to 23 percent. At the same time, the percentage of young people aged ten to nineteen jumped from 14 to 25. The parents aged similarly; those in the twenty-five-to-forty-four age bracket decreased from 38 percent of the population to 27 percent; and those in the forty-five-to-sixty-four category increased from 6 percent to 17 percent. The number of senior citizens increased almost imperceptibly, remaining at about 1 percent. The picture which emerges, therefore, is of a population aging in place, starting out as young families who ten years later have reached the "mature" family stage, when family size begins to drop.

The sons and daughters of the original Levittowners were getting ready to leave their Levitt homes in 1970. Many of their older brothers and sisters had left earlier; only a few stayed on after age eighteen.[54] As the total population remained unchanged between 1960 and 1970, those leaving the community during this period were replaced by others. Families declining in size were often replaced by younger families increasing in size.

Although precise data are not available, this population replacement appears to be weakening in the 1970s, as the population has reached a more advanced stage of aging in place. Household size in the Levittown homes seems to be dropping for at least two reasons. The first is that the teen population reached its peak about 1970 and now is in decline; some of the Levittown youth have been able to establish their own households in Levittown, but most have gone elsewhere, often into neighboring garden apartments. The second is that a large percentage of the adults in the "empty nest" stage of the life cycle seem to be staying in their Levitt homes, out of choice or for economic reasons.

Levittown is headed toward a demographic structure very different from the one with which it started. Even if the environment remains the same, the households will be smaller, the residents older, and the community less child- and youth-oriented. Levittown may even become something of a retirement community. How well this aged population may be expected to adapt to a community which was designed for young families is a subject discussed in later chapters.

The residential turnover during the 1960s resulted in a slight decline in the social-class level of the population in the sample census tract; higher-class families have been replaced by families lower in class standing. In 1960, 60 percent of the employed males were in working-class occupations, with the categories of craftsmen and foremen, and operatives, making up 54 percent of the total males employed, while 39 percent were in middle-class occupations, which included 14 percent professional and technical.[55] By 1970, the percentage of working-class occupations had jumped from 60 to 68 percent (and laborers from 4 to 6 percent), while middle-class occupations declined from 39 to 32 percent (professional and technical dropped from 14 to 11 percent).[56] At the same time the percentage of college graduates (both sexes) declined from 8 to 4 percent.[57]

The women of this Levittown tract worked in 1970 outside the home in larger numbers than formerly, commensurate with their reduced functions as mothers. Thirty percent of the females fourteen years of age and over were in the labor force in 1960; by 1970 the figure was 46 percent of females sixteen years and older.[58] In occupational level, they became more concentrated in

lower-middle-class occupations: 43 percent of the working women in 1970
were in clerical jobs, an increase from 38 percent in 1960; and 11 percent
were professional and technical, a decrease from 16 percent in 1960.[59]

The percentage of foreign stock fell during the decade from 20 to 14.[60] This
is partly accounted for by the new generation of young Levittowners, whose
children are one step further removed from foreign parentage. Foreign nationality as a cultural phenomenon has disappeared relatively quickly in Levittown, especially among youth. There is very little in the social structure to
sustain the foreign cultural heritage, and communities like Levittown, far
more than inner-city areas, represent the American melting pot.

A slightly higher percentage of recent immigrants to Levittown have come
from within the Philadelphia metropolitan area: 57 percent as compared to 54
percent in 1960.[61] The residents now not only come from places closer to
Levittown they also work closer to Levittown: the percentage working in
Bucks County has increased from 60 to 71, while those working in Philadelphia have declined from 29 to 19 percent.[62] Thus, jobs and housing have
become more closely related physically over the decade, and Levittowners
have become less dependent on Philadelphia as a source of income.

The automobile is still the overwhelming choice as a means of transportation to and from work—indeed it has grown in importance. It was the means
of transportation for 86 percent of the workers in 1960 and 91 percent in 1970,
while the use of bus, streetcar, subway, elevated train or railroad declined
from 8 to 5 percent.[63] At the same time, the number of families owning more
than one car jumped from 23 to 55 percent (8 percent in 1970 owned three
cars or more).[64] The number of cars to be found in this tract of Levittown
increased, therefore, from about 3,300 to over 4,600, or one car for every 2.6
persons.

In comparison, only 18 percent of the families in the Philadelphia area had
two or more cars. Twenty-three percent of the families in the Philadelphia
area had no car at all in 1970, while only 1 percent in the Levittown tract was
in this category.[65]

The Levittowner as the Average American

The demographic characteristics of the typical Levittown family are remarkably close to those of the statistically average American family drawn from the
1970 census,[66] as the following table indicates. The main differences are the
slightly larger size and value of the Levittowners' homes and the larger
number of cars to which he has access.

	Average American Family	Average Levittown Family (Data Approximate)
Location of residence	Metropolitan suburb	Metropolitan suburb
Race	White	White
Age of adult male	44	42
Age of adult female	41	39
Years of education completed	12.2	12.4
Number of children	2.35	2.2
Size of house	5 rooms	6 rooms
Value of house	$17,000	$22,000
Number of cars	1.25	1.8

The Levittown Area: Community System Characteristics

In many ways, Levittown is not a "real" community. It does not have its own separate government, or its own employment base, and even the major shopping center now lies outside of the Levittown area. In barest terms, Levittown is a large housing development, a dormitory suburb, and a place name: mail is addressed to Levittown, Pennsylvania, most Levittowners say they live in Levittown, and the term Levittown appears on maps.

Government Structure

The development called Levittown is divided into four separate jurisdictions of local government within the state of Pennsylvania and the county of Bucks: The townships of Bristol, Falls, and Middletown, and the borough of Tullytown (the distinction between a township and a borough is based on size and density). Each local government jurisdiction, with boundaries established years ago when the area was agricultural, has its own elected officials, its own tax rate, its own police force, and many other government functions. The school systems are also apportioned roughly along the lines of the governmental jurisdictions.

It is often difficult or impossible to know when one passes from one township to the next—in some cases the boundary runs through the middle of a Levittown neighborhood—but it makes a significant social and financial difference under which government the Levittown resident falls. Bristol township has the most problems, because it includes an older, built-up section of Lower Bucks County which has a large number of poor families. It also has

the highest real-estate tax rate of the four, and the highest percentage of
Levittown families with relatively low incomes. At the opposite extreme,
Middletown township has the fewest problems, the wealthiest Levittown
families, and the lowest tax rate. Thus the divisions within Levittown follow a
de facto principle found among most American communities—those with the
most problems have the fewest local resources with which to meet them.

During the early years, many Levittowners were very concerned about this
"fractionation" of local government. In order to get their fair share of services from the rural Republicans then dominant in local government offices,
and to insure coordinated local planning and development for Levittown, they
were eager to establish a governmental unity around what was a unified
housing development. Many volunteer experts in various fields of local government labored diligently in the early 1950s to prepare what came to be
called "The Blue Book"—"A Study of the Factors Involved in the Incorporation of Lower Bucks County, Pennsylvania."[67]

Nevertheless, a referendum to incorporate Levittown as a new, separate,
local-government jurisdiction was defeated. Not surprisingly, Bristol township residents were the predominant backers of the referendum; the other
townships, fearing increased taxes, especially school taxes, to pay for Bristol
township's special burdens, voted against separate incorporation.

Governmental incorporation for Levittown is virtually a dead issue today.
Given the existing fiscal and social realities, such as differences in tax rates
and income levels, the residents of Middletown, for example, could never be
induced to merge voluntarily with Bristol township. To a large extent, however, the residents of Levittown got what they wanted from the existing local
governments. In every township but one, Levittown residents make up a large
majority of the township's population, and thus the new suburbanites had the
votes to change the political coloration of local government offices from
solidly rural Republican to solidly urban Democratic. It is a commentary on
local government in America that, although Levittown has four governments
today instead of one, it has probably made little difference in Levittown's
growth, development, and problems over the years; one would be hard put to
identify any specific changes in the overall growth pattern or social structure
of Levittown which the consolidation of governments might have brought.

Employment Structure

Because there are almost no jobs, except for those furnished by schools and
shops, within the boundaries of Levittown itself, the community's degree of
economic independence or self-containment is very low. Levitt intended his
development to be a place to live, not to work; he assumed that most of his

home buyers would work in Philadelphia, Trenton, N.J. (a city of 104,000 population lying about five miles east of Levittown), or in the nearby Fairless Works of U.S. Steel Corporation. Levitt's assumptions about work places held true in the community's early years. A 1956 survey showed that two out of five residents of lower Bucks County worked within their home county, while 37.5 percent worked in the central business district and 25.3 percent in Trenton.[68] Over the years, however, the distance to work has diminished. In 1970, in the four townships which include Levittown, only about 14 percent of the residents work in Philadelphia, less than 10 percent work in Trenton, while 54 percent work within the Bucks County area.[69] In the sample census tract in Levittown, 71 percent work in Bucks County and 19 percent work in Philadelphia (of these, only 6 percent work in the central business district).[70] The three largest employers in the Lower Bucks area are the U.S. Steel Fairless Works with 9,000 employees, Rohm and Haas with 2,000 employees, and Minnesota Mining and Manufacturing with 1,560 persons, an estimated 30 percent of whom live in Levittown.[71]

Skilled factory work is probably the most characteristic working-class occupation. Many such jobs are in small concerns, distributed throughout the area surrounding Levittown. Almost all employees in Levittown drive to work; only 5 percent make use of public transportation to get to their places of work.[72]

Residential Facilities and Services

The Organization of Facilities and Services. The local governmental unit is but one facet of the administration of facilities and services in the American community. Typically, the U.S. resident is caught up in a complex network of geographically overlapping service districts, and the Levittown resident is no exception. In addition to services supplied by units at a higher level than the local government—county, state, and federal services in such areas as the courts, recreation, health and welfare, and planning—Levittown residents receive services from many nongovernmental jurisdictions at the local level. The schools of Levittown are run by three separate school districts, each independent of the others. Water and sewer facilities are run by the Lower Bucks County Joint Municipal Authority, established at the time Levittown was first built. The major public swimming pools and a few other recreational facilities in Levittown are run by the Levittown Public Recreation Association, a membership organization which, until very recently, was restricted to persons living in Levitt houses. Many welfare, "character-building," and health and medical research agencies are supported by the nongovernmental, nonprofit Bucks County United Fund. It is often difficult for the resident to find his way among this welter of organizations, and there is no single directory to which he can turn for guidance.[73]

Retail Establishments. Levitt's only venture into the retail field in Levittown was the planning and development of a sixty-store shopping center (originally called Shop-a-Rama) at a cost of $20 million. In its early years the center, adjacent to the offices of the Levitt Organization, provided the one community-wide focus and meeting ground for the development. Today, however, the center stands, looking undistinguished and slightly out of style, on what has become the edge of Levittown farthest from the newer and more wealthy sections of the community. There is growing concern about its future; the number of stores is down to about forty-five, and the center recently lost its large J. C. Penney outlet.

Since Levittown's inception, hundreds of retail stores have been built on scattered pieces of land throughout the area. Some stores stand by themselves; most exist in shopping complexes which range in size from a few stores to complete centers rivaling the original Levitt center in size. The stores provide needed "neighborhood services" to the lucky residents who happen to live near them; to the citizen at large, they often provide dramatic examples of commercial blight.

Most striking in the 1970s are the great number of these retail establishments going out of business, or on the verge of it. In some cases, entire shopping centers are in the process of gradual retail decline and abandonment. This is owing not so much to a decline in consumer purchasing power or to bad management as to the development of new, and usually larger, competing shopping centers nearby. The proliferation of retail establishments in the United States is checked only by the market forces of supply and demand and the regulations of local zoning boards. Zoning board directives, which can control the use of land in the public interest, may be weak or inconsistent, and typically show little concern for consequences outside of the board's jurisdiction. The fate of the aging, obsolescent, and bypassed shopping centers is never clear or definite; they may linger on marginally for years, or they may simply be abandoned, the hollow shell left standing indefinitely as a blight on the landscape. While an entire shopping center in Levittown has not yet been abandoned, many isolated commercial buildings have. The workings of the market in the retail field seem to generate two unfortunate side effects: the personal losses usually incurred by the losers in the competition, and the environmental blight which is the public's legacy.

The latest entry into the region's parade of shopping centers is the recently completed Oxford Valley Mall. Located on a huge piece of open land about one-half mile north of the Levittown boundary, the Mall consists of 124 shops plus four major department stores, surrounded by a massive parking lot which holds 8,000 cars. The Mall itself is fully enclosed and for pedestrians only. The shops are built on two levels, focusing on fountains, statuary, and sitting areas.

The Oxford Valley Mall stands in isolation, related to the environment around it by an elaborate network of access roads. During the day it appears from the outside like a huge fortress surrounded by a sea of cars. At night, it stands bleak and lonely in a vast, empty space of asphalt.

Once inside during business hours, however, the Mall is a world apart from its surroundings. The shopper is treated to a scene of strolling pedestrians, of gay colors and interesting interior spaces, and enjoys controlled temperature and clean air. The milieu of the automobile has been left behind. This is the only large environment in the Levittown area where one can be completely, if only temporarily, away from the auto. It is a world totally dominated by business and commerce, however—from this there is no retreat.

The full effect of this new shopping center on Levittown's retail economy is yet to be known, but it is expected that it will accelerate the obsolescence of the older shopping centers, leading to a further decline in retail sales. It is also having some interesting social consequences which will be discussed in the next two chapters. Most residents are very pleased with the Mall, especially middle-class adults and teenagers. Working-class adults tend to find it too expensive, however, compared to the smaller centers in the area.[74]

Schools. Schools rank second only to homes as the principal focus of interest and attention in Levittown. For many, schools were the drawing card in their move to the development, and schools rank very high in answer to the question: "What is important about Levittown?"[75] Indeed, interest in the schools has grown over the years as more children have reached school age, and as the early preoccupation with "house problems" has diminished.[76] Moreover, the main community issue in Levittown today is that world-wide modern phenomenon "the youth problem," and the schools naturally figure prominently in this issue. The schools are sometimes described as a battle-ground, as an insidious influence on the young, and as a source of disturbing social change.

While the typical adult in Levittown has very little direct contact with the school, for the child of school age it becomes almost as important as the home. It is at school that friends are made, peer groups formed, youth subcultures developed, and the attitudes and interests of the young heavily shaped. This is especially true for working-class youth, whose family life may be quite weak. The effects of the social climate within the school often pervade the nonschool hours.

There are within or immediately adjacent to the Levittown development twenty-one public schools and six parochial schools, many of which are on sites donated by the Levitt Organization. The public schools consist of fifteen elementary schools, three junior high schools, two senior high schools, and one vocational-technical high school. Levittown is a part of three mutually independent school districts. Because each school district includes many non-Levitt neighborhoods, a substantial portion of the Levittown school population goes to secondary schools located outside the development.

The public schools of Levittown seem little different from schools in other American suburbs. The culture of the schools is patterned strongly by inter-scholastic competition (mottos in the front hall of one high school: "Wilson cannot be topped"; "Through these doors pass the finest students in Bucks County"); sports competition is especially prominent. What are disturbing issues in middle-class schools become serious problems in those attended by the children of the working class, particularly drug use (estimated to involve over 50 percent of one high school's student body in the early 1970s),[77] truancy, and racial tensions in the one high school which has a sizable population of black students, from an area adjacent to Levittown. In the high school with the highest percentage of working-class students, 40 to 50 percent of the graduates go on to some form of higher education (including technical schools and two-year colleges); in the more middle-class high schools the percentage is higher.

Levittown differs somewhat from the typical U.S. suburb in the percentage of its youth, about 20 percent, who go to parochial schools run by the Roman Catholic church.[78] Parochial school enrollments have been dropping, however, due mainly to financial pressures on parents, but also to a declining interest in religion and to the growing inability of parochial schools, because of insufficient funds, to compete academically with the public schools. The parochial schools speak with pride about their firmer discipline and higher standard of student behavior; this is owing in large part to the fact that "behavior cases" are simply dropped by the parochial schools, whereas public schools are required to accept them in some fashion until age sixteen.

In addition to the Roman Catholic schools, a few private schools have been established in recent years for children whose parents have for one reason or another become dissatisfied with the public schools. Racial tension has apparently been one major source of such dissatisfaction. The number of children in such schools at the present time is extremely small. Smaller still is the number of Levittown youth who go to private schools outside the area; these youth are typically from the upper-middle-class sections of Levittown.

Religious Institutions. The church in Levittown plays a very significant role in the lives of its active members; it is a community within a community.[79] Put another way, it is a community within a noncommunity, for those who are church members have something that most other Levittowners do not have: a communal tie to a large number of people with whom many aspects of their lives may be shared. The church provides more than religious sustenance; indeed this may be one of its least important functions, although religious beliefs are the shared ideological binder which holds the group together. Church members meet their friends through church, and the church provides recreational and social activities throughout the week. In times of need, either physical or emotional, the church is there to help, with such assistance as a loan of money, a visit from the minister to a sick person, and personal and family counseling.

Levitt donated ground sites for most of the religious institutions in his development, and today there are over fifteen churches, temples, and synagogues within the area, with many other institutions in the surrounding environs which serve a portion of the Levittown population. Some of the churches were established in the early years of Levittown by the parent denominations, others were constructed later by "popular demand." It is not known precisely how many Levittowners are active church members, but the figure is probably about 50 percent, running slightly above the national average.[80]

The largest Protestant church in Levittown, a Presbyterian one, has about 1,500 adult members. Attendance at a typical Sunday service totals 500 persons, but the church also has many activities running throughout the week; Wednesday and Sunday evenings are especially big for teenage activities, for example. The minister has 800 counseling appointments each year. The church also acts as a meeting place for many local organizations, and even as a hangout for teenagers after school.

Although the social role of the religious institution is not unique to American society, it is more fully developed here than in any other advanced nation. This helps account for the U.S. ranking at the top among the Western nations in the percentage of the population that attends church or synagogue regularly.[81] The difference between the U.S. and Sweden in this respect is especially striking.

Recreational and Leisure Facilities. Recreation in Levittown is mostly a private activity of home and yard. Every Levittowner has a yard large enough for a small swimming pool, a badminton set, and a barbecue. The larger Levitt homes have a recreation room for such activities as Ping-Pong, billiards, and

board games. Virtually every home has a TV set, which in terms of time spent
is the most popular (and most passive) form of recreation in Levittown. Probably the most prominent public supplier of recreational services to youth in the
community today is the schools, which over the last few years have gradually
become more all-purpose institutions by opening in the evenings. Many
schools are now open six nights a week, with supervised activities in such
areas as basketball, swimming, and gymnastics. Attendance at these activities
is very disappointing to school officials, however, and they are at a loss to
account for this lack of interest. The youth complain that the activities are too
supervised, too difficult to get to in the evenings, and that they "have had
enough" of school during the day.

There is also within the Levittown area a system of parks and playgrounds
operated by the separate townships. The public facilities include tot lots,
playgrounds, ball fields, and undeveloped wooded areas. Data on the use of
these facilities are not available; the ball fields appear to be well utilized and
the tot lots underutilized; many wooded areas are used by teenagers but are
considered unsafe by older adults. A large and mostly undeveloped county
park, Mill Creek Valley Park, lies at one edge of Levittown.

Supervised recreational activities in Levittown are heavily oriented toward
the person with athletic talent and toward boys. Aside from school sports,
which are dominated by competitive teams, the most prominent sports activities are Little League baseball and, on a slightly lesser scale, Pop Warner
football—sports leagues geared to grade-school boys. Little League basball
was the first organized sports activity developed in Levittown, and it continues to be perhaps the most important community-wide activity in terms of
interest and publicity. Indeed, the community gained national attention in
1959–60 when its team won the world series in Little League baseball.
There is nothing comparable to the Little League organization for girls, and
there are few organized athletic activities for children with limited athletic
abilities. Consequently, the sports activities of Levittown, though highly visible, are limited to a very small portion of the youth population.

Adult sports activites are commonly initiated through the place of work;
there is interorganizational baseball competition among the work units in
many factories, for example. Beyond that, the Levittown adult turns to commercial sports facilities, the most popular of which is bowling. The several
bowling alleys in the Levittown area can be very lively places on a typical
week night, with team bowling and family bowling especially common.

In terms of time spent, another important leisure activity for many adults in
Levittown is drinking in the bars and cocktail lounges. As most restaurants in
Levittown do not serve liquor, the drinking of alcohol is relegated almost
exclusively to the home and to the many bars which dot the Levittown land-

scape. Most of the bars are in small shopping complexes; they remain open long after the other stores have closed for the night.

The Levittown bar is mainly a male habitat; in one bar I visited there were seventy-five males and one female. The men stop by for a drink on the way home from work and frequent the bars in the evening hours after dinner. Some bars are lively and noisy, with a great amount of male socializing; others are glum, with the men lined up in rows staring quietly at their half-filled glasses. Some of the bars are more family-oriented, with both husband and wife coming out for an evening, usually on weekends. Few of the bars have live entertainment, but almost all have the ever-present television set on in the background. Because of the distractions, it is extremely difficult to "follow" a complete TV show in a bar, and people do not go there for that purpose.

Levitt's main contribution to recreation in the area was the establishment, in 1953, of the Levittown Public Recreation Association (LPRA.), an organization of special interest because it is one of the few Levittown-wide organizations in existence and was in the early years an important bond between Levittown residents. The LPRA now controls five Olympic-size swimming pools—with adjacent pavilions, picnic areas, and playgrounds—and one baseball field; the first of the swimming pools was completed in 1959. While the capital cost of the facilities was paid by the Levitt organization, their upkeep and improvement are financed by annual fees; $30 per family, a reasonable fee for the ninety-two-day swimming season. The fee also entitles members to use the facilities and services of the LPRA's community center, discussed below, during the winter months.

In the early days of the LPRA, membership ran as high as 8,000 families—almost half of the families in Levittown. By 1973, membership had dropped to 4,600 families, an almost 50 percent decline that was due in part to the decrease in Levittown youth, now the almost exclusive users of the LPRA facilities.[82] Other causes are the proliferation of backyard swimming pools (it is estimated that more than 10 percent of Levittown households now have such pools), an increase in the availability of commercial swimming and other recreational facilities, and the recent evening opening of public schools for recreational purposes.[83] Keeping some children away from LPRA facilities are the poor maintenance and the growing number of youth problems. Though improvements have been made over the years, the financially hard-pressed LPRA has not been able to meet adequately, according to many residents, the high cost of maintenance and recurrent vandalism.

The great majority of pool users are between ten and fifteen years of age. Before the age of ten, a child cannot be at the pool without an adult or older teenager. After the age of fifteen, teenagers have access to cars and go further

afield for their activities, not wanting to hang out at a place associated with the
younger age-groups. During the winter months, however, when the pools are
closed, the pool areas have become major hangout places in Levittown for the
older teenagers. Adults are rather infrequent users of the pools, partly due to
the youth culture which prevails there. One of the pools has been left open
evenings for adult use, but pool use on these evenings is not high.

Levitt's old office building next to the Levittown shopping center, now the
headquarters of the LPRA, is the only general community center in Levittown. It is sometimes rented out for parties and wedding receptions (about ten
a year), it is used occasionally for such community activities as hobby and pet
shows, and it is the locus of a modest number of clubs and hobby activities,
such as photography and karate. Association officials are disappointed in the
very low participation rates for community center activities.

Several attempts have been made in recent years to utilize the community
center building as an after-school and weekend center. About 1970, the LPRA
made some alterations in its two-hundred-seat capacity main room and opened
it in February as "The Lounge." The hours were after-school 3:00 to 5:00,
Saturdays 1:00 to 5:00 and in the evening, and Sundays 1:00 to 5:00. On the
first few days after opening, daily attendance was about two hundred youths,
most of whom lived near the community center. "The Lounge" ran successfully for about three months, with only one or two serious incidents with
drinking and gambling. By April, however, regular attendance was down to
about thirty youths. After the summer closing, the center never again was able
to arouse much interest, and it finally closed. The community center building
is now open for youth in the afternoons, but only for sports. An active day
may find forty or fifty young people there, all of whom must be members of
the LPRA.

Over the years, the LPRA has also sponsored teen dances. An early survey
of Levittown residents indicated that most parents felt this was one of the most
important activities the association could sponsor for youth.[84] The association's success in this area has been very poor, however. Though some of the
dances drew crowds of over three hundred, the serious incidents which
arose—drinking, dope, gambling, weapons, and fights—caused the dances to
be discontinued.

Libraries. The history of the Levittown Public Library makes a fine case
study of the provision of residential services, American-style. No provision
for library services was made by any of the governmental units within which
Levittown falls, or by the Levitt organization, except for $200 which Levitt

gave toward a bookmobile. Instead of a bookmobile, however, a library was initiated by volunteers in a room in the community center. The library opened with four hundred books, all donated by private individuals.

When it began, the library was organizationally a branch of the Free Library of Fallsington, a nearby village. It soon became clear that the library would be unable to grow under these auspices, however, because a school board subsidy to the library facility in Fallsington restricted fund raising on the part of the Levittown branch. The connection with Fallsington was therefore severed, and the library went off entirely on its own with funds raised locally by volunteers. The "new" Levittown library—with 1,500 books—opened in 1954. In 1955, it moved to new quarters, the donated basement of a pharmacy in the Levittown shopping center, and in 1956 the library was legally incorporated.

The library continued to grow, almost entirely with volunteer assistance. A small, separate library building was constructed in 1958, and the name was changed to the Regional Public Library, serving each of the four townships. At this time the library hired its first professional librarian, who worked with 123 volunteers.

After a local fund drive, plus the acquisition of federal financial aid, a major new building addition was completed in 1965. Soon thereafter, and once the library was a firmly established community facility, it merged with the county library and became the Lower County Center of the Bucks County Free Library. In 1973, it had 57,000 volumes, twelve full-time, and two part-time employees. A success story, but one which was hard won by the diligent work of hundreds of dedicated volunteers. While Levittowners are proud that they have their own library, many feel that it is inadequate, and by conventional library service standards it assuredly is.

The Facilities and Services of Levittown: Some Conclusions

By North American standards, the facilities and services of Levittown are, in general, more than adequate. The schools are relatively new and seem to be of generally high quality, the churches are large and active, open space in Levittown is abundant, and the five community swimming pools are an important community asset. To these communal facilities must be added the many private facilities associated with the Levitt houses and yards. Why is it then, that the most common complaint of teenagers in Levittown is that "there is nothing to do here"?

This question will be discussed in the following chapters. What should be noted here are some of the ways in which Levittown falls short in its facilities

and services network, especially by European standards. Few of the facilities
are neighborhood-based; because of this they *seem* distant to the residents,
even though the actual time spent getting to them by car is not great. And the
necessity for a car sets up a double dependence situation: Not only must the
facility be available, but a car must also be available if the facility is to be
utilized. This situation holds true especially for retail facilities, the most
commonly used ones in any community.

Some important facilities are almost entirely absent in Levittown. There are
few child-care centers, few youth centers, and almost no facilities for the
elderly, the poor, the handicapped. This deficit places a special burden on
certain types of people in Levittown—on those persons, in fact, who are most
dependent on the resources of the local environment. Moreover, there are
almost no facilities or activities, except for those of religious institutions,
which involve all age groups together.

6

The People of Levittown

Patterns of Environmental Fit

Using the approach introduced and discussed in chapter 4, "The People of Vällingby," the lifestyles of Levittown residents are described in this chapter, and their relationships to the environment are explored from the point of view of the concept of environmental fit or congruence. From the household interview sample, cases have been selected which illustrate the range and types of environmental congruence found among adults in the community, followed by a description of the living patterns of Levittown's teenagers and a discussion of what most adults feel is the community's most serious problem—juvenile delinquency.

Environmental fit or congruence refers to the degree to which an environment accommodates the needs, goals, and patterns of social behavior of its residents. A situation of high congruence between a resident and his or her environment is one where there are few social or personal problems which are environmentally related and where there is both a feeling of contentment on the part of the resident with the environment as it is and a high evaluation of the environment in comparison with alternatives to it. At the other end of the scale, a situation of low congruence is one where many environmentally related problems and constraints on desired behavior are in evidence and where residents are discontented with their environment and evaluate it negatively. While the concept is complex and not easy to

apply empirically, it is useful in illuminating those characteristics of environments and of human behavior that are most closely interrelated.

Households Illustrating a High Degree of Congruence with the Environment

The Characteristic Levittown Household

Despite more demographic heterogeneity in Levittown than when the suburb
was first settled, one household and family type emerged from the demographic analysis as most characteristic of the community today, in the sense of
occurring more frequently than any other single type: The family of middle-
aged adults whose teenagers are leaving home. This is the type into which the
original Levittown settlers, who came as young families with children, now
fall. Within this category, eight of the households in the interview sample
were remarkably similar in life-style and attitudes toward Levittown, with
only minor variations in such characteristics as family size, place of origin,
and age. The common elements shared by most of these eight cases have been
put together, as was done for Vällingby in chapter 4, into a composite case—a
descriptive sketch of the characteristic Levittown household. The major dimensions of this composite type were often put forth by community informants in their discussions of the people of Levittown. Moreover, in many of
its demographic and social characteristics, this composite type is remarkably
close to the average American family, discussed in the last chapter.

The characteristic household consists of two married adults in their forties,
and two teenagers; a third, postteen, child has left home. This third child lives
near by, though in a garden apartment rather than a Levitt house, and continues to see his parents quite often.

Both adults work within the Lower Bucks County area, the man in a skilled
blue-collar (for example, pipe fitter in a factory) or lower-middle-class (for
example, insurance salesman) occupation, and the woman in a clerical, retail
sales, or teaching job. Each drives to his or her job, taking about twenty
minutes door-to-door. Both have finished high school but have had no more
than a year of college. They have lived in Levittown for about ten or twelve
years and grew up within the Philadelphia metropolitan area, where their
parents and relatives still live. Parents and relatives continue to play an
important role in their lives. Living as they do within easy driving distance,
visiting back and forth is frequent, especially on holidays, and the relatives
are important in a system of mutual aid.

Within the home, the parents share a bedroom and both teenage children
have separate bedrooms. There are two TV sets and two cars. The teenagers

travel to school by bus and have the use of the cars after school and in the evenings. The family has at least one pet, usually a dog or cat.

The adults' life-style centers around the home. Working long or irregular hours, the man complains that he has very little free time; his leisure time is spent at home in informal family activities, watching TV, or maintaining or improving the house or yard. The woman, who also complains of being pressed for time, follows a similar activity pattern, with interior maintenance and improvement replacing work on house and yard. One or two couples, in addition to parents and relatives, are seen socially, usually people met through work (often the husband's place of work). The social activities are informal: outdoor barbecues in the summer and after-dinner drinks; talk and card games during the winter months. The couple read the daily Lower Bucks County newspaper, subscribe to no more than one magazine, and seldom read books.

The characteristic family holds membership in a local church, and the adults attend Sunday services frequently. Except for the man's union or professional organization, they do not belong to any organizations or clubs in Levittown. One spouse may regularly participate in a single local activity outside the home, such as church, school, social service, or bowling; the other has no outside activities at all ("no time", "there is always too much to do around the house"). They seldom eat out in restaurants, seldom go to the movies, and almost never go into center-city Philadelphia or downtown Trenton for recreational or any other reasons. They get no regular exercise—either through walking (very few people walk any distance for any purpose in Levittown), bicycle riding (they do not own bikes), or sports activities.

Most of the nearby neighbors are known by name but not those who live more than four or five houses away. The neighbors are not typically seen socially, but the neighborhood is judged to be "friendly enough." Some of the neighbors can be counted on for help in an emergency. In nice weather, when people are in their yards, it is common to strike up a conversation over the back fence. But the neighborhood is not as social as it once was: "People come and go, you know, and there are so many newcomers now!"

Summer vacations are short, often only two weeks. Some men take no regular summer vacations at all, preferring long weekends at various times during the year. The vacation is commonly spent at home working on the house ("it's a time to catch up on necessary chores that we haven't had time to get to during the year"). If the family takes a vacation trip out of the area, it is seldom for more than a week and often for only three or four days, perhaps to the New Jersey shore.

The characteristic family moved to Levittown from a denser part of the metropolitan area in order to get a home of its own ("It's one of the best houses you could get for the money"), a piece of land, and a good place to raise their children. Both husband and wife participated in the decision and were in agreement about the move; neither has ever regretted it.

They are pleased to be living in Levittown and wouldn't mind living out their lives there; indeed, they have no plans to move. The qualities held most desirable about Levittown are those which initially attracted them to the community—the house, the yard, good schools; also, they feel that it is very "convenient" ("You have everything you need here, and it is near work and the big cities"). Levittown is much preferred over where they used to live.

If the adults were to move from Levittown, they would want a house similar to but larger than their Levitt house, on a larger lot with more open space around it. To obtain such a house would require relocating farther out into the country. Under no circumstances would they want to move into the city. "The city is hell," as one resident put it, and the less they see of it the better. There is a desire to be near "urban services," however, especially branches of downtown department stores.

Although the residents' attitudes toward Levittown are overwhelmingly positive, several "concerns" about the area are commonly expressed. The most important is that about youth and drugs. Levittown has had a mild outbreak of juvenile delinquency over the past five years, including drugs, vandalism, truancy, burglaries, auto thefts, and even some modest "gang fights" among teenage groups. Many parents are seriously concerned about these problems, especially, of course, if their own children are involved. They do not put the blame on Levittown, however ("You find the same problems everywhere, now"). The Levittowners are not clear about what has caused this increase in delinquency: moral laxness, loss of respect for authority, problems in the schools, and lack of discipline on the part of parents are frequently cited. They all agree on one thing: "It wasn't like this when we were young—times have changed."

Another concern, which ranks just behind the problems of youth, is the environmental changes which are taking place in the area. "It is gradually losing its country character." "There is so much traffic now, and so many new stores and businesses." The city is coming to Levittown, a realization which is held with displeasure.

It appears that this couple is congruent with the Levittown environment. Their life-style is not culturally rich by upper-middle-class standards, but is informal, friendly, and comfortable, just as they seem to wish. They have space for their family's needs; because most things they want are near them—work, shopping, schools, friends and relatives—they do not feel isolated; and their dependence on the car is a fully accepted way of life. When things go wrong with car, home, television set, or backyard swimming pool, they have the money to make repairs.

The characteristic Levittown adults have some concerns about life in Levittown but realize that the same things are happening all over the nation—rising crime and delinquency rates, over-commercialization, breakdown of morality and respect for authority. Indeed, they feel somewhat insulated from these trends in Levittown. Pride is taken in the fact that, within their own home, a bastion of decency, order, conformity, and trust has been created.

While many Levittown households do not match this composite household in such structural characteristics as family size, income level, and stage of the life cycle, the great majority of households interviewed shared a similar life-style, expressed the same attitudes toward Levittown, and seemed equally congruent with the environment. The following two cases indicate the range of variation of congruent households in the community.

Second-Generation Levittowners

While the most commonly occurring household type in Levittown today is an older version of the original Levittowners, next most common is the young family with small children, the second-generation Levittowners. These families, often younger than the original settlers were on their arrival in the community, are the typical replacements for the aging Levittown families that have moved on.

Mr. and Mrs. M. are an attractive, affable couple married three years. Each was born and raised in Levittown, although Mrs. M. moved to a larger house in a neighboring municipality at the age of eleven; both graduated five years ago from one of the Levittown high schools. They have a ten-month-old child and purchased their Levitt house a year and a half ago.

With two years of college, Mrs. M. worked before her son was born in a certified public accountant's office; Mr. M. completed his education with high school, worked for several years for the government, and has just started as a laborer at nearby U.S. Steel, five minutes from his home. He hopes to become an apprentice and eventually work his way up to a skilled, union-protected position. The family has two cars ("I would be lost without my own car," says Mrs. M.).

For the first few years of their married life the M.'s lived in apartments in the Levittown area. Their first apartment was "a disaster": noisy, damp, full of bugs, and with unfriendly neighbors. A second apartment was satisfactory but provided no place outside for a child to play except the parking lot. The decision to buy a Levitt house was a joint one. Both had grown up in the area, had liked it, and felt it was a good environment for child rearing; they now could afford payments on a house, and Mr. M. wanted a yard as a place to work on cars and boats. At first they were the only young couple in their new neighborhood.

Mr. and Mrs. M. have an active social life. About once a week friends, usually three or four couples, are invited for after-dinner cards and talk; Mrs. M. would like to have big parties but finds it too expensive. While several neighbors are included in their social gatherings, the M's best friends are former schoolmates. In addition, Mr. and Mrs. M. often visit with their own families. Mrs. M.'s father is dead, but she sees her mother every week, and often her three brothers and two sisters, all of whom live in the area. Mr. M. sees his parents and sister each week also, phoning them several times a week in addition.

The M.'s are irregular church attenders but regular bowlers on amateur teams, twice weekly. Mr. M. also plays weekly on a softball team during the spring and summer months. Unlike most older residents of Levittown, the couple take walks and go bike riding a great deal, now with a bicycle seat for the baby. Restaurants and moviegoing are limited to about once a month; the major form of passive entertainment is TV—three and a half hours per evening on the average, plus some daytime TV for Mrs. M. They subscribe to a wide assortment of magazines, including *Field and Stream, Ski, Boating, American Home,* and *Good Housekeeping.* They dream of owning a boat someday and of taking frequent ski trips.

Summer vacations are spent on short trips out of the area and in working on the house, for which they have big plans for improvements. They get to Philadelphia only for sports events ("It's not worth the aggravation to go there for shopping"); once a year they try to go to New York, especially for New Year's Eve. On these and similar occasions, family members are depended on for baby-sitting.

The M.'s are very happy with Levittown and have no plans to move, at least not for a long time. What do they like best about the community? "It is convenient; we have everything we need here; we can afford it; we have our family and friends here." Had they had more money, however, they might have looked for a larger house outside of Levittown. They plan to have three children at most ("only two if the next one is a girl"). Mrs. M. has no desire to return to work, although she enjoyed her job; she says she works full time as a mother and wife, and she has her bowling—"That's plenty for me."

This is a young working-class family which seems successfully to be leading a middle-class life-style. They have enough money (there must be a source of income supplemental to the husband's job as a laborer) to be able to afford a single-family house, two cars, an active social life, and a nonworking wife. Moreover, they have the benefit and security of having their parents and siblings nearby. By all appearances a very happy couple, there are few things lacking for them in Levittown. If their income increases, they may some day leave the community, but it will be only to get a larger house; they will seek to duplicate most of the characteristics of their present residential environment.

The Retired Couple

At the other end of the age spectrum from the M. family is the retired couple, a small but rapidly growing population segment in Levittown. While many older residents find life difficult in Levittown and are forced to leave, some have been successful in adapting to an environment which was designed for young families.

Mr. and Mrs. H., both still youthful looking and in good health, grew up on farms in a neighboring state but have lived in the Levittown area since young adulthood. As local farmers, they were residents of the area when Levitt arrived. They remember that time well: "We ate a lot of dirt and mud for several months, then the taxes jumped up like crazy . . . the old farmers here were sure that these new houses would be blown apart by the first big windstorm." A beautiful farming area was lost, they report, but the newcomers seemed to be nice people, and it was not long before they were accepted by the older residents. The oldtimers all agreed, however, that Levittown seemed a strange new way for people to live.

Mr. H. retired several years ago after several decades of employment at one of the region's largest automobile dealers. During the first years of Levittown, he also raised fruits and vegetables on his ten-acre plot and sold them at a roadside stand. The taxes on his property became so high, however, that he sold it ten years ago to a prospective shopping-center developer and moved into a Levitt house, picking one which had open space bordering the rear yard so as to give him a feeling of greater freedom and privacy.

Mr. and Mrs. H. live a quiet life in Levittown. Both are regular church attenders (Methodist) and were active in many church activities until recently, when their energy began to taper off; they maintain a religious home, with frequent reading of the Bible and other church literature. The man reads a lot (newspapers, magazines, and novels in addition to religious works), and takes a special interest in bowling twice a week. He maintains his interest in working the land through the care of a backyard garden, and he takes regular walks around the neighborhood with his dog. Every few months he attends a meeting of the Masons.

Mrs. H. devotes much of her time to housework, to sewing as a hobby, and to a few church activities. In amount of time spent, TV-watching is undoubtedly the major activity for both partners—the set is on all afternoon and evening and sometimes in the morning. On Friday evenings they regularly play pinochle with several couples who are former farmer-neighbors. For weekend leisure, Mr. and Mrs. H. take drives around Bucks County (both drive; they have one car), often ending up at nearby shopping malls where they sit and watch people.

They have a married son whom they visit once or twice a week; he lives in a nearby garden apartment and works for the same employer that his father did. Every six months, the H. couple drives down to their childhood home to visit a few relatives who still live there.

Mr. and Mrs. H. are content with their house, their lives, and Levittown. It is a nice-looking area, they say, and has all the city conveniences. "Anything you are looking for, you can find it in Levittown"; "The people keep their houses up nicely; the schools are good." "It has been fun to meet people who come from all over the country," they report. They feel their neighbors are friendly and helpful; mostly middle-aged couples live in their neighborhood, but there are other retired couples living nearby, two of whom are occasionally seen socially. Mr. and Mrs. H. can think of almost no aspect of Levittown they dislike—perhaps (on second thought) the traffic jams and lack of public transportation, but these don't often affect them directly.

Though some thought has been given to moving "back home," they say they will probably live here until they die. "More of our people are back home, and the pace of living is slower—you don't have to rush everywhere. . . . But our son is here in Levittown, and the medical care is much superior here." If they did move, the man would want another single-family house (for financial reasons, he says); the woman would consider an apartment (easier to maintain).   ·

This couple seems as well suited to Levittown as is the couple with young children. Their life-style as a retired couple might even be seen as an enviable one. But it depends heavily on their good health, maintenance of an adequate income, their continuing ability to drive a car, and the proximity of their son. Each of these considerations could change suddenly, with possible drastic effects.

The main life-style variations to be found in Levittown, apart from those attached to stages of the life cycle, are based on social-class differences.[1] The composite description of the characteristic Levittown household referred mainly to an upper-lower-class or lower-middle-class family. The middle- or upper-middle-class Levittowners are found in larger houses, with more facilities, in neighborhoods of more expensive homes. They tend to be involved in more activities outside the home, such as clubs and organizations, and to go to "the city" slightly more often, for shopping or perhaps entertainment; they eat out more in restaurants and take longer and more expensive vacations. At home, upper-middle-class families engage in more formal entertaining (such as dinner parties) and subscribe to a larger number of magazines than working-class families. Working-class families tend to be less congruent with the environment than middle-class families for reasons explored in the next section.

Households Illustrating a Low Degree of Congruence with the Environment

The Problem Family in Levittown: A Constructed Type

While the characteristic household discussed above was a composite based on features common to a number of families in Levittown, for the discussion of incongruence a "constructed type" has been developed consisting of a combination of the main problematic traits found among families in the community.[2] The purpose of a constructed type is to provide a coherent description or explanation of a phenomenon by reducing its diversity and complexity through "selection, limitation, combination and accentuation."[3] No family in the household sample had all of the negative traits which are included in this constructed type, but each trait was found in at least one family, and several families had many of them. While the following portrayal therefore exaggerates the severity of problems found in any single Levittown family, it points up the nature and range of difficulties which many families face, emphasizing the ways in which these difficulties are environmentally related. As in the case of the characteristic family, the major dimensions of this constructed type frequently were raised by Levittown informants when they discussed family problems in the community.

The problem-family in Levittown is very large: four, five, or more children cause the relatively small Levitt houses to burst at the seams. The children do not have their own bedrooms, they have inadequate indoor play and study space, and they have—by American standards—little privacy. Further, they are always "getting in their parents' hair," and their parents, in turn, have little space in which to lead their own adult lives. The teenagers in such a situation tend to stay away from home as much as possible, hanging out on the streets or visiting friends.

The adults were born and raised either in a low-status working-class district of Philadelphia or in a working-class coal or steel town in upstate Pennsylvania. Place of origin affects their attitudes about Levittown somewhat (the small-town Pennsylvanians are more likely to have negative views of Levittown and to talk vaguely about moving "back home"; the Philadelphians virtually never talk of moving back); but the life-styles of the two working-class groups appear to be quite similar.

The father/husband in the family works very long hours and is seldom home. Overtime work and moonlighting are common in Levittown, and some men have shift work. The shift worker's schedule is very different from that of the rest of his family, and it is constantly changing—sometimes it is the evening shift, then the early morning hours, and occasionally the normal workday.

The man's main role in the family is economic provider. When home, he remains passive and detached from most home and family activities, spending a great amount of time in front of the television set, typically watching sports events with a can of beer in hand. Sometimes he hangs out in the evenings at his favorite bar, doing about what he would be doing at home but in a situation more congenial to him. The man expresses hostile attitudes toward society and feels misused by it. He is in a "rat race," and has to spend most of his time just trying to make ends meet at a job which is personally unfulfilling. At the same time, he would rather be on the job than around the house because of the deterioration in his family life and the resultant feelings of guilt about it. This man appears edgy, defensive, quick to anger, and "turned-off" to much of life, but he gets some satisfactions from being a provider, from "bonding" with his male friends, from television, and from the sense of superiority which he derives from leading a basically disciplined and hardworking life, in contrast, he feels, to many in society around him.

The mother/wife is either "stuck at home" with the kids and no means of transportation (the family can only afford one car, which the husband drives to work), or she holds a full- or part-time job in order to make ends meet. With a full-time job she is under great pressure in the performance of her twin roles, for she must also continue to attend to her housewife and mother functions with little extra help from her overburdened husband. The woman feels resentful of her situation, neglected by her husband, anxious and guilty about her own contribution to their deteriorating family life, and somewhat out of control of the situation—which is dependent very strongly on her husband's occupation and income level. If she is "just a housewife," she feels bored and perhaps lonely in addition.

This family is marked by serious financial insecurity. It is not poor but is living above its means, and the man's continued employment is always problematic. The adults "make do" from week to week; food shopping is done by the woman in bulk the day after payday, to make sure there will be enough money to cover this necessity; she has carefully been following the ads, to get the best buys. Clothing purchases are made mainly during times of sales. The family is heavily in debt from buying things on time: cars, home furnishings, television sets, and of course the house itself. The family wants to have the material things that a middle-class, suburban family should have and that most of the other families on the block have, but this leads to a constant struggle—not only to buy these things, but to maintain them. If an emergency occurs, such as the serious illness of a family member, financial disaster can strike.

The next most serious family problem after finances is the teenagers. They are not doing well in school, are sometimes in trouble with school authorities and police, seldom are at home (''We don't know where they are, they never tell us''), are sullen and uncommunicative with their parents (''You just can't talk to them''), and are regular users of dope or alcohol. To their parents, they appear shiftless, lazy, insolent, aimless, and generally uncontrollable (''We just don't know what to do about them''). The parents are at a loss to explain why their teenage children have become the way they are. They don't openly blame themselves, and they talk generally about a breakdown in morality and respect for authority, about bad influences among their children's peers, and about drug pushers (''people from outside the community who come in here and . . .''). They seem certain about one thing: Times have changed a lot since they were young (''Most of these problems didn't exist then . . . kids had respect for their elders . . . drugs weren't available . . .'').

The psychological brunt of the family's difficulties with its teenage members falls on the mother. Unlike many other women in Levittown, the woman of this family does not have parents and close relatives to rely on. Her parents and relatives may be dead or living too far away; sometimes she is estranged from them. This leaves a wide gap in her life, for she has few close friends on whom she can rely in the way she would on a parent, brother, or sister. If not employed, she is in no activity outside the home where she could meet potential friends (she finds it difficult to make new friends anyway), and she long ago has dropped girl friends from her premarital days, for reasons of geographic distance if for no other. The single source of primary relationships for this woman has become the neighborhood. She frequently drops in and out of the neighbors' houses, and relies on them for advice, assistance, and social contact. The neighbors are virtually the only focus of her social life; when she has an informal get-together with ''friends,'' these friends are at the same time her neighbors.

The neighbors can be a tremendous assist to her life; without them she would indeed be in a very bad way. But there are drawbacks. She did not choose her neighbors; they simply happen to live near her, and she may not always be satisfied with her lot, for the choice is very limited. The neighbors are not secure friends; she or they could move away at any time. Most important, the neighbors tend to have the same problems that she does. This provides a commonality that can enhance their relationships, but it also helps to mire the woman still further in her anxiety-filled existence. The neighborhood becomes an extension of her own family: She is still left with the need to get away from it all for a while, to gain perspective on her situation, to learn from older people who may have successfully mastered these problems, and to find social outlets which can help her attain a greater measure of self-respect.

Apart from the neighbors, the woman has no social life and even no social contacts (unless she holds a job). She complains that her husband never takes her out ("He's too busy"), they never eat in a restaurant ("It costs too much"), she does not belong to any club or organization, she does not participate with others in any organized activity. She is an irregular church attender ("My husband never wants to go"). The woman seldom leaves Levittown for even short periods of time; she doesn't ever get a vacation. Her husband may get a few weeks' vacation in the summer, but this time is spent fixing the house. If they do take a trip ("it's very difficult and expensive with such a large family"), it is for only a few days, perhaps a long weekend at the shore. These trips are often times when serious family fights occur; the family members are not used to being so physically close to one another and having only each other to relate to. The extensive arguments reinforce the husband's notion that they never should have taken the trip to begin with, and he will refuse to go the following year. Life for the family at home centers around the TV set. It is on from morning to night, with different family members viewing it at different times; many members say that it is their favorite activity.

This family's problems are compounded by a breakdown in the marriage relationship of the adults. They are in their forties, overweight, and losing their youthful attractiveness; the "crisis of the 40s" hits them with full force. The man knows that he is going no further in his job; indeed, he will be lucky to hang on to what he has. The woman knows that she must give up dreams of higher status; she is stuck at this level for the rest of her life. To the man, the woman has lost her sexual attractiveness. With a concern over his fading sexual prowess, he starts to "look around"; he may have an affair or perhaps leave his wife entirely. The woman experiences a similar sexual distaste for the man—and she usually has no sexual alternatives, even if she wants some. So she "lets herself go," and the role of sex in her life virtually comes to an end. Without sex, the quality of the marriage sinks even lower.

With the marriage in a rut, the teenagers in difficulty, and the family in financial straits, it is not surprising that personal and social tragedies may follow. Alcoholism is reportedly common in Levittown; divorce and separation are increasing. But even without these manifest social and personal problems, the life-style of the problem family becomes extremely unrewarding and unfulfilling—the family settles down to a life of "quiet desperation."

In many outward appearances, the Levittown problem family may seem little different in basic structure from the more successful family. But several structural differences are crucial, in my judgment, in accounting for the lower quality of life which the problem family has: the lower income and educational levels of the adults, the larger family size, and the fewer relatives available for regular social interaction and mutual assistance.

Levittown is designed for the relatively self-sufficient family. Each house has a sizable amount of private space and facilities, while the community as a whole has a limited amount of collective space and facilities. For those families that are economically and culturally self-sufficient, the Levittown life is very satisfactory. They can provide within the home many of the things which in other settings are provided by the community.

It is those families lacking this self-sufficiency that have trouble. Especially important is economic self-sufficiency, which affects things as various as the length of time the husband must work each day, the number and length of vacations that a family may take, access to commercial recreational facilities, and the ability to afford a needed second car. There is little in Levittown outside the home that the poor family can rely on in time of need.

Size of family drastically affects the household's real income level. The larger families in Levittown tend to be the poorer ones; though the head of a large family makes the same salary as his next-door neighbor, his family's ability to pay for needed services is much lower. Further, many extra burdens are imposed on his wife.

Poor families must rely heavily on relatives for mutual aid, sense of belonging, and psychological support. The poor families that seem to be worst-off in Levittown are those where necessary extended family ties, particularly on the woman's side, do not exist. These kinship ties are very difficult adequately to replace.

In addition to this set of difficulties associated with problem families in Levittown, I encountered in the household interviews three distinct patterns of incongruence among the women of the community. The most common was the situation of high dependency, which the following three actual cases exemplify.

The Dependent Woman

Mrs. H. is a short, overweight woman who appears quite affable, with a ready smile. Now in her fifties, she has lived in Levittown for fifteen years and was born and raised in what is presently a slum area of the nearby city of Trenton, N.J. Her two daughters were raised in Levittown; one is now married and lives in a neighboring state (but sees her mother once a month), the other lives with her but will soon marry and move to another part of Levittown.

Mrs. H.'s husband died nine months ago. He left two cars, a very low mortgage on the house, but little money (he was the driver of a door-to-door delivery truck). This woman's life has suddenly changed from one of financial security to great financial insecurity. Since her husband's death she has been working at home taking in sewing and mending work, but this does not bring her enough income. She is desperately looking for a job; her daughter is helping her out financially until she can find one.

One of Mrs. H.'s biggest problems is that she can not drive; she has flunked the driving test three times ("I just get too nervous"). This means that the job she takes must either be within walking distance or along the route of the one bus line which runs near her home. There are very few places of employment within walking distance, though she once worked at the closest establishment to her—a delicatessen which is a thirty-five-minute walk.

Her sewing keeps her busy ("I would rather do it than anything"), and she spends the whole day in front of the TV set, except when she has visitors. She almost never goes out in the evenings and never takes trips out of Levittown. Mrs. H. is completely dependent on others to transport her to those places where she must go—food shopping, the doctor, and church.

In many ways Mrs. H. considers herself quite fortunate, however. She is social with her neighbors, active at her church (and deeply religious), and can count on the assistance of her two daughters and of a sister who lives in Trenton. But she is worried about her younger daughter's forthcoming marriage and move, as this will leave her alone for the first time.

Mrs. H. thinks the world of Levittown; she never wants to live anywhere else. She hates Trenton, where she grew up, and feels extremely fortunate that she was able "to get out in time." Stating that the transportation situation is her problem, she can think of no changes that would make Levittown a better community. She says she is quite happy and never feels bored.

There are many respects in which Mrs. H. can be considered incongruent with the Levittown environment. The lack of public transportation will keep her employment situation problematic, maintenance of the house will tax her ingenuity and her resources, her home-bound life will offer little variety, and she will find it difficult to make ends meet financially. If she gets by, she will do so through a high dependence on others, a life-style which is always a precarious one. The Levittown environment exacerbates her dependent status, yet a move from Levittown might not help her much. The environment to which she moved might be worse for her in other respects, and she would lose her neighbor-friends, who have now become extremely important in her life.

Mrs. V. is a thin, nervous woman in her late thirties. Her husband left her three months ago to live with a waitress who works at the luncheonette near where he works, after telling his wife that he no longer loved her. Mrs. V. and her husband are currently locked in a desperate struggle over support payments. He is harrassing her in various ways to get her to leave the house and thus save himself some money. She refuses to grant him a divorce, and their relationship is one of deep bitterness. They have two children, ages eleven and fourteen.

Their marriage and family life before he left had some of the traits of the maladapted family described above. The man worked irregular hours and, with much overtime employment (or "so he claimed"), was seldom at home. The family infrequently ate meals together; when they did, mealtimes were often scenes of anger and antagonism. Their vacations were no longer than two or three days away from home (the recent ones had ended in great unpleasantness), and the family had no social life apart from the informal dropping by of neighbors. The woman did not work, was not a member of any club or organization, and had dropped out of church.

From the perspective of today, however, Mrs. V. regards those as the pleasant years. She can not work because of ill health and is therefore completely dependent financially on her missing husband; she spends much of her life begging, cajoling, or trying legally to force him to give her food money, make payments on the home bills, provide clothing for the children, and so on. To make matters worse, she does not drive and has no car. She is learning how to drive (she tried to learn once before but had an accident), and wants her husband to provide her with a car. Until her transportation situation is resolved, she must depend on neighbors and nearby relatives to give her lifts, plus use the community taxicab, leading to frequent demands on her husband for taxi money, which he feels are excessive.

The children of this family have been strongly affected by the marital breakup. The son is doing poorly in school, and his mother says, "You just can't talk to him anymore." The daughter is failing in school, has frequent headaches for which she takes tranquilizers, and spends much of her time sitting in front of the TV set; she is soon to begin counseling, at the recommendation of school authorities.

In spite of these difficulties, Mrs. V. likes Levittown very much, especially her neighborhood and neighbors, several of whom have been of great assistance to her; she would deeply regret having to move. Yet, as in the last case, some elements of the Levittown environment surely exacerbate this woman's tragic, dependent situation, increasing her feelings of helplessness and loss of self-respect. As her own problems mount, she will be able to provide less and less nurturance and guidance for her children, and there is little in the environment to help compensate for this.

Mrs. S. is a wispy, fragile woman in her early forties who speaks with a frail voice; though not totally sightless, her vision is enough impaired for her to be considered legally blind and qualify for special state benefits. She has lived in Levittown for eight years and has one daughter left at home. Her life now is almost totally home bound because her husband works "all the time," is home very seldom, and consequently is not able to take her many places. She has few friends, almost never goes out, and sees little of the neighbors.

Mrs. S. has two special interests in life. She breeds dogs and has on the premises three large dogs as well as seven other pets. While obtaining great satisfaction from this enterprise, she is constantly on the edge of legality because she lives in a residential district where dog breeding is not permitted, and she is frequently at odds with her neighbors over the nuisance that the dogs create. As a second major interest, she has permitted her home and yard to become a kind of informal youth center, which again creates enough of a nuisance to generate the animosity of neighbors, some of whom occasionally phone the police. It is common for as many as twenty teenagers to hang out after school on her property and in her home ("Mom's really great," says her daughter, "the others in the neighborhood don't want to have anything to do with us"). As long as the young people stay on her property, keep out of the street, maintain a reasonable noise level, and have her permission, there is nothing that the police can do to stop this daily pattern of social interaction. This does not assuage the neighbors, however, who sometimes make life difficult for her.

Mrs. S. appears resigned to her situation in life. She has nothing negative to say about Levittown and much prefers it to the places she has lived in the past. She might prefer a larger house, however ("for the sake of the dogs").

Again, the Levittown environment does not provide much support for this highly dependent person. Her life probably would be more full and well rounded in a small town. A rural area might also be preferable, for she would at least have insulation from the neighbors. She is presently living her life, to some extent, through the teenagers. While this brings her undoubted satisfactions (and she provides a youth facility which the community has failed to provide), it is not clear what, if anything, will fill the gap left in her life when her daughter leaves home in a few years.

The Trapped Housewife

The trapped housewife is a frequently cited suburban problem type, centering on feelings of isolation, boredom, and resentfulness. I expected to find more housewives with these feelings than I did; just two or three of the women in my sample fit into this category, only one of whom could be called a serious case. However, this environmentally related problem is most commonly

found in mothers of young children, and only six of the women in my sample
were at this stage of life.

Mrs. W. is a young and attractive mother of a two-year-old son. She
and her husband moved to Levittown three years ago from a Philadelphia
row house; her husband is a construction worker.

When asked what she does in a typical day, Mrs. W. says "the same
old stuff"—cleaning, washing, taking care of the infant. When asked
about her life, she replies sarcastically, "I really have an exciting life."
While she goes out occasionally with her husband, her life centers around
her women friends in the neighborhood ("We're in and out of each
other's houses a lot"). Her mother is dead and her father is in a nursing
home. She says she feels bored and finds that there is very little to do in
Levittown. She can't get out at all during the day because her husband
drives their one car to work.

By comparison, her husband is very active—in semi-pro football in the
fall (three times a week in the evenings) and Little League (working with
boys) in the spring; he frequently goes off on long weekend hunting
trips with his buddies and visits his parents and relatives in Philadelphia often. He appears to be much more "engaged" and contented
than his wife. His wife is seldom included in his activities.

In this case, the wife's difficulties seem particularly related to immobility,
the lack of variety in her life, the solitary and routine nature of her work day,
and her husband's inattentiveness. A young mother is highly dependent on the
local environment for stimulation and variety in her life, and little of either
exists in Levittown. Mrs. W.'s neighbors provide needed adult social contacts
during the day, but they face the same predicaments that she does and hence
are not able to provide the occasional diversion and relief that she needs.
Further, this woman does not have parents on whom she can rely for baby-
sitting, for advice about childrearing, and for simply "getting things off her
shoulders." Her lack of daily satisfaction stands in sharp contrast to the
activities of her husband, which further aggravates her feelings of being
"trapped."

The trapped housewife problem is more commonly discussed in connection
with the college-educated woman who finds herself as a young mother in
relative isolation, doing menial work, after intellectually exciting college
years filled with dreams about a fulfilling career. No such woman turned up in
my household sample, but several of the middle-class women I did interview,
who had raised their families in Levittown, told me they had occasionally had
strong feelings of isolation and boredom when they were young mothers. The
following comment by a Levittown mother and wife of a professional man,
which was included in an article about the community written at the time of

the twentieth-birthday celebration, expresses the feelings of one housewife
who feels trapped by the environment:[4]

> Intricate networks of paved roads and busy highways. Red, green, and
> yellow traffic lights quietly bloom on and off, on and off to miles of
> harassed backed-up traffic. And the houses cover the landscape. And that
> woman in the tiny house back there has older children who are trying to
> get off to all corners of the earth away from this undigested mass of
> houses, houses. And she is too depressed to know what she wants.
> She's been so busy raising her children in that safe incubator that she
> just has made no contacts anywhere outside Levittown activities. She is
> just a loner. Trapped in the beautiful park she helped create in the midst
> of megalopolis.

The Lonely Woman

The third distinct environmentally related problem or type of incongruence
found among the women of Levittown is loneliness. Loneliness seems to rank
behind dependency and boredom in prevalence; only one case of admitted
loneliness was uncovered in my twenty-five-household sample.

> Mrs. H. is an assertive, well-dressed, professional-looking woman who
> has been separated from her husband for five years. She lives with her
> daughter, age thirteen and was an original owner in Levittown; she has
> lived in the same house and neighborhood for twenty-one years. Since
> she was first married she has held a job, taking off only a year and a half
> for the birth of her child.
> Her job (a responsible position in the food services area) is out of the
> Levittown area and involves a large amount of driving; she works long
> hours and arrives home each day tired. When her daughter was younger,
> she was left under the care of some friends in the neighborhood while the
> woman was at work. These same friends have helped her, since her sep-
> aration, with home maintenance problems.
> Mrs. H. is a regular church-attender, but is in no other clubs, organiza-
> tions, or activities. Her parents are both dead, and she has no relatives
> living nearby. She used to be social with the neighbors on each side of
> her, but both families moved away. Other than the members of the one
> family who help with her daughter and house, she has almost no friends.
> She has virtually no social life and does no home entertaining except
> perhaps at Christmas. Her evenings are spent watching TV, talking to her
> daughter, and reading a few magazines.
> Mrs. H. appears tired and rather sad, although she tries to maintain a
> cheerful disposition. She likes her work, but at home she feels bored,
> would like to go out more, and feels that her life is rather dull and unin-

teresting. She can't think of anything she dislikes about Levittown ("I have always liked it, especially the fact that it is so convenient"). She does plan to move into an apartment when her daughter leaves home, however ("Home maintenance gets to be a burden as you grow older"), and she hopes to retire to her small hometown in a neighboring state.

The Levittown neighborhood appears much less than ideal for this woman. With few relatives and no husband, she is heavily dependent on friends, yet she has little time left over from her long workday to meet and cultivate any. Her work cuts her off from the kind of regular, spontaneous interaction that is necessary to turn neighbors into friends. The other activities of Levittown require preplanning on her part, yet she feels too tired and doesn't want to get "involved" again after a long day's work. Mrs. H. might be happier in an environmental setting which provided her with more potential sources of friends and more stimulation and variety, for example, places nearby where she could go unescorted in the evening for diversion, recreation, and companionship.

The Teenager in Levittown

Teenagers appear to be considerably less enthusiastic about the Levittown environment than their parents: about 25 percent of the young people in my sample would prefer to live elsewhere or want to "get out of Levittown" when they set up their own homes. The discrepancy between negative teen attitudes and the positive opinions of their parents may seem natural in view of the fact that the community was freely chosen by their parents but that for teenagers it was something they simply were born into. But the issue runs much more deeply. The great majority of teenagers felt that the community was "nice" or "O.K.," mentioning most often qualities which differentiated it from city areas: "quiet, and not crowded," and "no real gangs or problems like the city." (The second most important positive aspect mentioned was "my friends are here," which says little about the environment.) The teenagers joined their parents, therefore, in feeling that Levittown was a pretty good place to live and that it certainly was better than most alternatives—especially cities.

But nearly 50 percent of the teenagers in my sample said they often felt bored, a response given by only two or three of the adult women. Many Americans feel that boredom is a common affliction of this nation's teenagers, having something to do with the teenage subculture, the schools, and changes in the larger society. It is also, I believe, strongly related to characteristics of the local environment (this will be discussed more fully in chapter 8). It is instructive to look at what the teenagers of Levittown view as the causes of their boredom and at the distinguishing characteristics between those teenagers who are bored and those who are not bored.

On the reasons for their boredom the teenagers are unanimous—there is "nothing to do" in Levittown. That is, there are few facilities in Levittown to which the teenager can go for his leisure-time activities; there are few things "going on" in Levittown for the teenager. Important corollaries of this opinion are that many of the best leisure-time facilities in the community are commercial, and their high costs prohibit much use by the youths from lower-income families; also, due to the lack of public transportation, it is very difficult to get to what facilities there are. One teenager summed up his situation: "There's not much to do here, and those things there are to do cost money; also, there's no way to get to them." Some parents share this view of life in Levittown for teenagers: "This area is just for adults, the kids have been left out."

Other adults, however, feel that there is plenty to do for kids in the community—"It's just that they don't want to do them." This view is often enunciated by the officials in youth-serving institutions, who point to the many supervised activities which the schools sponsor in the afternoons and evenings. The main Levittown high school is open six evenings a week, for example. Yet these activities are very poorly attended, and the youth leaders are typically unable to explain why. The teenagers assert that the activities are *too* supervised and that they have had enough school supervision during the regular school day. Also, the schools are often too far away—sometimes eight miles or more—to get to easily in the evenings.

Three distinct teenage life-styles can be discerned in Levittown, oriented to the three "pulls" of home, school, and street. The *home-centered* teenagers are those who return home after school, stay in their rooms or visit the homes of one or two close friends, do their homework, watch TV, listen to records, talk on the telephone, and lead relatively quiet lives. They are normally on good terms with their families, who in turn have a high degree of family solidarity. The home is relatively rich in social and cultural resources—books and magazines, stereos, play equipment, and so on.

The *school-centered* life-style consists of active participation in after-school activities, typically competitive sports for boys and sports-related activities (cheerleading and pom-pom) for girls. Teenagers with this life-style are somewhat more extroverted and socially outgoing than the home-centered group (for example, they date more), and they find their days are active and busy. They are supportive of the school and filled with "school spirit." Their opinions of Levittown tend to be favorable. A variant of this life-style is the church-centered group consisting of those whose after-school lives are wrapped up in church youth activities. This is not a large group in Levittown, but it is one which stands out because its members seem well adjusted and lead their lives somewhat apart from the rest of the community.

Those who are turned off by school and home (and also church) take up the *street-centered* life-style. Their after-school lives are spent "hanging out" in Levittown neighborhoods, chatting and "fooling around" in groups of varying sizes. While disinterested in after-school activities (usually they are not interested in school at all and are the weaker students, academically), they also do not feel comfortable staying at home, since often they are at odds with one or both parents. They are highly peer-group-oriented and mistrustful or hostile toward authority; they are commonly characterized by parents as lazy and lethargic, aimless and goalless, and undisciplined.

The size of the street-centered group in Levittown is a matter of great concern to the youth authorities. Although estimates vary widely, and precise data are unavailable, the group probably consists of no more than 25 percent of Levittown youth. But it is within this group that Levittown has its youth problems, the most widely discussed social problem area in the community.

"Hanging out" has become a normal activity in the teen years, and its quality as an activity varies depending on the environmental conditions under which it takes place; but even at its best it does not provide a solution to the problem of boredom or an answer to the need for "something to do." Like watching television, it is only in one sense *doing* something; many teenagers and most parents, indeed, regard it as doing nothing.

What, then, do bored teenagers say they want to do that they are unable to do in Levittown. The response is virtually unanimous: they want a youth center that is easily accessible without a car, that has free or inexpensive recreational facilities, and that they can use for talking, dancing, and eating. Further, the youth center, unlike the school, should be structured to a large extent by teen values and interests; adult supervision should be, at the very least, disguised.

What distinguishes the bored from the nonbored youth in Levittown? Generally speaking, the nonbored are actively engaged in productive, interesting, or personally rewarding after-school activities, whereas the bored are not. The great majority of the street-centered group feel bored, and they are the ones most negative and hostile toward their community. Within the other two groups the school-centered youth are probably least bored. They are "plugged in" to an activity which the community regards as very important; they have social status, friends, and little free time to worry about.

More boredom is found in the home-centered youth, though it varies from time to time and season to season (*most* Levittown youth seem to feel bored during the summer months). The least bored among the home-centered seem

to be those youth with strong family ties, a few close friends, strong academic
or intellectual interests, or a hobby. Sometimes boredom is expressed rather
intellectually, however; the youth aspires to bigger things with more variety,
challenge, and excitement. Levittown is dull and parochial by contrast. The
bored youth of the home-centered group turn to TV in place of hanging out,
spending long hours (perhaps five or six) each day in front of the tube.

Juvenile Delinquency in Levittown

The delinquency problem in Levittown is not as serious as it is in most of
America's cities, but it is a concern to most residents and for many it is their
greatest community concern. Furthermore, the problem has grown rapidly in
recent years, partly due to an increase in the size of Levittown's teenage
population.

The most serious concern is drugs. Hard data on drug use by Levittown
teenagers are not available, but the most frequent estimate in the spring of
1974 was about 50 percent (split evenly between boys and girls), given by a
police official, a school official, and a high school student body president.
Drug use consists almost entirely of soft drugs, mostly marijuana; a drug user
is considered to be a person who takes drugs "when the opportunity arises,"
especially on weekends, at parties, and at hang-out areas. A much higher
percentage of Levittown youth seem to have tried drugs at one time or
another; eight out of ten was one school official's estimate.

Parents and youth officials are at a loss for explanations to account for this
problem, except that drugs have become widely available in the last few years
and have replaced the alcohol which was prevalent in their day (there is some
evidence that the drug problem is now subsiding in Levittown and that youth
are returning to alcohol, bringing to many adults a sigh of relief). They are at
an even greater loss for a solution. The main efforts have been educational,
such as special antidrug programs in the schools, and law enforcement, including a strong move to catch the pushers, many of whom are fellow students. Parents of teenagers have feelings of fear and resignation about the
problem: "Parents just have to hold their breath and hope that nothing goes
wrong"; "Keep your fingers crossed."

Most drug users are not delinquent in any legal sense other than that of
illegally possessing drugs; the use of drugs seems more a symptom of boredom and alienation than of overt, antisocial hostility and criminal behavior.
But the amount of delinquent behavior in Levittown is regarded by officials as
quite high—the most common estimate was that 10 percent of the teenagers
are real "problem cases"—and these officials hold that most of the delinquents are drawn from the ranks of the drug users. According to police, the

most serious crimes in Levittown, such as burglary, are committed typically by youth who need money to support their habit (except for burglaries in the wealthy sections of the community, where professional, out-of-town burglars have become a growing menace); the less serious offenses, such as vandalism, are commonly committed by youth "who have been given a false sense of courage by pot or alcohol." Some police officials feel that if the use of drugs and alcohol by Levittown youth could be curtailed, delinquency rates would drop precipitously.

There is surprisingly little hard data about delinquency in Levittown; no records at all are ordinarily kept about many delinquent acts, out of concern for the youth's reputation and future. The extent and even the nature of delinquent acts must be derived from off-the-record statements of public officials and youth leaders, from newspaper reports, and from the teenagers themselves. Vandalism has become perhaps the most common type of delinquency. Evidence of vandalism can easily be seen in Levittown: broken and defaced signs, graffiti on walls, damaged public telephones. The facilities that have been hit hardest are schools: in 1972, vandals were responsible for $100,000 in damage in four representative school districts in Lower Bucks County.[5] Homeowners are also frequently targets. Many cases have been reported of homes which have been severely damaged after the owners reported to police that they were being bothered by gangs of youth who were hanging out in the vicinity; homes located near natural hang-out areas, such as street corners or small parks, are especially subject to this problem.

Other common forms of delinquency in Levittown are home burglaries (the burglars typically come on foot and take small items), shoplifting, theft from vehicles, and auto theft. The complaints against youth that are most often filed with the police by adults are for loitering and disturbing the peace, usually stemming from hang-out groups that get out of bounds. Of growing concern to police and school authorities is the problem of runaways—youth who leave home and school without telling anyone where they are going. Most runaway episodes are for several days only, but the frequency and duration have been increasing. In one Levittown township (1970 population, 67,498), the number of recorded runaways increased from 298 in 1967 to 388 in 1973.[6]

The amount of juvenile delinquency in Levittown is not out of line with other areas of Bucks County. Indeed, within the Philadelphia metropolitan area, the Levittown ranking is low. Most Levittowners are quick to point out that "the same problems exist everywhere." Nevertheless, the rate of delinquency is much higher than it was a few years ago and growing rapidly, although the teen population is now in decline. Many parents point to a decrease in discipline in the home as a root cause of delinquency. "Childrearing used to be more strict"; "Kids are very unsupervised now, mothers don't look after them." Others blame the schools: "too large," "too heterogeneous," "not enough personal attention," "bad elements are allowed to take over." Youth officials suggest that a fundamental change has taken place in the amount of time that parents spend with their children: "Both parents work and are seldom home; when they are home, they are too tired to really communicate with their children." The youth tend also to give this factor prominence; in one study of youth in the Levittown area, 88 percent of the youth surveyed regarded "communication between adults and youth" a major problem—the highest percentage among the factors which were raised.[7] The "communication" referred to is of course not only in amount but in content, and not only with parents but with other adults of significance in the lives of youth.

The social causes of the kind of delinquency found in Levittown are extremely complex. The Levittown delinquents are to be found mostly in the hang-out groups, those groups whose members claim a high degree of boredom and are the most common users of drugs. Nationally, the fifteen-year-old age group contributes the largest share of delinquents. Characteristics of the residential environment may be only marginally involved as causal factors in delinquency; nevertheless, because teenagers are more affected by the environment than any other age group, it is important to examine some of the ways in which environmental elements may be involved. This will be done in chapter 8.

Patterns of Environmental Fit in Levittown:
Some Conclusions

Levittown started more than twenty years ago with an enthusiastic group of citizens: young couples who needed space for their growing families, liked the idea of owning their own home, and realized that a Levitt house was a "best buy." These families were home-centered, had reasonably good incomes, were upwardly mobile, and seem quickly to have become well adapted to the rather sedentary, anonymous, and truncated community in which they found themselves. Many of these families are still living in Levittown, their children now gone; others moved on, or up, and were replaced by families who are more heterogeneous in class, ethnicity, and stage of the life cycle than the original residents.

Levittown has not turned into a physical or social slum, as some predicted. It is still a best buy in the area, with houses which are generally well maintained, a luxuriant landscape, and a physical plan which works reasonably well for most residents, providing safety and security, stable property values, peace and quiet—attributes which are dearly sought by many Americans. The typical Levittowners have average or above incomes, they have reasonably steady employment, they work hard, and their families are structurally intact.

Yet Levittown does not seem to work as well for its residents today as it did at the beginning; it is not the environment which has changed, but the people. Levittown was designed for the mobile, middle-class family with young children. As long as the family remained strong, Levittown was a reasonably good environment for the young child—safe, spacious, with plenty of playmates nearby, and good elementary schools, often within walking distance along traffic-depressed streets. If anyone suffered it was the mother, whose world consisted of little else but home, child, and husband. But the early years of children are always hard on mothers, and few would probably have wished to give up the space, privacy, safety, and schools for an environment which was more convenient or exciting—and this was the choice often perceived by the Levittown mothers.

In the early years of Levittown the teenager, the elderly person, the widowed and divorced female head of household, the working-class woman living in tight financial straits and cut off from relatives, were unfamiliar figures. Today, they have become common, and the environment is not as congruent with them as with their predecessors. For adults in anything but a fully functioning, economically secure family system, Levittown may be an invitation to trouble; it provides great opportunity to the self-sufficient family but little sustenance and support to the family which is not self-sufficient.

For teenagers, Levittown has some serious drawbacks. If their family proves inadequate to meet their needs, they have few alternatives. And it is an uncommon family which can provide all of the things which a complete and well-rounded community could offer—facilities, a sense of participation in ongoing community activities, places where teenagers and adults can spontaneously meet, and a chance to observe life as it is lived outside of living room and yard.

7

Vällingby and Levittown

A Structural Comparison

Vällingby and Levittown were chosen for this inquiry to represent suburbs that differed significantly in major environmental characteristics yet that were built to house similar types of people. How comparable are the two communities in these terms? Drawing on the detailed descriptions in chapters 3 and 5, this chapter summarizes the main similarities and differences in the built-environments, community systems, and demographic structures of the two communities.[1]

Built-Environment and Community System Characteristics

Both communities are "packaged" and planned suburbs, built by a single developer or government planning group. Each was constructed in the 1950s (the main shopping center opened in Levittown in 1953, in Vällingby in 1954) and consisted of approximately the same number of dwelling units (17,311 in Levittown, 18,850 in Vällingby). Each suburb is located on the edge of its metropolitan area, but in this regard two important differences must be noted. Philadelphia, as the twenty-third largest city in the world, is substantially larger than Stockholm, which ranks one hundred twenty-fifth; the Philadelphia urbanized area had a population of about 4,355,000 in 1970, compared to 1,350,000 for the Stockholm urbanized area.[2] And Levittown is located farther from the center of its metropolitan region, about twenty-two miles from downtown Philadelphia, while Vällingby is only eight miles from downtown Stockholm. (The travel times are forty-five minutes and twenty-seven minutes, respectively, based on public transportation.) These differences in scale are accentuated by the fact that Levittown is located within the vast Eastern seaboard megalopolis which stretches from Boston to Washington (indeed, Levittown is really a suburb of *two* metropolises—Philadelphia, Pennsylvania, and Trenton, New Jersey), while Stockholm stands in virtual isolation, surrounded mainly by fields and forests.

The ties of each suburb to its parent city are dissimilar. Levittown lies in governmental jurisdictions that are independent of the city of Philadelphia. The suburb is linked to Philadelphia by a high-speed transit line, but only a very small percentage of Levittowners actually commute to work in the city. Though the economy of the Levittown area is one segment of the Philadelphia metropolitan area economy, the political and social climate of Levittown bears scant resemblance to the counterpart climate of the area's central-city or hub.

Vällingby is a fully integrated part of its parent city of Stockholm. It falls under the jurisdiction of Stockholm's city government, a large percentage of its working residents commute downtown by high-speed transit, and its cultural, recreational, and social ties to central-city Stockholm are relatively strong.

The Levittown area contains more heavy industry than Vällingby, the Vällingby industrial base consisting mostly of light and service industries. Commensurate with its weaker tie to the city, a larger number of Levittown's workers are employed in its suburban vicinity—about two-thirds to three-quarters, while perhaps less than half of Vällingby workers are employed in the suburbs. The travel distances are somewhat longer for residents of the U.S. suburb, however, because of the differences in the scale of each metropolitan area. Further, over 25 percent of Vällingby workers are employed within their home community, whereas there are few jobs within the boundaries of Levittown. The journey to work in terms of average travel time appears roughly comparable in each community (about twenty-five minutes); firm data are not available, but it is probable that travel time for the journey to work has decreased over the years for each community's employees, due to the substantial growth in the number of locally based jobs.

Though travel times are similar, the means of transportation are not. The automobile is used by 91 percent of Levittown workers, with only 5 percent commuting by collective means of transportation. In Vällingby, 29 percent of workers commute by automobile, 47 percent use collective means of transportation, and 15 percent walk to work. In Levittown 99 percent of the households have at least one car, and over 55 percent have more than one. By comparison, about 40 percent of Vällingby households have no car at all, while very few have more than one.

In summary, neither suburb closely resembles the prototype of a dormitory community whose working residents commute long distances to the central city, though each was closer to this type when first built. In Levittown, few workers are employed within the community; most work nearby at jobs which in many cases have been decentralized, moving from city locations to suburban districts. The jobs are more scattered than in Stockholm and the distances to them are greater, but these impediments are partially overcome by the automobile, which provides relatively fast door-to-door transportation. In Vällingby, a higher percentage commutes to the downtown area (with door-to-door travel times of perhaps forty-five minutes), but this is offset by the clustering of a large number of jobs within Vällingby, a significant percentage of which can be reached by foot or bicycle (ten-to-fiteen-minute travel times). In Vällingby, compared to Levittown, many more work places are available to persons who can not or do not want to drive.

The size of Levittown in land area is about three times that of Vällingby, while the number of dwelling units is roughly equal. As a result, there is a gross residential density in Levittown of 3 dwelling units per acre, compared to 10.5 units per acre in Vällingby. Due to the smaller household sizes in Vällingby, however, the contrast in residential densities measured in terms of population rather than in dwelling units is not as large: 12 persons per acre in Levittown and 24 persons per acre in Vällingby. Both are well below typical urban densities. The land that is not built on in Levittown is mostly split up into private yards; its counterpart in Vällingby is almost entirely public space.

All of the Levittown dwelling units are single-family, detached, privately owned homes; they average five and one-half rooms in size, including a kitchen, and contain 4.2 persons. Ninety-two percent of the Vällingby dwelling units are in multifamily housing, mostly owned by public authorities (the remaining 8 percent are in privately owned, mostly attached, single-family houses). The typical multifamily unit is a garden-type apartment building of three stories, although about a quarter of Vällingby's dwelling units are in six-to-ten-story, elevator-serviced, high-rise apartment buildings. The average Vällingby dwelling unit is slightly more than three rooms in size, including kitchen (each unit has additional storage space in the basement), and it contains 2.5 persons. Thus the present number of persons per room unit in each community is quite comparable—.60 in Levittown and .77 in Vällingby, although the differential was greater at the time the communities were first built, when Vällingby household sizes were larger.

The site plan of Levittown consists of seven or eight superblocks, each of which is bounded by major arterial roadways and is divided into five or six named neighborhoods. Within the neighborhoods, the street system was designed so as to be an impediment to through traffic. The elementary schools, swimming pools, and small parks are distributed in a relatively planned way among the superblocks; most other facilities are not. Retail services, for example, are haphazardly scattered throughout the area without particular regard to shopper convenience and need, and many of the major shopping centers are on the area's periphery. The only services that are within a reasonable walking distance of most Levittowners are elementary schools, small parks, and sometimes playgrounds or wooded areas. The typical pedestrian environment in Levittown consists solely of houses, private yards, and streets. There is no separate circulation system for pedestrians; a large portion of Levittown does not even have sidewalks along the roadways.

Vällingby's site plan consists of six superblocks strung out along the subway line like beads on a string. Each superblock or city district (except for one, which is slightly off to the side of the subway line) focuses on a commercial and cultural center, or centrum, located at a subway stop. These centrums contain most of the retail services in Vällingby, plus some social and cultural services such as a theater, restaurants, health and welfare clinics, churches, and youth centers. Some of the centrums contain additional employment facilities, such as government agencies and insurance companies. Every Vällingby dweller is within reasonable walking distance of a centrum and its subway stop, which are no more than about a thousand yards away.

The largest centrum, Vällingby proper, serves an area which extends beyond the boundaries of Vällingby. Additional retail services are located within Vällingby but outside the centrum in smaller neighborhood centers and as isolated "convenience shops" on the ground floors of apartment buildings. Elementary schools, day-care centers, and parks and playgrounds are distributed in an organized fashion among the residential areas.

The city districts of Vällingby are separated from one another by green belts which contain the principal arteries of the automobile circulation system, the interior of the districts being mainly oriented to pedestrian traffic. There is a relatively complete pedestrian circulation system that is separate from the automobile system; most Vällingby apartment buildings face the pedestrian ways, automobiles being kept to the rear of the buildings and generally to the periphery of the districts (the Radburn plan). The pedestrian ways typically pass through the public open spaces which make up a large portion of the land area in each district.

As built-environments, then, Levittown and Vällingby are virtually at opposite ends of a continuum in many important respects. Levittown is a low-density, automobile-oriented environment consisting of single-family houses on privately owned land; Vällingby is a high-density, pedestrian-oriented environment consisting of multifamily housing on publicly owned and utilized land. Levittown's site plan is unfocused; Vällingby's is sharply focused on the centrums and subway stops. Partly owing to the intentional localization of facilities which is an aspect of its design, Vällingby contains many more residential services than Levittown: public transportation, youth centers, day-care centers, public meeting rooms, and playgrounds and play parks. Finally, in comparison with Levittown, Vällingby is both more closely tied and accessible to the city, and in closer proximity to "nature"—woods, lakes, open fields. This favorable situation is also due partly to Vällingby's high density, public-transportation-oriented design (which permits a location closer to the city center and at the same time enables open space to be preserved), but also to the differences in scale and location between the Stockholm and Philadelphia metropolitan areas.

Both suburban environments have remained over the years at a relatively high level of environmental quality; indeed their appearance has improved as the growth of vegetation has softened the original harsh lines of new construction. The only major environmental change in Vällingby has been the expansion of some facilities, notably the main Vällingby centrum, and the addition of others, such as the swimming and sports hall built in 1972. Because of weaker land-use controls in the United States, Levittown and surroundings have changed much more than Vällingby in the twenty years, often in ways which are regarded negatively by the residents. The major changes in Levittown have been the unplanned development of garden apartments and commercial centers on scattered sites throughout the area and the residential, commercial, and industrial development of land surrounding the community. These changes have generated much traffic congestion on the main thoroughfares of Levittown, a condition which the residents view with displeasure. Other changes have been the emergence of new residential services, most of which are outside the Levittown area; the many alterations and additions to Levittown houses; and the sharp increase in the average number of automobiles per household.

The adults in both communities today seem well pleased with their surroundings, but there are some indications that today's Levittowners like their environment slightly less well than the original settlers, whereas the residents' opinion about Vällingby has improved slightly over the years. These opinion changes may be partly due, however, to changes in the demographic structure of each community.

Demographic Characteristics

In their early years, the two communities more closely resembled one another

demographically than they do today; the demographic structure of each suburb has altered more than the built-environment in the twenty-year period, and
these changes have been in somewhat divergent directions. Vällingby's peak
population occurred about 1960, when the number of residents totalled
58,701. In the same year Levittown, with 9 percent fewer dwelling units, had
a larger population—about 68,000. The difference is accounted for by the
smaller size of Vällingby families and households: 3.0 persons per household,
compared to 4.2 in Levittown (1960). The smaller Swedish household size
was not enough to prevent Vällingby from being comparatively overcrowded,
however, because its dwelling units were not as large as Levittown's; the
average number of persons per room in 1960 was 0.94, versus 0.76 in the
U.S. suburb.

In age and stage of the life cycle, the original residents of the two suburbs
were similar: 79 percent of the Vällingby population and 85 percent of the
Levittown population were in the young-family age groups; 35 percent of the
Vällingby population was under the age of sixteen, compared to about 45
percent (under age fifteen) in Levittown, a difference which is consistent with
the smaller Swedish family size; while 44 percent of Vällingby residents were
between the ages of twenty-one and forty-four, compared to about 40 percent
(between twenty and forty-four) in Levittown.

Since 1960, the demographic structure in the two communities has di-
verged. While the total number of residents in Levitt houses remained about
the same in 1970, the Vällingby population decreased from 58,701 to 47,606.
By 1972, it had dropped still further to 43,189; at the present time it may be
below 40,000. How is one to account for this interesting difference?

There are several possible explanations. First, the Vällingby population has
advanced faster through the stages of the family life cycle, mainly due to
lower birth rates and smaller family sizes. The peak teenage population in
Vällingby occurred in the late 1960s; by 1970, many teenagers were already
leaving home (and were leaving no younger brothers or sisters behind). In the
early 1970s , the outmigration of Vällingby youth accelerated; by the late
1970s the relatively youth-free population will become stabilized. This explanation asserts that Levittown is merely lagging behind Vällingby, and that
Levittown faces the same eventual depopulation. Though total population
figures for Levittown in the years after 1970 are unavailable, the peak teenage
population in Levittown occurred in the early 1970s, and there probably is an
outmigration of youth at the present time. (The schools and other youth-
serving institutions in Levittown have not felt the impact as strongly as in
Vällingby, because of the new residential developments within and around
Levittown.)

A second explanation complements the first but implies that Vällingby's long-run depopulation will be more severe than Levittown's. There has been an outmigration of large families from Vällingby and their replacement by smaller household units. In 1970, 26 percent of all Vällingby dwelling units were inhabited by a single person (and 53 percent by no more than two persons), compared to only 3 percent in Levittown.[3] The average size of new dwelling units built in the Stockholm area since 1960 has been larger than those of Vällingby, prompting larger families to prefer the new suburbs; Vällingby, at the same time, has attracted households whose needs for space are not as great.

By 1970, therefore, not only had Vällingby fallen behind Levittown in population size, but the makeup of the population had also altered. The percentage of Vällingby residents in the young-family age groups had dropped from 79 to 50 percent; while in Levittown the decline was much less steep—from 85 to 68 percent. Half of the Levittown population was under the age of twenty-one, while in Vällingby less than one-third was below this age.[4] Thus, over time, Vällingby's population has become much more heterogeneous than Levittown's in terms of age groups and household types, partly as a natural consequence of the small size of Vällingby's dwelling units; 57 percent are two rooms plus a kitchen, and smaller. None of the Levittown homes are that small.

In view of the normal maturation of the population that has taken place in each suburb, it can be said that the match between household and dwelling-unit sizes in Vällingby has improved over the years (partly due to initial overcrowding), whereas Levittown is on the verge of a mismatch. As the youth leave, two adults (sometimes only one) will find themselves inhabiting a three- or four-bedroom home. As the expense becomes too great, they will be forced to move, leaving their friends and neighbors behind. This appears to be happening less than might be expected, however, because the houses are not large by U.S. standards, and it is often financially advantageous for older people to stay rather than rent an apartment.

While cross-cultural comparisons of social class are difficult to make, and my data were limited to occupational classifications, the residents of Levittown and Vällingby appear very similar in social-class level and distribution. The only data on social class in Vällingby are from 1966, showing 11 percent upper middle class, 57 percent middle class, and 32 percent working class. By comparison, Levittown in 1960 was 20 percent upper middle class, 30 percent middle class, and 49 percent working class. The actual class distributions in the two suburbs are more similar than these data indicate, however, because the Swedish system classifies "technicians" as middle class rather than upper middle class, as they would be classified in the U.S., and "foremen and craftsmen" are classified as middle rather than working class.[5] This accounts for the bulging middle class in the Swedish data. Further, the Swedish data consider both females and males, whereas the U.S. data are restricted to males. If this variation were compensated for, the U.S. distribution would shift upward in class level and thus become more similar to the Swedish pattern.

There are indications that both suburbs have slightly declined in average class level since their inception; each is more working class now than it was a decade ago. The reason is apparently the same in each community; the common process of urban neighborhood change is being followed, in which higher-class families move on to new housing (usually farther from the city center), and their dwellings are taken by persons of a lower class level. Because these suburbs were among the first to be built after the wartime housing shortages of the 1940s, and higher-class families had few other housing alternatives, the process of neighborhood change may be accentuated in these communities. The wealthier families lived in them temporarily and moved as soon as more expensive housing was constructed.

There are some dissimilarities between the two suburbs vis-à-vis their class standing relative to the parent cities and societies. The class distribution in Vällingby is very similar to that of Stockholm as a whole, while Levittown's is shifted considerably upward compared to that of the city of Philadelphia. In addition, the average class levels of Vällingby and Stockholm as a whole are slightly above the national average, whereas Levittown's class level is just at the U.S. national average and Philadelphia's is below it.

Residents of the two communities differ significantly in ethnicity. Other races are an insignificant component of each community's population, but Levittown is more heterogeneous than Vällingby in religion and national origin. Levittown has a sizable Roman Catholic population (perhaps over 40 percent) and a sizable Jewish minority (about 10 percent); the Protestant population is divided among numerous denominations. The overwhelming majority of Vällingby residents, on the other hand, are of the Swedish Lutheran faith. About 10 to 15 percent of Levittowners are of foreign birth, or of foreign or mixed parentage; the comparable figure for Vällingby is less than 5 percent.

An important dimension of ethnic, class, age, and life-cycle heterogeneity within a community is the geographic distribution of residents in terms of these characteristics, or residential differentiation. The two communities show some interesting variations in this regard.

Residential differentiation by social class is greater in Levittown. In 1960, the two class-extreme census tracts varied by 82 percent middle and upper middle class in the one and 39 percent in the other, a gap which may have widened over the years. In Vällingby, middle- and upper-middle-class families predominate in the single-family-house areas (which are close to, but set off from, the apartment areas) and in the private apartment buildings (which are intermixed with the buildings owned by public corporations). Because of differences in scale, the day-to-day interaction among persons of different class levels is higher in Vällingby; they shop in the same markets, walk the same paths, and use the same facilities. In contrast, a large portion of Levittown's upper middle class lives in one of the four Levittown governmental jurisdictions, where they have almost no contact with residents of the other governmental units.

Levittown has almost no internal differentiation by age and stage of the life cycle, however; the geographic distribution of persons in this regard is almost random (excluding the garden apartments). In Vällingby, where age and life-cycle stage heterogeneity is much greater, the residential differentiation of these statuses is also comparatively high. High-rise buildings, which have smaller dwelling units, tend to have more young, single, and elderly persons. Some residential buildings are specialized, such as the pensioners' housing and "hotels" for young single persons. These buildings are intermixed with other types, however, and Vällingby residents of all ages and life stages use many of the same services, facilities, and public spaces.

In summary, today's residents of the two suburbs are not demographically as similar as might ideally be desirable for this kind of research, but they were much closer at each community's inception, and they remain equivalent in the important dimension of social class. The largest dissimilarities are the smaller size of the current Vällingby population and its greater heterogeneity, by age and life-cycle stage, together with Levittown's more pronounced heterogeneity by religion and national origin.

8

The Social Impact of the Residential Environment

A Comparison of Living Patterns in Vällingby and Levittown

Winston Churchill once said: "We shape our buildings, and afterwards our buildings shape us."[1] The issue of environmental effects on behavior, or environmental determinism, was first broached in chapter 4, where the congruence, or environmental fit, between Vällingby residents and their milieu was considered, an approach repeated for Levittown in chapter 6. The emphasis in these chapters was on the degree to which the respective environments were able to *accommodate* the preexisting values and behavior patterns of their residents; stronger relationships which imply causality were not stressed. But as useful as the concept of congruence may be, man-environment interaction includes not only accommodative relationships but also causal ones, patterns of influence or effect which flow in both directions: people have great influence over the environment, but the environment also has some influence on people.

More than it may appear at first glance, however, the relationship between environmental congruence and environmental influence is a close one. This can be seen by asking what happens when situations of environmental incongruence are maintained over time. Don't people, in the process of adjusting to environmental possibilities and constraints, modify their own behavior? It is not stretching a point too far to suggest that environmental influence is the dynamic aspect of environmental congruence. As William Ittelson and his coauthors have stated:[2]

> When we observe behavioral changes which seem to be caused by
> some environment, this change is the result of an interaction between
> prior behavioral needs and values and the setting's capacities to meet
> those needs. The environment does not determine the types of
> behaviors which occur, it only operates in conjunction or distinction with
> the values and needs which people are trying to realize in that environ-
> ment.

The pattern of environmental influence not only operates in situations
which we would label incongruent; on a day-to-day basis, over long periods
of time, people are quietly and subtly adjusting their own behaviors, values,
and even needs to the characteristics of the environments in which they find
themselves. Many and perhaps most of these adjustments may be of little
importance both for the individuals involved and for the society around them;
and the adjustments will often be overwhelmed by the more powerful
influences of nonenvironmental factors such as family, income level, religious beliefs, or messages from the mass media. But some may also have
lasting personal and social significance, more than is commonly realized.

The focus of this sociological inquiry is on two groups of people with
similar needs, values, and aspirations, who found themselves living in residential environments which were notably different in character. Over time, in
what ways have their lives been influenced by the special characteristics of
their environments, and which environmental factors stand out as being the
most influential in shaping their behavior? These are the questions to which
the present chapter is addressed.

Cross-cultural research is hazardous at best; findings which seem convinc-
ing can be distorted by a variety of factors stemming from the noncomparabil-
ity of cultures and the lack of understanding an observer from one culture may
have of the other. In the present inquiry, the difficulties engendered by cross-
cultural research are compounded by a lack of quantitative data and the nature
of the subject matter, one of the most sensitive and subtle areas of sociological
investigation. This chapter is written, therefore, with some trepidation; I have
been at times almost painfully aware of these difficulties. Yet it is also written
with confidence, a confidence which comes from the belief that I have a
reasonably good knowledge of both cultures and an understanding of each
suburb that has been built up by a "triangulation" of data sources—resident
interviews, informant interviews, discussions with outside experts, existing
data, personal observations, and the literature on suburbs and other residential
environments in both Swedish and English.

There are, and can be, few "hard" scientific findings about a subject matter as complex as this one. Nevertheless, much knowledge of importance may be gained by a careful examination and analysis of the wealth of data assembled and by a sorting out of those notable differences that come into relief through a cross-cultural comparison of two case studies. In addition, I have not hesitated to give opinions and insights which appear reasonable, feeling that, in a field as young and undeveloped as this one, these would prove useful in stimulating thought, providing research ideas, and promoting interest.

The Living Patterns of Adult Family Members

In each suburb today there exists a core of families containing middle-aged adults and teenage children, some of whom were original settlers of their communities and most of whom have lived there for many years. The attitudes and life styles of these families were portrayed in chapters 4 and 6 under the heading "the characteristic household." Drawing from the interviews with these and other comparable households, from existing data sources, and from personal observation, a comparison is made in this section of the activity patterns of adults in each suburb who are of similar social-class level and stage of the life cycle, exploring the ways in which differences in living patterns may be related to differences in the environments.

Work

Almost all women in Vällingby of working age hold jobs; in my sample of twenty-five households only one full-time housewife was encountered, the mother of a young child. In Levittown, the percentage of women of working age who hold jobs is lower; in the household sample there were ten full-time housewives, including several middle-aged women with no children at home, the type who are seldom found not gainfully employed in Sweden. What accounts for this striking difference? The explanation is mainly to be found in the economic and social systems of the two nations. In Sweden the working woman has long had greater public acceptance; many American men spoke, for example, of how they hoped their wives would never have to go to work—they were clearly opposed to the idea. Moreover, Swedish work life is structured in ways which greatly benefit the working woman, with such features as childbirth leaves, leaves for the care of sick children, flexible working hours, and long summer vacations.

Characteristics of the Vällingby environment also seem to play a role, however, by making it easier for a woman to work. Indeed, in many ways the Vällingby environment is ideal from the working woman's point of view. A large job market in the vicinity is easily reached by public transportation; home maintenance activities are at a minimum; and the community provides excellent day-care services in the immediate vicinity of the dwelling units. At the same time, there is little incentive for the Vällingby woman to be a full-time housewife. The apartment is small, with only a limited number of ways in which it can be modified; and there is little neighborhood social life.

In comparison, many features of Levittown make the life of a working woman there a greater struggle. It is more difficult to find suitable employment within reasonable commuting distance; there is almost total dependence on the automobile (what happens if she can't drive, can't afford a car, or the car breaks down?); and the working woman often finds it difficult to juggle the demands of her job and her high-maintenance home. If she has children, public day-care facilities are lacking and private alternatives are not always easily or satisfactorily arranged. At the same time, Levittown provides more incentive for a woman to be "just a housewife"; The stay-at-home woman in Levittown can be active in maintaining and improving her relatively spacious home and yard, and often there are neighbors similarly situated with whom she can socialize during the day. Moreover, because of her husband's long work hours, it is often necessary for the American woman to curtail her own work life if home and children are to be properly cared for.

Levittown may provide women greater flexibility in choosing between home or job, because the environment can be adapted to either role; in Vällingby the housewife, especially one with no children, is like a fish out of water. Yet the life of a full-time housewife seems not always to be freely chosen by those Levittown women who find themselves in this role. A number of the housewives I interviewed would prefer to work; yet not only do they find the logistics difficult, but also their husbands are opposed. These appeared to be the most bored women in Levittown; they feel their life is routine, without variety or stimulation, and unrewarding. As the women's movement succeeds in creating more national awareness of this problem, the number of such women will grow, and the boredom may change to active resentment.

With the percentage of gainfully employed women in the U.S. sharply rising, the relative disadvantages of the Levittown environment for the working woman are increasing. For the woman who can't afford a second car, who has difficulty in making child-care arrangements, or who has specialized employment needs, Levittown can become a noose around her neck. The percentage of working women in every advanced society has grown rapidly in recent years, suggesting that the full-time housewife soon may become a thing of the past. If this is to be the case, communities like Levittown may drop considerably in appeal.

Major differences in the work lives of the men in the two suburbs were not expected, but some significant ones came to light. The men of Levittown work longer hours than the men of Vällingby. While number of hours in the average work day is similar in the two countries, the men of Levittown were involved in more overtime work, moonlighting, long hours of semiprofessional and business employment, and weekend work; some men did shift work, which often involved long and irregular hours. Further, a common complaint by Levittown men (and about men by women) was that they had no time for activities outside work and that they were always tired after work. The Vällingby man, by contrast, appears relaxed and less "at odds" in the relationship between the work and nonwork phases of his life.

As in the case of the working woman, the differences in male work life is accounted for mainly by dissimilarities between the occupational systems and work environments of the two societies. For example, there is a greater struggle in the U.S. to "get ahead"—and to keep from falling behind. The personal income gained through work is essential in Levittown for many emergencies of life, such as illness, for which one receives government aid in Sweden. And the work environments in the U.S. may be more stressful; Sweden has become noted among the industrialized nations for efforts to improve the quality of its occupational milieus.

Yet the residential environment can make two contributions to longer work hours and to the stress of work. First, the total time away from home for work purposes is affected by the length of the journey to work, a factor which has led in the U.S. to the common complaint about the absent "suburban father." In these two suburbs, however, the journeys to work seemed about equal in length, and considerably less than the suburban stereotype would lead one to expect. Second, the environment can influence the resident to work longer hours so as to earn more money for such high-expense items as home maintenance and improvement, transportation, private recreational facilities, and for "keeping up with the Joneses." Environments differ, in other words, in the extent to which they throw costs onto the individual householder and in the degree to which they encourage residents to live above their means.

There are subtle ways in which the Levittown environment may encourage the kind of overwork which leaves some Levittown men tired, resentful, and with little time for other important activities in life. Home maintenance costs are high, and the environment virtually requires the ownership and upkeep of two or more cars by many families. Moreover, there is pressure to provide private recreational facilities and equipment, such as backyard swimming pools, Ping-Pong and pool tables, and multiple television sets. Such purchases, of course, represent a widespread desire for a higher standard of living, but this may be undesirably escalated in some families by the inadequacy of alternative public facilities and by the need many residents feel to withdraw into their private worlds, a need based partly on an underlying concern that "there is not much out there" in the community and on the recognition that one's quality of life depends heavily on the extent to which the microenvironment is embellished with private possessions.

Further, pressures to spend money for private improvements are increased by the competition among some Levittown residents to "keep up with the neighbors," a competition which is accentuated in the low-density suburb by what one suburban expert has called the "visibility principle."[3] A characteristic feature of the U.S. suburb is the relative ease of observation residents have of their neighbors' overt behavior and life-style. The private yards, automobiles, and home exteriors are continually "open for inspection" and, due to the larger amount of neighboring, even the home interiors are more "exposed" than in an apartment environment. While the visibility principle also is characteristic of small towns, because of their greater heterogeneity of age and class and a more rigid class stratification system, the principle does not seem to promote as much open competition as it does in suburbs. Life in Levittown is something like a track race: the residents of each neighborhood are all relatively equal at the start, even to the point of having look-alike houses; later, it is not difficult to spot those who are clearly ahead and those who have fallen behind. The one position leads to high personal status, pride, and satisfaction; the other to low status, low self-esteem, anxiety, and frustration.

Far more than their Swedish counterparts, the U.S. single-family detached house and the suburban environment lend themselves to status-seeking. The house is flexible and it comes in numerous levels of quality; the suburbs have become highly differentiated in terms of income level, making it relatively easy to tell a person's class level by knowing his address. The U.S. suburban house, and as much as possible the surrounding residential environment, are set up to display class position, and high positions are zealously fought for and jealously protected in the fluid class structure of American society. In the Swedish suburb the situation is muted: apartments are not very flexible; the housing market is tighter, making it more difficult for persons of higher class to jockey for position; and residential differentiation by social class is retarded by the more stringent government control of land use.

It would be easy to overemphasize status-striving as a force in American suburban life and as a cause of overwork among men. Most home maintenance and improvement and home equipment purchases in Levittown are doubtless desired on grounds other than status; many of the overworked men are merely trying to keep up with house payments, not improve their house so as to be as good as some neighbor. Yet some status-striving does seem involved in the complex of factors which generate the comparatively less desirable work situation of Levittown men.

Socializing

The U.S. residents seem slightly more "social" than the Swedes; they themselves give, or go to, more parties or other social occasions through the course of a year and see socially a larger number of people outside of the members of their own households. Moreover, social occasions in Levittown tend to be more informal. The pattern of dropping by for an unplanned social activity is common in Levittown, while in Vällingby social occasions are more planned and formal, typically organized around a meal.

In both communities, social occasions are most commonly spent with relatives, the holidays being almost always an extended family get-together. Because they come from larger families (one grew up in a family of thirteen children), the Levittowners have more close relatives, and these relatives seem to live a shorter distance away than the relatives of families living in Vällingby. (A large portion of the relatives of Levittowners in my household sample lived within the greater Philadelphia area.) In addition to visiting, most residents in each community maintained frequent contact with relatives—especially their parents—by phone and letter.

After relatives, the second major source of persons with whom the residents in each community socialize is work associates; there were no apparent differences between the suburbs in this regard. Other sources mentioned were friends from childhood, school classmates, church associates, and neighbors. Church associates were listed as a source of friends by some Levittowners but by no one in Vällingby.

The neighborhood was not a major source of close friends for most residents in either community, but it was more important in Levittown than in Vällingby, and for some in Levittown, who had few other alternatives, it was quite important. It is not uncommon for a group of neighbors to socialize back and forth in Levittown, especially during the summer months, when neighbors will drop over for a barbecue, a drink, or a game of cards. The incidence of social neighboring seems to have declined over the years, however, as residents have been able to choose friends outside the neighborhood with whom they have more in common.[4]

In Vällingby, socializing with neighbors is minimal. There are several possible environmental causes for Vällingby's lower level of neighboring. The need for neighbors is less in an apartment situation. Much neighboring in the U.S. suburb arises over home and yard maintenance activities and young children, neither of which was a major factor with these Swedish families.

There are fewer places in Vällingby to meet and get acquainted with neighbors; conversations can not take place over the backyard fence, for example. And apartment living seems to retard neighboring due to psychological feelings generated by close physical proximity; there is a greater fear of getting "stuck" in a neighboring relationship, of having fewer lines of retreat.[5] For similar reasons, neighboring is less in Vällingby's high-rise buildings than in the garden apartments.[6]

In summary, the difference between the two suburbs in the amount of socializing and social life is associated with the larger kinship network of the Levittowners and their access to two sources of friends that were not utilized in Vällingby—neighbors and church associates. Because informality in social activities is most common with relatives who live close by and with neighbors, the higher incidence of informal activities in Levittown may be partly accounted for by the greater prominence of these groups in the residents' lives.[7] In addition, the larger size of the Levittown living space and the availability of a private yard may promote informality; less advanced planning is required to make guests comfortable and to provide them with social activities than in the small apartment with limited facilities.

Home Care, Maintenance, and Improvement

The requirements for care of the dwelling unit are important in accounting for differences in the way the residents of the two suburbs allocate their time, money, and energies. The Levittowner lavishes great care on his home. A large block of the man's time, especially on weekends and vacations, is spent working on the house. Many Levittowners are in the middle of home improvements, or speak animatedly about home improvement plans; much of the work is do-it-yourself, a substitution of the householder's time for money ("sweat equity"). While most men say they enjoy this kind of work, it involves the displacement of time from other spheres of life; Levittown men cite home maintenance and improvement almost as often as their regular work as a reason why they have so little time. Much of the home maintenance is a necessity; many Levittowners could not afford to live in their houses if all maintenance work had to be done by outside service people.

The Vällingby resident also carefully attends to the dwelling unit—but this is only home care, not home maintenance and improvement. The interior of the Vällingby apartment is typically immaculate (a Swedish cultural trait), but home maintenance is handled by the apartment managers, and home improvement is, for the most part, not possible. Some Vällingby dwellers complain about this; they want to be able to maintain, modify, and expand their dwelling as they see fit. Since they can not, however, the Vällingby men must allocate their time to other activities. This may help to account for the greater amount of time Vällingby men spend in active interaction with family members.

Social Participation

The term "social participation" refers to outside-of-work participation in clubs, organizations, church activities, and other community affairs. Because Sweden and the U.S. are considered to have the highest organizational density of any societies in the world, it was surprising to find such low organizational participation in both samples. Working people in each suburb were usually nominal members of their union or trade and professional associations, and the parents of younger children were occasionally involved in school affairs. But aside from the involvement of Levittown residents in religious activities there was little involvement of residents in either suburb in any club, organization, or community activity outside of the work sphere. The residents' nonwork lives were organized around home, family, and the pursuit of individual activities. This low level of community participation, however, is typical of members of the urban working class.[8]

Eighty percent of the Levittown sample were church or synagogue members, and two-thirds of those were regular attenders of religious services versus only 8 percent attenders in Vällingby. Thus, religious activities play a much more significant role in Levittown than in Vällingby, though less than a quarter of the Levittown sample participated in religious activities beyond the weekly Sunday service.

Political participation was low in each suburb, reflecting again the working-class status of the residents. In the household sample, only one politically active person was encountered in Levittown, and none in Vällingby.

Recreation and the Use of Leisure Time

The differences in this sphere were greater than in any of the others that have been discussed, and it is an aspect of life in which the residential environment apparently has marked effects. It is important to recall at the outset that Vällingby residents, especially men, have *more* leisure time. The difference is even greater when summer vacations are included in the comparison: Vällingby workers averaged about four weeks, Levittown workers two or three weeks; several Levittown men stated that they had no summer vacation at all.

The most common leisure-time activity for Levittown residents is TV viewing—an average of two or three hours each evening, compared to about one hour an evening by Vällingby residents. Almost all Levittowners watch a great deal of television; some housewives have the set on continuously from morning until bedtime. Many Vällingby households, in contrast, watched little if any television. This dissimilarity is certainly related to the amount and types of TV programming in each nation. Sweden has only two TV channels, and general television programs are ordinarily not on the air during the day; evening programming includes fewer entertainment and more public affairs programs than in the U.S. Many Swedish respondents criticized the television fare as being dull and uninteresting, as well as limited.

But one suspects that another factor is also involved in this difference in the amount of time allocated to TV viewing. A paramount characteristic of TV viewing as a leisure-time pursuit is that it is passive, requiring no effort on the part of the participant. The overworked Levittown resident appears tired and more in need than the Vällingby resident of something which is relaxing and at the same time effortless.

What do Vällingby males do instead? Compared to their Levittown counterparts, they participate more in active recreation, such as walking and bike riding, and spend more time interacting with their families, especially their children. In neither community do the men often engage in active, year-round sports activities, such as tennis or swimming, or in other forms of regular strenuous exercise, such as jogging; but the Swedish men do much more walking and bike riding. In contrast, the Levittown men do almost no walking or bicycling either for exercise or pleasure; the only exercise most get during their leisure time is in "working around the house." This variance between the physical recreations of men in the two suburbs seems closely related to differences in the physical environment: Vällingby is designed for walking and bike riding; Levittown is designed solely for the automobile. [9]

Swimming during the summer months, however, was relatively popular among adults in both suburbs; boating was also popular in Vällingby because of the availability of facilities in the area. Bowling was engaged in by a portion of the Levittown men, especially the working-class men. The men of both nations seemed to read the same amount, to participate to the same extent in clubs and organizations, and to go out to movies and sport events about equally.

Another notable difference between the residents of the two suburbs is the use of summer vacations: the Swedes have relatively long and regular vacations, while the Americans' are shorter and more irregular. About 40 percent of the Vällingby households in my sample, and most of the families with children, owned a summer cottage where most of their vacation was spent plus many weekends during the warmer months of the year. There is little doubt that the second home is partly made possible by the minimization of expenditures on the first home. A number of families stated that, if they moved to a single-family house, they would not be able to afford a summer cottage.

Although at their summer cottage only about one month each year, Swedes typically invest a great deal of emotion and energy in it. The cottage makes apartment living through the dark winter months more bearable and gives a complete change of scene each year. The summer cottage provides an outlet for two activities which are limited in apartment life: informal neighboring and socializing, and home maintenance and improvement. The same families tend to return each year to the summer cottage areas, and the missed neighboring in the winter apartment is compensated for during the summer months. Because the summer-cottage owner invests much time and energy in working on his dwelling, neighboring often centers around home maintenance and improvement activities. The summer neighbors are often relatives; it is common for the Swedish extended family to reassemble this way once a year.[10]

For many Swedes, therefore, the summer cottage provides a complement to the apartment; the residential environment is split between two places and each, with its special merits, helps to offset the disadvantages of the other. Many Swedes would prefer to live the year round at their summer place, yet their desire for a good job and for urban services such as good schools and hospitals prompts continuing metropolitan-area residence. The higher urban incomes, plus the relatively inexpensive urban living arrangements, make the two-home way of life financially possible.

The ownership of two homes is widely regarded in the U.S. as a very desirable circumstance, but it is restricted mainly to middle- and upper-class families. Many Levittowners long for an annual change of scene, and the leading choice is "the woods," though some prefer "the shore." Yet only one Levittown household in my mainly working-class sample owned a second home, one handed down by their family. The physical opportunity is available, with the Pennsylvania mountains and New Jersey shore areas not far away, but with the expenses of their current housing and life-style there is little money left over. If summer vacations in the U.S. grow in length, this disadvantage will come into sharper focus.

Shopping

The shopping patterns of the residents of each environment are of contrasting types. In Levittown, bulk purchases of food are made on a weekly or biweekly basis by car, supplemented by an occasional purchase of perishables. In Vällingby, the typical pattern is daily shopping on foot. The Swedish householder commonly purchases food on the way home from work, buying only what can be carried by hand, usually enough for several meals only. This may be supplemented by occasional bulk purchases if a car is available.

The difference between the two patterns of shopping is strongly related to environmental characteristics. There are fewer supermarkets in Sweden, fewer households have cars, and there is less food storage space within the residence unit. Sweden appears to be shifting to the American pattern of shopping, however; some younger Vällingby residents, for example, make bulk purchases by car on a weekly basis outside of the community.

The problem in Levittown, on the other hand, is the lack of neighborhood shops within walking distance; a loaf of bread entails an automobile trip, often of a sizable distance. This limits shoppers to drivers, a problem in some families, and restricts the shopping participation of children.

Shopping often seems to be a more pleasurable experience for the Vällingby resident, especially nonfood shopping. Trips made to downtown Stockholm were ordinarily for the purpose of shopping, for example, but shopping as a semirecreational experience—sometimes combined with a meal out or a movie. A recent survey of Stockholm residents showed that one-fourth of all weekday shopping trips and one-third of all Saturday shopping trips do not involve any purchases (the Stockholmer makes, on the average, seven to nine visits to a store each week).[11] The Levittowners' trips to the new shopping malls may also be recreational shopping trips, but they usually do not involve as many nonshopping activities and pleasures.

Summary

A living pattern comparison between the adult family members in the two residential environments reveals many similarities. Both groups are strongly familistic: their lives center on home and family and are organized in terms of family values; they maintain close ties with parents and other relatives. A career orientation is not strong, the job being merely a means to a satisfying nonwork life; they are not attuned to the life-style sometimes called consumership—having fun, with few family responsibilities. The adults are not active in community affairs, nor are they "culture consumers" with a strong concern for the arts, fine restaurants, and intellectual life. Their roots are small-town and rural rather than urban and cosmopolitan, and their cultural, social, and environmental preferences direct them away from the city rather than toward it. In each of these respects they are typical of the urban working- and lower-middle-class population in most advanced societies.

Yet there are also some notable differences, some of which are at least marginally related to characteristics of the residential environment. One is in the work life: the Levittown men work longer hours and have less free time;

the Levittown women are much more likely to be full-time housewives. In Vällingby, the man has fewer environmental pressures to make ends meet, while the Vällingby woman has more opportunities for gainful employment and her employment takes some of the pressure off the man.

Other major differences are in socializing patterns and in the use of leisure time. The Levittown men, who have less leisure time, use it more passively, with the exception of home maintenance activities. Neighboring and informal socializing are more common in Levittown.

The life-style of Vällingby adults seems to involve a better integration of home, work, and leisure for both sexes; one sphere is not in competition with the other, and among the spheres there appears to be relatively little role-conflict. In contrast, many Levittown men complained about the lack of leisure time, and their wives commented on the man's inattention to home and family matters. The Levittown housewife expressed a desire to work and to "get out of the home" for longer periods of time, while the working woman of Levittown showed some tension in juggling the twin demands of home and employment.

The Residential Environment and the Child

What does a child need in order to grow up and be a confident, loving, and productive adult? While the answer can not definitely be known, it would almost surely include good parenting and a happy family life; schools that motivate and inspire to learn; play space and facilities that are safe; appropriate and challenging contact with peers; and a social environment that gives the opportunity to learn how the world functions.

The residential environment can be influential in the life of the child through its effect on each of these factors. The adequacy of parenting is affected by the community in which parents find themselves; the quality of schools is heavily determined by demographic characteristics of the environment (the number and types of children, the income and educational levels of the parents); contacts with peers are environmentally shaped; and the residential environment *is* the social environment for most children.

Though the physical results are quite different, both Vällingby and Levittown were specifically designed with the child in mind. In neither suburb today is the rearing of young children regarded by the residents as a particular problem, except that there is some concern in Levittown about a decline in discipline and a rise of permissiveness. Yet some strong impressions about the impact of each environment on the child, and on childrearing, emerged through talks with helping professionals and school officials and from personal interviews and observations. While one recognizes the dangers of cultural bias, insufficient knowledge, and the lack of comparable statistical data, these impressions should nevertheless be passed along because of the great importance of the topic and the likelihood that nothing more than impressions will soon be forthcoming.

The world of the preschool child in Levittown consists of the home and the yard, with an occasional trip to the shopping center. If the family can afford it, the home and yard will contain adequate play facilities—enough to keep the child occupied. The environment is safe: the child has freedom of movement indoors and out, yet the mother has ease of observation and control. Indeed, the appropriateness of this kind of environment for young children is a major reason so many young families in America desire to live in the suburbs.

As the child grows older, his geographic range is extended to include the neighborhood. He typically is able to find suitable playmates in the neighborhood, and he can spend time playing in houses other than his own. The neighborhood has been designed to limit through traffic; it provides a reasonably safe play environment by American standards. When the child reaches school age, he is often able to walk to the neighborhood primary school and to extend the range within which he may regularly see friends, many of whom are now school associates. This range is extended still further by the bicycle, which almost every Levittown child has.

The environment of the Levittown child, therefore, provides companions, play space and facilities, proximity of schools, fresh air, and relative safety; by contrast with inner-city areas, Levittown is a Garden of Eden for the child. Nevertheless, there are some important environmental deficiencies. There are very few hard surfaces, other than streets, of the kind that are necessary for many children's games and activities. Consequently, the children play on the streets at a relatively early age. Moreover, the child must cross the street to visit many of his friends (children, like adults, tend to have many more friends from those houses that face their own across a street than they do from those houses whose rear yards connect with their own). Although through traffic has been limited, the streets were not designed for children's play or use, and are hazardous. A Swedish study showed that children up to the age of about ten do not yet have the combined motor and intellectual development necessary to handle themselves safely around moving automobiles, even when well trained in safety rules.[12]

Because the young child needs adult supervision in street crossings, a key age for the Levittown child is the age at which he is allowed to make these crossings on his own. This age seems to have declined over the years. In the early years of Levittown it was six or seven, now it is four or five (this is cited by some parents as an example of the decline in discipline and rise in permissiveness).

This decline is an indication of a more general environmental problem in the neighborhood; once the child leaves his house and yard, it is very difficult to supervise him. The child's environment of front sidewalk and street is only occasionally frequented by adults; when the child is out of sight of his own home, he is often beyond the supervision of adults and thrown into the company solely of his peers.

Some parents try to overcome this problem by laying down and enforcing strict rules about where the child may play, or by regularly making appointments for the child to play at friends' houses, and only at those houses. Both of these strategies are burdensome to the harried suburban mother, however, which leads to their frequent bypass or avoidance.

Another deficiency in Levittown from the child's point of view should be suggested by this discussion; it is lacking in variety, community, activity, action, and unusual events which are of natural interest to children. The environment has few stimuli, and it seldom changes. Day after day the child sees the same cars, the same houses, the same friends, and the same handful of adults. He sees little of adult work life, community life, or the life of many age groups other than his own. The most exciting event is the automobile trip to the shopping center. The Levittown child is, to a large extent, isolated from society.

Many parents compensate for this lack of environmental variety by transporting their children to interesting places, but many more do not, or can not. Moreover, there are many advantages to the child's being able to go to and explore interesting places on his own at older ages. His very high dependence on parental transportation becomes a major problem for both parent and child.

The most important factor in a child's socialization is good parenting—parents who provide close contact and who interact with the child in a way which is loving, supportive, and educational. Here, too, the residential environment may have some important, though indirect, influences. My strong impression is that Levittown parents spend much less time *interacting* with their children than do the parents of Vällingby.[13] The case of the fathers has already been discussed. The fathers of Levittown work longer hours, spend more time maintaining the home, watch more television, have shorter vacations, and seem more tired during their leisure hours. These factors, several of which are related to environmental characteristics, cut in seriously to the amount of time fathers have to spend with their children. Some of the time they do spend is low-quality interaction, such as interaction while driving an automobile. The fathers' interaction is curtailed further by the greater prevalence of polarized sex roles in American society, with norms holding that children are mainly the woman's responsibility.

In an earlier era, the home during the day was a beehive of cooperative activity—grandparents, aunts and uncles, fathers home for lunch. In the Levittown environment, child care is almost entirely the responsibility of a single person—the child's mother. Today's U.S. suburban woman spends the day in relative isolation, save for a few neighbors whose predicament is the same as her own. She gets no help in either child care or housework. It is not that her burdens are unnecessarily heavy, but that her routine is boring, often thankless, and with seldom a break. Though she cares greatly about her children, it sometimes becomes difficult under these circumstances to adequately fulfill her child-care responsibilities, especially if she has a large family. The incessant round of supervision, stimulation, discipline, education, and physical care of children, without help or even positive reinforcement, can become a burden far heavier than most people—especially men—imagine, or than many women who are not isolated with young children appreciate. It is a situation which leads some women to withdraw emotionally in their interaction with children or to seek avenues of escape, such as constant television watching. Because of their situation, it is probable that Levittown mothers, like their husbands, also have less interaction with children than their Swedish counterparts, although most Vällingby mothers are employed outside the home.

The environmental situation of parents, perhaps more than any other factor, leads to the overpermissiveness that many Levittown parents are concerned about. Overpermissiveness is a form of neglect; parents are simply too busy, tired, anxious, or preoccupied to interact as fully with their children as is desirable. The parents' environmental situation also appears to generate a decline in family activities—activities in which all members of the family jointly interact in some pleasurable or productive way. Mothers have had enough of the children during the day; when father finally comes home, it is her time to spend alone with him and not in some joint family pursuit. This is unfortunate, because family activities are among the most pleasurable, important, and rewarding experiences in a child's life.

Though in many respects a satisfactory environment for childrearing, then, Levittown is not without some limitations and deficiencies. How does Vällingby compare?

The Vällingby environment has four main differences that are significant for child rearing: it substitutes public for private space, it has completely separate pedestrian and vehicular areas, it has more variety and diversity, and it has many neighborhood-based services and facilities which assist both mother and child.

There are drawbacks to apartment living with children, and the parents of Vällingby are well aware of them. The substitution of public for private space means that the child has less internal play space in the home and no private yard, particularly a problem for large families. The child who is able to go out to a fenced private yard will be allowed more freedom at an earlier age than the child who must go out to a public area, especially in view of the fact that the mother of the ground-level dwelling is in a better position to observe and supervise the child than the mother in an apartment. In addition, the small apartment sometimes leads parents to restrict the visiting of children's playmates, particularly when the mother is concerned about neatness and order in the apartment. It is the rare Vällingby parent of young children who doesn't wish for somewhat more space within the dwelling unit.

The limitation of private space in Vällingby is offset by a relative abundance of public space. Private yards have been collected together, as it were, to form large public yards. Because the public space was designed for pedestrians only, it is as safe as the U.S. private yard and at the same time larger, more diversified, and containing a much wider variety of play areas and facilities than the individual family could possibly afford. The Vällingby child often has an attractive area as large as a block in which he may freely roam. The area contains sand boxes, wading ponds, playground equipment, play houses, indoor recreation centers, rocks, hills, and trees, and benches for sitting.

For the older child, beginning at ages six or seven, the play area is much safer than an area of comparable size in Levittown, even though in both cases the child is far beyond the observational range of the parent. The reason is that the public areas of Vällingby contain, at most hours of the day, many adults who can act as informal supervisors—adults use the pedestrian areas of Vällingby almost as much as children. Further, mothers will commonly be found in the play areas devoting their time to the supervision of a young child and at the same time able, if necessary, to assist the other children playing nearby.

The play areas of Vällingby provide more interest, more challenge, and more variety and "action" than their Levittown counterparts. With the possible exception of preschoolers, who often play in protected areas, children of different age groups are more in contact with one another; and the environment changes regularly as new faces (rather than new cars) continually pass by. There are hard surfaces for skating and ball games, rocks for hide-and-seek, and paths for running.

The greatest asset of all, however, is the supervised play park. Scattered through Vällingby are eleven park-like playgrounds, described in chapter 3, which provide daily activities, such as games, arts and crafts, and athletics, supervised by well-trained personnel. The parks also provide morning baby-sitting for children under five. Standard procedure for mothers of youngsters in this age group is to leave the children in the play park for two or three hours while they do their shopping and cleaning. Such services go a long way to make up for the relative lack of private space in Vällingby. The child has more diversified environments, and the mother has temporary relief from the burdens and responsibilities of child care.

Vällingby mothers have a real opportunity to take a job, at least part time, if they wish to; located in every neighborhood is a day-care center which will take care of their children during working hours. (Not every child can get into a day-care center at once, however; in most Swedish suburbs, including Vällingby, there are still not enough openings to meet the demand.) I am not in a position to assess the long-run consequences for the child of being raised each weekday by the professionals in a day-care center rather than by his own mother. I can only say, based on my own observations and experiences, that the Vällingby day-care centers provide an experience for the child that is loving, supportive, and at the same time challenging. The staff are well trained, the facility is designed to provide an environment which is most appropriate for the child, and the program is carefully supervised. The child of the day-care center probably has more interaction each day with adults as well as with peers than the child who is alone with his own mother. Moreover, the center is structured to strengthen the role of the family rather than to detract from it. It is commonly located in close proximity to the child's dwelling unit, and the staff try constructively to assist the parents in their child-rearing functions rather than to replace them.

On the whole, the child of Vällingby seems less isolated from the larger society and its concerns than the Levittown child. He or she comes into contact with more adults (and adults who have a greater age spread), sees more work places, because of the proximity of offices and small industries as well as shops, and goes to the city more often.

The most important difference for the child between Vällingby and Levittown, however, is the greater parental contact, especially with fathers. As discussed above, family activities, such as taking walks together, are more common, and the father has fewer obligations and distractions to reduce the interaction he has with his children, in both quality and quantity. Vällingby mothers, because they do not carry the same psychological burdens as the mothers of Levittown, may also have better relations with their children and enjoy them more. The process of childrearing seems less filled with anxiety for Vällingby parents. I believe this is due partly to the fact that they know they can count, to a much higher degree than Levittown parents, on the local environment and community as sources of support.

The Teenager in the Residential Environment

Teenagers spend a larger portion of their time in the local residential environment than almost any other age group. This fact lies behind the growing body of opinion which holds that teenagers may be the group most affected by environmental characteristics. It should not be surprising, then, that the impact of the environment on teenagers was pointed up more sharply in this inquiry than it was for any of the other age groups that were considered.[14]

The adolescent years are difficult in every modern society, both for the adolescents themselves and for their parents, and the question of how society can successfully bring its young into adulthood has no easy answers. In earlier times, the child became an adult in a few short years by fully assuming adult work roles soon after puberty. He quickly came to share adult responsibilities, duties, and rights. The stage of life called adolescence emerged with the rise of mass education and the consequent delay of the start of work life. This stage of life has lengthened over the years and become more differentiated from adult life-stages in values, goals, and interests.[15] The differentiation has led to the formation of distinct adolescent subcultures which are sometimes in conflict with the subcultures of adults, contributing to what is sometimes called the generation gap.

By all indications, the adolescent years in Sweden are not as problematic as they are in the U.S., and the generation gap seems narrower. This probably is due mainly to dissimilarities between the two societies in their educational, employment, and family systems. In a comparison of Danish and U.S. socialization of adolescents, for example,* a striking difference in family structure was found: "American families are much more often authoritarian than are families of Danish adolescents. It is the American parent rather than the adolescent (or the two together) who is likely to make most decisions."[16] Moreover, "in the United States, it is the mother who is most likely to voice the family directives, and to back them with discipline."

In Danish families, by contrast, both parents frequently share responsibilities.[17] These differences in family structure, which the authors of the study suggest are related to larger sociocultural dissimilarities, seem to be a cause of another striking cross-cultural difference: Danish adolescents showed a much stronger sense of independence from family influence, and

*The Danish socialization and family systems are similar to the Swedish.

this independence was associated not with rebelliousness but with closeness to parents and positive attitudes toward them.[18]

As another example, the Swedish educational system may put less pressure on adolescents than the U.S. system. The number of youth who go on to higher education is much less in Sweden than in the U.S., thus reducing the tension that arises during the high school years over the need to go to college; this is compensated for in Sweden by a more vigorous and accepted program of vocational instruction at the high-school level for youth of all classes.

While sociocultural variations can account for many of the differences between adolescent behavior in the two suburbs, it was surprising how strongly the environmental situation of youth was emphasized in discussions about youth problems with adolescents, their parents, and youth-serving personnel in each nation. Moreover, the most noteworthy attitudinal difference between residents of the two environments was found among adolescents. About one-quarter of the Levittown youth expressed a dislike for their environment, and almost half of them stated they were bored,[19] while the Vällingby youth were overwhelmingly satisfied with their environment, liking it even better than their parents, and boredom was a negligible factor for them. What environmental characteristics may help to account for these differences?

The Adolescent in Levittown

The youth of Levittown are in general agreement that in their community there is too little to do, a lack of transportation, and some of the recreational facilities cost too much. The lack of things to do is somewhat paradoxical because Levittown is by U.S. standards well supplied with recreational and other facilities, including swimming pools, neighborhood schools, parks and playgrounds, and baseball fields. But it is often overlooked that these facilities are used mainly by preteens. Use of the swimming pools is highest in ages ten, eleven, and twelve and drops off precipitously among youth in the early teen years, who don't want to be associated with facilities which are primarily used by younger age groups. By age sixteen, when many Levittown youth get drivers' licences and cars, pool use often stops completely. In addition, the pool season is only ninety-two days, or one-quarter of the year. The schools close by in the neighborhood are all primary schools, while the high schools and middle schools are often beyond the usual walking or biking distance of Levittown teens and hence outside of their normal after-school orbits. Parks and playgrounds are mainly for adults and young children; they are used by teenagers mainly for hanging out—standing around in small cliques for purposes of social interaction. Ball fields and basketball courts are sometimes used by teenagers, but most sports activities for this age group take place under school auspices, where they are geared mainly to the serious, competitive athlete and not to the part-time amateur.

Thus the teenagers turn from public recreational facilities to commercial ones, particularly to bowling alleys and skating rinks. The use of commercial facilities is enhanced by the fact that they are the most lively places in town; on any evening they contain an actively engaged group of Levittowners—often of many different age groups—who show a deep interest in what they are doing. The participants seem happy, are jovial with one another, and make the facility an exciting place to spend time. But the facility costs money, more of it than many teenagers can afford on any but a very irregular basis.

The use of those few facilities that are truly available and appropriate for teenagers in Levittown is seriously undermined by the lack of public transportation. This is a chronic complaint of Levittown teenagers and of their parents as well. A mother of seven children noted: ''If you had more things for kids here it wouldn't do much good, because there would be no way to get them there.'' The lack of public transportation cuts deeply into the life style of most teenagers, and may contribute as much to their feelings of boredom as the lack of facilities.

The greatest feelings of boredom in Levittown are experienced by thirteen- to sixteen-year-olds, and it seems likely that these feelings are related to the special consequences which transportation deficiencies have for this age group. After age twelve or thirteen, the youth's environmental orbit widens considerably; going out in the evening becomes important, new recreational and social facilities are utilized, and friends are drawn from a much larger territory because the neighborhood-based schools have been left behind and classmates in the larger schools live in neighborhoods that may be distant from one another. While the needs of the fourteen-year-old Levittowner are very different from the ten-year-old, however, the means of transportation which each has available are identical. Walking is usually impractical, because the destination is too far away. Bike riding is sometimes feasible, but is not as commonly used by teenagers as by younger children. The reasons are many, and include the fact that bikes are a symbol of childhood and are stolen easily and often. In addition, bicycles are generally impractical in poor weather, unsafe at night, and involve risk in going long distances and crossing major thoroughfares in a community as dominated by the automobile as Levittown.

This leaves the third means, dependence on an adult, usually the mother, a means which often proves unsatisfactory both for parent and child. The constant round of chauffeuring is the self-professed bane of many suburban mothers, including those of Levittown. But only the lucky child has regular access to such a parent-chauffeur: 25 percent of the women in my sample could not drive; about 40 percent of the Levittowners have only one car, usually driven to work by the man; and many mothers of teenagers hold jobs, thus greatly limiting the time they have available for their child's transportation needs.

Thus the youth of early teen years face continual frustration in reaching places in Levittown which may be of interest; the boredom of "too little to do" is affected not only by a lack of facilities and activities but also by a lack of accessibility to them. Moreover, the youths' transportation, frustrations, and boredom are compounded by the great dependence on parents for something as vital as transportation, which comes at a time when the teenager is striving for greater independence. The situation can lead to deep, underlying resentment on both sides and adds to the confusion and sometimes hostility that often seem to mark parent-teenage relationships in the U.S.

Hanging Out. The teenager in Levittown who has nothing to do spends his time, when he is not watching television, "hanging out." Because a surprisingly large number of Levittown youth spend time hanging out, and it is these youth who are widely regarded as one of the major problems in the community, the social phenomenon of hanging out may be an important key to an understanding of the malaise of the teen years. It is not a practice limited to teenagers. Old people hang out in city parks and watch the world pass by; small-town people may sit in the shade, chat with one another, and watch their fellow residents go and come. Hanging out is usually a passive activity, done in the company of peers, and best performed in an area where the group can both see and be seen. It is a partly social function, relaxed companionship with peers, and partly an attempt to be where something interesting or exciting may happen.

A problem in environments like Levittown is that interesting or exciting happenings seldom occur. Hanging out typically takes place on street corners in purely residential areas, in parks and wooded areas which are adjacent to residences, and at the swimming pool areas when they are closed for the season. None of these locales provides any interest or excitement whatsoever beyond that generated by the teenagers themselves. Most of these hangouts are places for escape rather than places where passive stimulation can take place. They are places where teenagers are even more "outside" of community life than they are in their own homes and where they must rely solely on their own imaginations and fantasies for "something interesting to do"—the bored leading the bored.

Some hangouts in Levittown do provide more stimulation and activity—school parking lots, neighborhood shopping centers, and isolated snack and short-order places. Yet these, too, have serious limitations. The school parking lot attracts only a select group of automobile-oriented peers; the neighborhood shopping center is often unsatisfactory because the shopkeepers fight to keep the youth away (maintaining that the youth hurt business) and because the main "life" is the coming and going of cars, principally with adults on shopping expeditions; the snack places usually can be reached only by automobile, thus limiting some of the value they might have.

The stark reality for the Levittown teenager is that there is no satisfactory place within the community where he can go to see and be seen and to watch the world go by. Much of the real world—the world of commerce and industry—is either widely scattered within Levittown or outside the area entirely; adults can reach it, but teenagers can not. Moreover, there is no central collecting point within Levittown (comparable to Main Street in a small town) where the residents gather, interact, and conduct their daily affairs. The shopping centers tend to be utilized solely for commercial purposes; they have few subsidiary social functions, however much the shopowners may wish otherwise.

The teen hangout groups in Levittown consist usually of youth who live in the same neighborhood, rather than peers met in high school who happen to share common interests. This is symptomatic of a more general problem in communities built like Levittown: because of the lack of transportation, it is difficult to make and maintain friendships with peers in high school who share common interests. The high school draws students from such a large geographic area that the chances are great that friends met in school will live very far away and be inaccessible during after-school hours and on weekends. This geographic fact of life throws the child back onto the neighborhood, where peer interaction may have to take place among youth who have little in common save for the locational tie, or in some cases there is no suitable friend available at all. The territorial bond is important among Levittown's hangout groups; in some areas there are gangs who take the name of their neighborhood, and there have even been some fights, though not very serious ones, over the protection of gang turf. The bond which geography provides is a weak one, almost ersatz, for it signifies nothing very real—one geographic area in Levittown is very similar to the next.

The desirability of Levittown for teenagers has improved somewhat in recent years through the development of large, enclosed, pedestrian-mall shopping centers, several of which are located within easy driving distance of most Levittowners. The new Oxford Valley Mall was described and briefly discussed in chapter 5. I encountered few Levittown teenagers who did not find these malls delightful places to spend some time. They incorporate many of the attributes of a highly desirable place to hang out: pleasant, pedestrian-oriented surroundings, a constant change of scene as people come and go, and many standing and sitting areas where one can see and be seen. Moreover, they are not just teen ghettos but include people of all ages and many walks of life.

Although the malls have become a frequent destination for Levittown teenagers and are a significant environmental improvement from the teen point of view, they are not without some serious limitations. They are difficult to get to, requiring a special trip. The Oxford Valley Mall has recently initiated a bus service that serves part of Levittown, but the malls are relatively inaccessible to most teenagers who do not have access to an automobile. They are also completely commercial in character—a kind of ersatz downtown whose sole intended function is the buying and selling of merchandise. Because of this, the shopowners do not always take kindly to the teenagers' use of the malls for social purposes. Large groups of teenagers are prevented from forming by the mall security officials; small groups of teenagers are frequently told to "move on." Finally, the mall is of limited use to the teenager because it is *only* a place to hang out; as one youth put it, "all you can do is walk around." In other words, there is really nothing to do there, either—as in the rest of the Levittown area.

In summary, life in Levittown is lived within the home and not out in the community. The environment outside of the home is relatively lifeless; it consists of the automobile in transit and the teenager on foot. While reasonably well suited to the automobile, it is poorly suited to the teenager. The teenager must count on the home for stimulus, activity, and excitement. For those who must count on the environment, life appears dull, uninteresting, and boring. This may be the Achilles' heel of suburban life. The environment seems to work well for those who have satisfying "microcommunities" within their own homes and for those who are able regularly to leave the environment. For others, the environment can be more sterile and lifeless than the remotest small town. Teenagers make up a large percentage of these "others"; they appear to suffer most from the underside of suburban life.

Youth Centers in Levittown? The teenagers of Levittown often put forth a rather straightforward environmental solution to their problem of boredom—they would like to have a youth center. The request by teenagers for such a facility is so commonly heard that one wonders why it is not answered. There appear to be three main reasons: first, youth centers are very expensive, and they seem to lose out in the incessant battle over scarce tax dollars and voluntary contributions; second, it is difficult within the American system of local government to determine what institution should administer such general community facilities (welfare? recreation? education? some new youth authority?); third, they have been tried on a limited basis and have failed. An example was cited in chapter 5—the Levittown Public Recreation Association made several attempts which had to be abandoned after some teenagers became unruly. Some parents and youth leaders fear such centers; they are difficult to control and may easily become unmanageable.

Yet youth centers have been run successfully in many communities in the United States, as well as in Europe, as the Vällingby case indicates; they are difficult but not impossible enterprises to manage. The first youth centers of Levittown inevitably will face the problem of grappling with the immense pent-up energy which exists—"you give the kids a place of their own and they go wild." This is a very different situation from the community with established youth centers in each neighborhood, centers which the children have grown up with and which have become regular habitats for neighborhood youth.

Youth centers may seem an artificial solution to a complex problem, and the idea of segregating "troubled" youth into a clubhouse, as opposed to integrating them into the community, is regarded in some quarters as undesirable. The youth centers appear artificial because they are not "productive" social clubs, yet they may be a necessary answer to an already artificial community, one in which there is very little real community life to plug into. The two main focal points for youth in the U.S. suburb are home and school, and there are many youth who simply do not feel comfortable in either of these environments—for a wide variety of reasons ranging from unhappy, belligerent parents to a distaste for school work in a society which places a great premium on academic achievement. The main alternative for these youth is the street, and street life represents in many U.S. communities a third force (often the strongest one) in addition to home and school. The youth center must be thought of as an alternative to the street; in the comparison, I believe that it is a much superior alternative.

One main ingredient for the success of youth centers is the structuring of their activities, for the most part, by the values and norms of the youth themselves rather than by those of the adult leaders. In this way the center becomes a true alternative to home and school rather than an extension of them, and it maintains some of the character of street life which is most attractive to youth. Yet the control of disruptive behavior is equally important, otherwise the consequences can be worse than those of street life, where youth at least cluster in groups that are usually so small as to render them benign. Adult social control must be ever-present but as little oppressive as possible. This very delicate handling of the social control function is the principal managerial problem in youth centers both in the U.S. and abroad.

The second major problem of the youth center administration is getting youth to come, a problem that may seem strange in view of the strong desire of youth to have a center in the first place. At the heart of the problem is the presence of teenage cliques: small groups of teenagers who are continually in one another's company, who have developed their own subculture, and who often manifest hostility to rival groups. As one Levittown police official put it: "No general facility would work because youth are so splintered into cliques." Because cliques are already established, with strong interclique rivalries and hostilities, this social organization would become superimposed onto a new youth center. A dominant clique may quickly "gain control" of the new center, declare it as their territory (as they have done with their outside locales), and resent the intrusion of other cliques and even adults. Many teenagers, then, would naturally become reluctant to intrude in "foreign territory"; it is like, as one teenager put it, "walking into a stranger's living room."

This problem has been a most serious one in many new youth centers, but it should not be thought of as irremediable. It is likely that strong cliques are generated partly by the absence of a general facility within which youth can relate on their own terms; they are forced by the pressure of social circumstances to link together in a close-knit pattern of social organization in search of unity and meaning. Looking at the other side of the coin, one has reason to believe that the presence of a network of youth centers, which are accessible and active, can alter the social circumstances to such a degree that the power of the clique system is diminished. Thus the very important efforts of youth center personnel to reduce the dependence of teenagers on cliques is reinforced by the presence of the facility itself.

The usefulness of a youth center can extend well beyond the function of keeping youth occupied and off the street. It can become an important center for teen counseling in problems of sex, health, drugs, social relationships, and financial matters, a function which is lacking in many communities in the U.S. Teenagers often need some place to go, and someone to talk to, other than at home or school, for impartial advice and moral support. The center can also be used as an employment exchange for part-time jobs: the availability of part-time work, especially in the summer, is one of the best solutions to the problem of teenage idleness.

The Role of the Automobile. In addition to differences in environmental attitudes and feelings of boredom among the teenagers in the two suburbs, the consequences of the automobile for teenagers in the United States were strongly highlighted in the cross-national comparison. While the Vällingby teenager can not by law drive until age eighteen and few Swedish teenagers own or have access to cars, transportation deficiencies in Levittown conspire to virtually force the American teenager, at least the teenage boy, to learn to drive at age sixteen (the minimum legal driving age in the state of Pennsylvania) and to hope for a car of his own. As a means of transportation, of course, the impact of the car is far-reaching. Suddenly, a whole new world opens up: a world of faraway places, a world of adults, a world of privacy in which one can escape the reach of authority. The limitations of the old environment can be transcended; the youth can now touch the "real" world. It is no wonder that boredom among Levittown's youth decreases significantly after the age of sixteen. Not all Levittown youth get their own car at age sixteen, however; most rely on borrowing their parents' car, or on hitching up with the lucky friend who owns one.

The consequences of the automobile extend deeply into teen subculture and parent-teen relationships. The car in Levittown suddenly provides, at age sixteen, the independence, especially for boys, that in the previous years was dearly sought for and denied. The use of a car is a big ego-builder for boys, and the new-found freedom is often abused. Many parents mark "the year he got his license" as the beginning of trouble; "after that, we lost touch with him, we never knew where he was, we couldn't control him anymore." In many respects, the automobile gives teenagers too much independence, too abruptly, and at too early an age. Evidence for this judgment can be seen in the number of automobile injuries and deaths incurred by teenagers, which in the U.S. is extremely high (I was surprised at how many of the teenagers encountered in Levittown had been involved in serious accidents), and in the importance of the car for juvenile delinquency, to be discussed below.

Because the car is a virtual necessity in Levittown, and in view of the fact that not all teenagers possess one, it becomes one of the most significant (and more significant because scarce) status symbols in teen culture. The boy who has one gains high status; girls find it useful to link up with such boys so as to be assured (but usually to the regret of their parents) that they have transportation, as well as a measure of independence from adults. Those teenagers who don't have a car feel deprived and often bitter; some of the most vicious antagonisms between teenagers and their parents arise over the use or purchase of a car. This has become increasingly true for girls as well as boys; girls need a car as much as their brothers, but their parents show greater reluctance to grant permission.

Some of the principal values in the teen subcultures of suburban areas are symbolized, and to some extent generated, by the automobile: freedom, independence from adult authority, but also speed, power, and physical appearance. In a comparative survey of Danish and American adolescents, the researchers concluded: "One gets the impression that the American is much more concerned with status and power, while the Dane is much more content with individual happiness and self-expression."[20] The same impression came from my comparison with Swedish youth.

While teen culture in the U.S. is shaped by factors of much greater significance than the automobile, and many of the values noted above are characteristic of American culture as a whole and widely promulgated through the mass media, the sociocultural impact of the automobile on teen life in the U.S. may be underestimated. With the problems of youth in America deepening, this impact deserves much more national attention as well as the careful consideration of social scientists.

The Adolescent in Vällingby

The principal advantages of the Vällingby residential environment for teenagers are the availability and accessibility of a great diversity of facilities and other environmental elements. The Vällingby teenager is within close walking distance of one major and several minor shopping centers, schools, sports facilities and areas, woods, trails and sitting areas, several employment zones, and youth centers. Other facilities and services are easily accessible by low-cost public transportation. Vällingby is environmentally much "richer" than Levittown; there is more going on, more to stimulate interest, and more frequent changes of scene.

Teenagers are the most frequent pedestrians of the modern world; their needs for spatial range are great at the same time that their means of transportation are often primitive. Vällingby is a pedestrian-oriented environment, not only for teenagers but for all age groups. This means that teenagers are not dispossessed, for lack of transportation, from facilities and services that are available to adults; they do not become second-class citizens in the environment.

Owing to the appropriateness of the community for teenagers, Vällingby youth can be more actively involved than their Levittown counterparts in things outside the home, and at the same time less dependent on parents. Not only is the Vällingby teenager less dependent on parents for transportation and for use of the home for youth-related activities but also for money, due to the presence of numerous facilities and services in Vällingby which are low-cost or free. Thus the Vällingby teenager is more independent of his parents at an earlier age—a goal for which most teenagers strive. This does not mean that affective ties with parents are weaker, however. On the contrary, there is reason to believe that these ties are stronger, because conflicts between child and parent over dependency are lessened.

While it is true that adolescents want and need some places to be by themselves, places which they can call their own, the heavier burden in modern societies is to find ways to include them in ongoing community activities, to prevent feelings of functionlessness, meaninglessness, and social isolation. One way frequently advocated, and perhaps the best one, is the provision of part-time jobs or other productive activities in the community; neither Sweden nor the U.S. has been very successful at this. But the design of the environment can also make a useful contribution. In Vällingby, the teenager is more in contact with the round of functions necessary for the successful operation of every community and with the diversity of people who make up the society; because his community is more than society's dormitory, he does not feel as detached from society. Also, environmental stratification by age groups is not as apparent in Vällingby as in Levittown; few public places or facilities are used exclusively by teens, and, where they are, the proximity of adults and younger children is a constant reality.

On the other hand, the Vällingby teenager lacks the private space which is in the possession of most Levittown youth. Fewer Vällingby teenagers have private bedrooms or recreation rooms, and almost none have private yard space. Thus the Vällingby teenager is less able to conduct certain activities in his family surroundings, a problem for some teenagers, particularly those from large families where parents necessarily have a special concern about order and neatness in the home. This lack of private space is thought by some Swedes to force teenagers outside, where they may end up hanging out on street corners and getting into trouble. A more likely reason for hanging out, however, is the teenager's desire to get on "netural ground," away from home and school, and to a place where something is "going on." Conflicts with parents, of course, can make a major contribution.

Although comparative statistical data are not available, my impression is that a lower percentage of teens hang out in Vällingby than in Levittown. The hanging-out process in Vällingby is strongly affected by the youth centers, described in chapter 3; many Vällingby teens who are attracted to the hanging-out style of life spend their time instead at these centers. While only a small percentage of Vällingby teens use the services of the youth center, those who do tend, by all appearances, to be the type that in Levittown claim boredom—working-class youth who have limited familial internal resources. Since boredom among Vällingby youth seems a much less serious problem than it is in Levittown, additional weight can be given to the judgment, expressed by Levittown youth, that adequate youth centers would relieve teenagers of many problems and anxieties. Indeed, the few bored teenagers whom I interviewed in Vällingby were very disgruntled and troubled youth whose behavior (especially drunkenness and drug abuse) had caused them to be banned from the youth centers. Since they were in no other community activities and for one reason or another could not find a job, they felt—quite properly—that they had nothing to do.

In many ways, participation at the youth centers can be considered a form of hanging out. But it is hanging out in a variety of activities that are not available to the youth in the street. Further, it is hanging out away from public view—something that many adults in these areas have come to consider a distinct advantage.

To summarize, all three major components of the residential environment seem involved in Vällingby's advantageous qualities from a teenager's point of view: the structure of the built-environment, especially its pedestrian orientation and central focus; the structure of residential facilities and services, especially public transportation and the youth centers; and the demographic structure. Also important is Vällingby's location: near enough to the city for frequent excursions (which teenagers take more often than their parents), yet also close to the countryside, for its recreational opportunities.

The teenagers in both suburbs preferred country living to city living; most of those who indicated a desire to move from their present residential location preferred a more rural area, although several in each community opted for a more urban way of life. This may seem to conflict with the "prescription" for teenagers given above of a more heterogeneous and lively environment; but I do not think it does in reality. The rural environment brings its own special joys, challenges, and excitements. These are difficult to compare with the urban virtues, though they serve similar needs and purposes. Moreover, there is some reason to believe that the teenagers' rural preference is not solidly grounded. In Sweden there is a strong nostalgia about rural living, yet many Vällingby teenagers did not seem to enjoy their months at the summer cottage; indeed they commonly would stay in town by themselves during summer vacation when they reached the age of about fifteen or sixteen. In the United States, a desire for urban living is virtually snuffed out by the cloud of anxiety, fear, and hopelessness which hangs over many U.S. cities.

The Social Control of Teenagers

The adolescent years have become associated with acts of antisocial behavior that range from minor rule-breaking to seasoned criminality; most common, perhaps, are acts of vandalism against public and private property. While only a small percentage of youth is typically involved in such delinquency, it has become a widespread and growing concern in both Sweden and the U.S., as well as in every other advanced society. It is important to look not only at the attributes of the environment which promote positive behavior among teenagers, therefore, but also at those which retard delinquent acts. Delinquent acts are much less frequent and severe in Vällingby than in Levittown, even taking into consideration the difference in size of juvenile populations. Environmental dissimilarities may help to account for part of the variation.

There is reason to believe that much antisocial behavior by juveniles is peer-motivated, stemming from pressures within the peer group for challenge, excitement, or bravery. Because of this, the process of hanging out should be looked at closely in environmental studies; it is apparently within hangout groups that most antisocial acts are generated. Most youth authorities would probably agree on the great importance of an adult presence in the lives and activities of young people. As a factor which retards delinquency, this presence may be especially important in the public hangouts where youth congregate.

Most Vällingby hangout places, especially the centrums and the subway stops, are locales where adults pass by and even intermingle at every hour of the day and evening. Even the hangouts apart from the main centers of activity are not far from the continual surveillance of adult pedestrians. From the point of view of many Vällingby adults, the daily visual presence of groups of unkempt teenagers is an unpleasant experience; some even express sharp animosity and fear. From a social-control perspective, however, it may be a not wholly undesirable situation; because teenagers know they are "being watched," antisocial activities are probably inhibited. Further, the teenagers know that informal surveillance can lead quickly to formal action by the authorities. (This process is often stalled, according to some Swedish experts, by the reluctance of many urban Swedes to intervene.)

By contrast, the youth of Levittown have a feeling that the streets and public spaces are theirs, and theirs alone. It is their "turf" by virtue of the fact that they and no one else are using it, though the police frequently try to disrupt this feeling by keeping groups of youth "moving along." Most of the hangout spots in Levittown, while not geographically isolated, are functionally isolated from the informal observation of adults. Those members of the community who are in a position to observe, do so from passing cars or nearby homes, each of which has barriers that retard the progression from observation to informal social control such as direct intervention or phoning the police. An additional barrier is the sharp distinction in Levittown between public and private property. The Levittowner looks out for his own private property; he is much less concerned about what happens on public property.

Just as important for social control as the surveillance of hangout areas is the continuous presence of adult pedestrians in the environments where acts of vandalism take place. Vällingby has fewer spaces which, because of geographic or functional isolation from adults, are natural targets for the malicious acts of youth. In Levittown, on the other hand, the public facilities that are frequent targets of malicious acts, such as schools, are more isolated: at night, for example, schools are a no-man's-land, completely dead spaces where surveillance is minimal, though some now are forced to employ a night watchman.

The great geographic mobility of the Vällingby teenager, due to public transportation, has been discussed as a community advantage, but some Swedes regard it as a two-edged sword. Isn't open access to a large downtown area an invitation to trouble, compared with the situation in Levittown in which the younger teenagers are more restricted to their local community? There is no doubt that suburban teenagers "on the loose" in downtown Stockholm have become a problem in recent years. Bunches of youth, unsupervised by any adult, are regular nighttime inhabitants of downtown subway stations, where they are sometimes noisy, rowdy, and occasionally drunk. From a social-control point of view, however, this situation may be preferable to that of Levittown, where the older teenagers are out for the evening in cars. The motorized Levittown youth has even greater freedom of movement; he has much more privacy in the automobile than the Swede has in the subway, creating a greater potential for peer-enforced rule-breaking; and his activities take place in greater isolation from adults, often in peer-dominated automobile hangouts in remote places. Moreover, the Vällingby teenager is relatively safe from the serious injuries and high mortality rates associated with the automobile which have become familiar characteristics of teenage life in North America.

Just as important for social control as an adult presence in the lives and activities of teenagers is the willingness of those adults present to intervene. There is evidence to indicate that environments differ significantly in this respect.[21] It is partly a matter of scale; one is less likely to intervene with strangers than with people who are known or familiar. But environmental settings of the same scale can differ, in terms of the willingness of their residents to intervene, depending on how socially cohesive or integrated these residents are with one another. Social cohesion is affected by such community characteristics as demographic heterogeneity, rate of residential mobility, and the presence of the physical symbols of a distinct community such as strong focal points and boundaries that all residents recognize.

Many Swedes believe that urban residents in Sweden show great reluctance to intervene in the kind of situations which have been discussed, especially when compared to small-town residents, whose social climate is more intimate and involved. While the data are lacking which would permit a comparative assessment of the willingness to intervene in Vällingby and Levittown, my impression is that it is about equal in the two communities. Vällingby has more physical symbols of community and lower residential mobility, but the residential areas are denser—a higher percentage of the people encountered each day are strangers. Fewer strangers are encountered in Levittown, but the community has little social, cultural, or political cohesion.

An additional element in every adequate social-control structure is agreement on the norms that are to be enforced. In communities that lack cohesion there may be disagreement over important norms, or inadequate communication about the norms that do exist, creating problems in the socialization and social control of young people.[22] Community-wide norms concerning the discipline of children, such as the time they must come in at night, the places they are allowed to go in the community, the material possessions they may have and at what ages, may be weak or unenforced; to the degree that they are, the power to set norms tends to fall into the hands of the teenagers ("everybody else is doing it"). The concerned parent comes to feel very alone, in the face of a highly organized community of adolescents, and there develops a relative powerlessness of adults to control their own children that can become a contributing factor to juvenile delinquency. Communities in which this kind of adult powerlessness seems especially strong are those in which there is high demographic heterogeneity in class and ethnicity, so that many different norms of childrearing, discipline, and proper teen conduct prevail; and those in which there is little communication among residents, for example, where there is no newspaper, no political structure, or no common school board.

Both Vällingby and Levittown have some of the characteristics which lead to adult powerlessness; Vällingby with its lack of communication channels and Levittown with its ethnic and class diversity. Yet the problem seemed more pronounced in Levittown. In Vällingby, lack of a strong local community is counterbalanced by the extreme cultural homogeneity of the residents; all Swedes, they share a common set of norms about matters relating to youth. The ethnic and class diversity in Levittown, together with the lack of communication channels, has generated an adult powerlessness in dealing with youth that many parents feel and sense is growing. In its first few years, Levittown had a stronger sense of community because of its newness; also class heterogeneity was less and adolescents were fewer. That Levittown is divided into four political jurisdictions and three school districts, and now contains many unassimilated residents such as those in the garden apartments, exacerbates the situation.

Juvenile delinquency and disruptive and inappropriate behavior by teenagers are not *caused* by the environment. Most social science theories locate the causes of delinquency in the emotional setting of the family and the social structure of the society. But the qualities of the environment likely make a contribution to the process of delinquent activity. Communities and environments *do* differ in their rates of delinquency, and the differences probably can not be attributed solely to the character of the families who live there or to the larger social systems which shape their lives.[23]

Selected Aspects of Environment and Behavior

In the foregoing discussion of adults, children, and teenagers in the residential environment, many important environment-behavior relationships have been explored. It seems useful, however, to summarize the findings and insights of this inquiry in regard to several environment-behavior topics which loom large in the minds of planners, architects, and other environmental designers, and which figure prominently as research foci in the environmental social sciences.

Social Relationships among Adults

Architects and planners frequently put forth the proposition that the design of the environment has important consequences for the social relationships of its residents. It is said that environmental design can affect the amount of contact people have with others, the development of friendships and feelings of friendliness, and the establishment of cooperative groupings and sense of community.[24] Such propositions are based on the well-founded assumption that the character of the environment determines to some degree what type of people will live there, whether rich or poor, young or old, married with children or single, and the accessibility that they will have to one another.[25] Some architects feel that these social effects are the most important set of human consequences that an environment may have. Did these social consequences show up in the present comparison between environments with very different spatial distribution of people, facilities, and paths of contact?

Not all social interaction consists of social relationships; such relationships involve interaction between two or more persons in which a relatively stable set of social expectations develop.[26] Further, social relationships vary greatly in the significance they have for those involved; some are essential for a sense of personal well-being; others are trivial and without much meaning. In a denser environment, there is naturally interaction with more people each day than in a less dense situation; one may even have more social relationships. The important question is, however, what effect does the environment have on those social relationships that are of greatest human significance?

In a major contribution to our knowledge in this area, Harvard sociologist Robert S. Weiss recently has identified four social functions or needs which social relationships serve; he suggests that the lack of social relationships in any of these four functional areas leads to personal and social difficulty of various kinds.[27] The functions, which provide a framework for the following discussion, are intimacy, social integration, reassurance of worth, and assistance and help.

Intimacy. Intimate social relationships (or social relations which serve the function of intimacy) are those in which one can freely express feelings without self-consciousness; they depend on trust, feelings of emotional solidarity, and ready access; they often take a long time to become established. A lack of intimate relationships leads to feelings of emotional isolation and loneliness.

The sources of intimate relationships are typically a marriage partner; a close relative such as a brother, sister, parent or child; or a very close friend. A person generally has only one or two intimate relationships, but those are extremely important to him. Perhaps the most satisfactory and lifelong intimate is the spouse, though in some marriages the relationship is not an intimate one (the classic example is the working-class woman who is more intimate with her own mother than with her husband). Unmarried adults may substitute a roommate, lover, or other close friend, or may remain emotionally tied to their parents.

The presence or quality of intimate relationships is not strongly associated with characteristics of a residential environment. These relationships depend on long contact over time, together with the personal ability to be emotionally close to someone. Several environmental influences are worth mentioning, however. The environment provides a pool of *potential* intimates. For this reason, the divorced or separated, or the single adult in search of a mate, is better off in the Vällingby environment than in Levittown; more persons in Vällingby are the type from which intimate friends can be drawn. The environment can also affect existing intimate relationships through contributing to the breakup of families or the splitting up of persons joined by intimate bonds. A diversity of housing types, for example, is desirable to avoid splitting relatives who desire physical proximity but have different needs for housing; and to permit young intimates to set up their own households.

The loneliness that stems from a deficiency in intimate relationships is probably more widespread in Vällingby than in Levittown, because there is a much higher percentage of persons in Vällingby outside of the family stages of the life cycle, especially the single elderly and single young adults, persons often without intimate partners. In the Levittown environment, however, such persons would probably be even worse-off, because the pool of potential intimates is less.

It has been noted that neighboring is a more common form of interaction in Levittown. This might be expected to improve Levittown's comparative position vis-à-vis intimate relationships, but the neighboring relationship appears seldom to be a truly intimate one. The neighboring relationship is important for several of the other functions, however, to be discussed below.

Social Integration. Each individual has a need to belong—to participate with others in common endeavors, to share ideas, information, and experiences, to feel that others agree with his objectives and goals. The need to belong can find expression in specific social relationships—friendships and companionships with other like-minded persons—and in more general or diffuse ties to groups, community, and society.

While intimacy relationships concern the sharing of the deepest and most personal emotions, the social integration relationships involve one's ties to the larger social world—the feeling that one is "plugged in" to an ongoing social order. When there is an absence of this kind of relationship, feelings of social isolation, boredom, and disinterest are generated. For men and working women, work associates provide the major source of social integration relationships. Housewives turn more frequently to friends from school, community organizations, and church, or to neighbors, who may in one sense be "work associates."

Social integration is especially problematic for the housewife in many modern settings. The work of the housewife-mother in earlier historical periods was conducted in the presence of many other adults with an atmosphere of cooperation and companionship. Today, she often finds herself isolated from community concerns and from others with whom she can share ideas and interests. For the stay-at-home housewife the neighboring role has a special significance, as the neighbor is often the only person to whom she has regular access during the day.

Levittown has a comparative advantage over Vällingby in this regard; a housewife-mother is more likely to be able to engage in neighboring relationships and is more likely to have other housewife-mothers living next door with whom she can share experiences. In Vällingby, on the other hand, the need for this type of social integration is less because most women work. Moreover, if a woman does stay home, it is easier for her to get "beyond" the neighboring role. The availability of public transportation and child-care services provides the opportunity to widen the universe of potential daytime friends.

Reassurance of Worth. This function is served by those relationships which attest to the individual's competence in major roles: worker, housewife, student, community participant. The main sources for the relationship are associates and superiors in the various activity groups; a lack of such relationships leads to feelings of low self-esteem. Again, the modern housewife is most vulnerable to a deprivation in this area—she has the fewest ready-made associates. The neighbors may be of less value to her in this regard; they are too much "in the same boat," and also, being randomly selected, they may not provide support. Husbands and parents are very important sources of reassurance, but if these relationships break down or are absent, it is very important that she be able to find reassurance of some kind in the wider community.

It is probable that working women have greater reassurance of worth than housewives in modern societies, other things being equal. Owing to the higher percentage of working women in Vällingby, that community may have a comparative advantage over Levittown in respect to this relationship. Because so few nonworking housewives were interviewed in Vällingby, however, a comparative assessment of the reassurance of worth provided housewives in each environment is not possible.

Assistance and Help. Every household needs assistance and help in the forms of service, resources (including financial resources), and specialized information and knowledge. Lack of social relationships or other resources through which these needs may be met leads to feelings of anxiety, vulnerability, and overdependence. Higher-income households are able to get much assistance and help from commercial sources: service and tradespeople, banks, professionals, books, and so on. Lower-income families rely heavily on friends, neighbors, and especially relatives. Only relatives can commonly be relied on for more than limited assistance and help; this is one reason the very poor are imbedded in a close-knit network of kinship interaction and relationships.[28]

Working- and lower-middle-class families fall between these two extremes. They are often cut off from relatives but do not have the money of the upper-middle-class family to pay for commercial services. Neighbors become important, therefore, especially in single-family-house areas where needs for services are great.

Vällingby households can rely less on neighbors for aid and assistance. But their needs are also less because of apartment living, and more of their needs are met publicly through facilities and services located in the neighborhoods (such as day care, baby-sitting services, and public transportation). In chapter

6, the dependent Levittown woman was discussed—one of the least congruent types in Levittown. Her needs for assistance are great—home maintenance, child care, transportation, and even loans of money. Typically, without a husband and cut off from relatives, she survives through the cooperation of neighbors and friends in the close vicinity. While Levittown is a satisfactory environment for the self-sufficient household, it is a daily problem for her. The Vällingby environment would ease her life, both in cutting down her needs for aid and assistance and in providing alternative sources to the sometimes precarious and unreliable relationships with neighbors and friends.

Because the issues are complex, the value judgments difficult, and the data scarce, no attempt will be made to assess how Levittown and Vällingby compare overall as generators or reinforcers of these important social relationships. It might be useful, however, to summarize the major ways in which social relationships are affected by characteristics of the residential environment:

1. By reducing the need for some relationships. An example is Vällingby's reduction of the need to secure aid and assistance from friends and relatives through the provision of neighborhood-based services.

2. By providing a larger body of persons who are potential candidates for a social relationship. This potential is affected by the demographic structure of the community. Are there enough possible marriage partners and persons of similar age, interest, and outlook on life? (It is the search for this potentiality which has generated more homogeneous communities in the U.S.—for the elderly, the young singles, young families, and so on.)

3. By providing awareness of and access to persons who are likely candidates for a social relationship. From this perspective, it is usually desirable to place as neighbors persons who share the same values, a consideration which can be influenced by the clustering of dwelling units of a common type. Further, the design of buildings and site plans can affect awareness and accessibility by the provision of facilities and areas where people of like-mindedness may spontaneously meet.

4. By enabling social relationships to continue after they have become established. For example, communities dominated by a single housing type or age group often make almost mandatory a move from the community if one's need for housing space or age group changes. Such a move often entails the abandonment of friendships, which are sensitive to propinquity and frequent contact. The community that is more diversified in housing types enables a change in housing without a major change in residential location.

In regard to each of these ways, the consequences of the environment are greater for those whose lives are relatively restricted to the local area—

especially housewives—and least for those, such as middle-class professional people, whose highly mobile living patterns enable them to transcend the local area in which they have their major place of residence.

The Environment and Mental Health

The relationship between characteristics of the environment and emotional traits of residents is a complex one about which there is little solid knowledge.[29] Although this relationship was not a major focus of this inquiry, several insights into the relationship were gained which are of some interest. Most of the sample of residents of both communities stated that they were generally contented with life and pleased with their environment. But the men of Levittown appeared noticeably more edgy, irritable, tired, and annoyed with their lives. It seems reasonable to attribute these traits, in part, to the work and environmental pressures that have been discussed above.

The least contented women of Levittown were the nonworking mothers of younger children, especially those lower on the socioeconomic ladder. *Boredom* seems the most appropriate way to characterize the psychological state of some of these mothers. Their lives lacked stimulus, variety, non-child-associated activity, and feelings of contribution and accomplishment.[30] Their Vällingby counterparts, on the other hand, were much more likely to work outside the home, to have less home care, and to have superior day-care services for their children; they also had much smaller families.[31] Further, the Vällingby residential environment provides more stimulation, diversity, and accessibility.

While boredom among women may be less in Vällingby, *loneliness* appears to be greater. The Levittown women who have few other sources of friends can generally rely on the neighborhood to provide them with some suitable adults with whom they can share information, feelings, and confidences. Though loneliness is commonly referred to as a psychological trait among Swedes in general, the loneliness of Vällingby women may be heightened by their inability to depend on the neighbors for social interaction and social relationships.

The Social Functions of the Neighborhood

The planners of both Vällingby and Levittown subdivided their developments into distinct neighborhoods, each physically demarcated from the others, organized around facilities, and with its own name. In each nation the planners sought to establish social units through physical means, units with which residents could easily identify and in which patterns of community life could be established.[32] Levittown's planners, following the neighborhood planning ideology of the time which originated in Great Britain, designed their community with forty neighborhoods, averaging 1,500 to 2,000 persons in size, and focusing on an elementary school.

Although advocates of the neighborhood principle in planning and not unmindful of the need to promote social interaction in urban settings, Vällingby's planners favored neighborhoods of a much larger scale than Levittown's, in which people were housed more closely together so as to permit efficient public servicing at a high quality level. They divided Vällingby into six, pedestrian-oriented geographic units, each of which centers on a shopping-services complex and originally contained about 10,000 persons.

How successful were the planners in achieving new units of social structure through the physical design of neighborhoods? Does one neighborhood pattern have advantages over the other?

In neither suburb has social structure tended to follow neighborhood lines. Levittown neighborhoods have generated a few sparsely attended women's clubs in the upper-middle-class areas and parents' organizations connected with the elementary schools. Religious institutions, governmental units, most clubs and organizations, and trading areas of shopping centers are not related to the named neighborhoods of Levittown. Levittown adults without children in elementary schools seem to have no more tendency to socially interact with those in their own neighborhood than with persons in other neighborhoods, if near neighbors are excepted. Most residents, however, quickly identify their place of residence with the neighborhood name. As would be expected, those in higher-class districts more readily associate residence with neighborhood. The few objections to the neighborhood units concern the paucity of neighborhood services, especially shopping.

The functions and use of the neighborhood in Levittown are strongly affected by the dominance of the automobile. Throughout most of history the neighborhood has been defined by walking distance. Yet this dimension of the neighborhood applies only to about a half-block of houses in Levittown, for beyond a half-block adult Levittowners feel compelled to drive. Once in the car the neighborhood localization of facilities and services becomes much less significant; people are willing to drive a few extra minutes, if necessary, to permit the choice of a better shop, a less crowded recreation facility, or a more desired church or club.[33] Because most daily activity and work patterns disregard neighborhood boundaries, the growth of neighborhood-based social networks is made less likely, especially in the presence of ethnic heterogeneity and high rates of residential mobility.

Although it seems to have received no special consideration by the planners, the microneighborhood, or immediate vicinity of a person's home, has more social importance in Levittown. Personal knowledge of coresidents, ranging from name only to neighboring relationships, extends among houses side by side and facing one another across the streets for no more than about half a block, forming individual social networks of perhaps ten to twenty-five households. These networks are relatively weak, sometimes nonexistent, in upper-middle-class areas: several households were encountered that neither had contact with neighbors nor knew neighbors' names after a residence of two years. But in the working-class districts these microneighborhood social networks are often in evidence.

In the low-density U.S. suburb, elementary-school-sized neighborhoods like those designed for Levittown appear destined for social functionlessness. But social functionlessness does not mean that the neighborhood idea necessarily should be abandoned in suburban planning. Neighborhoods of 1,500 to 2,500 persons arise naturally in the planning of elementary school districts and park systems. They also seem dictated by traffic planning considerations; the efficient planning of intermediate collector streets leads to neighborhoods of a size similar to that suggested by the optimum size of elementary schools. Neighborhoods which make sense in school, traffic, and recreational planning also provide residents with at least a minimum "sense of place"—a feeling of identity with a geographic unit.

There are some social drawbacks to the neighborhood design of Levittown, however. Basic to neighborhood planning of this kind is the separation of neighborhoods from one another by green belts or buffer strips. While this enhances the geographic identity of the neighborhoods and adds to the community's open space, it also spreads the development more widely over the landscape, so that people live still farther apart from one another. The resulting distances are a special problem for those who don't drive—teenagers, the elderly, the handicapped, and many women. Friends met in church, high school, or voluntary organizations within Levittown find it difficult to get to one another.[34] Because the intensification by buffer zones of the physical identity of the neighborhoods offers few social advantages and these buffer zones are seldom used for leisure-time purposes, a more socially desirable physical design might be to aggregate the open space into large areas on a community's periphery, where it could be better enjoyed for recreation while leaving the residents with easier access to one another.

A good case can be made for site plans in low-density suburbs which include measures to stimulate the formation of social networks at the microneighborhood level. Although not every suburbanite wants or needs additional contacts with neighbors, such contacts are often desired by, and necessary to, housewives and others whose dependence on the locality grouping is very high. At the neighborhood scale of from five or ten to perhaps fifty or sixty households, the use of cul-de-sac and short loop streets, the provision of central meeting places, recreational facilities and other focal points, and the presence of firm geographic boundaries would probably promote social contacts, especially if the housing clusters contained residents who were homogeneous in class, age, and life-style.[35]

Conclusions about the social functions of neighborhoods in Vällingby are similar to those drawn for Levittown. As service areas, the larger neighborhood districts of Vällingby have worked well, but as the physical bases of social structure they have been no more successful than the neighborhoods of Levittown. Residents identify with the Vällingby districts to the extent of naming them when asked where they live, but the districts fail to encapsulate many of the activities of their lives; they work, seek entertainment, and often have their friends elsewhere.[36] The functions of the districts are limited to shopping, local recreation, and some clubs and organizations. Because the districts have limited functions does not mean, as in the case of Levittown, that the neighborhood design is a poor one, but it adds evidence to the proposition that the creation of "community" can not be accomplished by physical design alone.

The Vällingby counterpart of the Levittown half-block, the more socially meaningful microneighborhood unit, is the apartment building stairwell, consisting of six households in the typical garden apartment. This is the sociospatial unit within which most Vällingby dwellers know the names of their coresidents, though in a surprising number of cases the names are not known and there is very limited social interaction.

In Vällingby, as in Levittown, the level on which to concentrate if some stimulus to social interaction is desired is not the neighborhood or district but the building or building cluster. Many of the interviewed Vällingby residents expressed a wish and even a need for more neighbor contact. Some longed for the equivalent of a block party; others seemed to require something like an introduction service. The promotion, in each building, of greater homogeneity by class and stage of the life cycle would probably do more than any other measure in reducing Vällingby's social contact problem, but some success might also come from providing more facilities and spaces where spontaneous contact among residents could take place and by having garden apartment buildings of smaller size arranged not in the common rows but in building clusters—the garden apartment equivalent of the loop streets and cul-de-sacs of single-family-house areas.

9

Implications for Urban Housing and Development Policy in Sweden and the United States

Stockholm Suburban Development after Vällingby

In the almost twenty years since the completion of Vällingby, Stockholm and the other cities and towns of Sweden have undertaken a program of residential construction which in output per capita is unrivaled by any other nation in the world.[1] The serious shortage of urban housing, which lasted into the 1970s, prompted the Swedish national government to give high priority to the housing sector. While about 50,000 new housing units were completed each year in Sweden in the early 1950s, by the mid-1960s this figure had jumped to over 100,000, mostly due to national financial assistance.[2] The 1965 national parliament had put forth a policy of building one million new dwellings in the following ten-year period, a policy which had the backing of all shades of the political spectrum and which, by 1974, had been achieved.

Government policy, as stated by the 1967 parliament, was that "the whole population should be provided with sound, spacious, well planned and appropriately equipped dwellings of good quality at a reasonable cost."[3] This policy dictated the continued production of mostly multifamily units in Sweden's urban areas and even in the smaller towns. By 1970, single-family houses made up only about 30 percent of Swedish new housing construction, a figure not very different from that in the 1950s; in Stockholm and the other large cities the percentage was only half that amount.[4] Thus the basic planning decisions which led to the development of Vällingby were continued: high-density suburban housing typically tied to the cities by high-quality public transportation systems. The later suburbs of Stockholm also followed many of the design concepts pioneered by Vällingby: the separation of pedestrian from vehicular traffic; the grouping together of housing units into clusters of about 10,000 persons, each served by a major commercial and cultural centrum; the provision, at a high level of quality, of local services such as play parks and day-care centers; and the arrangement of housing units so that most residents could live within five hundred meters of the centrum and subway stop, with the single-family houses located on the periphery.

But most of the Stockholm suburbs which followed Vällingby differ significantly from it in density, building type, architectural design, and environmental appearance—and also, often, in demographic structure. These differences have become the focus in Sweden, over the past ten years, of a barrage of criticism from persons in all walks of life; indeed, it sometimes seems difficult in Sweden today to find persons who feel positive toward the recent suburbs, although a number of studies and investigations have shown that the majority of residents are by no means unhappy or even negative about their new suburban milieu.[5]

The critics refer to the newer suburbs with such phrases as "inhuman environments," "brutal destroyers of the landscape," "social disaster areas," "architectural monstrosities," and "concrete jungles."[6] When it was first built, some of the same phrases were applied to Vällingby; but they are not heard today. Is it just a matter, then, of the relative newness of the recent suburbs? Will the critics be mollified when these suburbs settle in and mature? Undoubtedly this will to some extent be the case; much of the criticism has focused on the lack of services, the sparsity of vegetation, and the rawness of the milieu, factors which will improve with time. One of the earliest targets of criticism, Skärholmen (completed in 1968), already in the past few years seems to have grown significantly in popularity as a place to live.[7]

Yet more deeply rooted differences between the early suburbs—Vällingby and Farsta—and the later ones are hard to deny. From the perspective of the present, the early suburbs seem more closely tied to their counterparts of the thirties and forties than to the suburbs which followed them. The differences which exist make the later environments, in my opinion, considerably less desirable than their predecessors as places to live. While I disagree with much of the criticism which they have generated, I agree with the critics, and with many in Sweden today, that in the effort to produce an abundance of dwelling units in a brief period of time, mistakes were made; housing environments were developed which have serious flaws, and Sweden will have to live with these flaws for many years to come.

To be sure, the demographic structure of the later suburbs differs from that of Vällingby, and some of the criticism has been indirectly focused on the residents rather than the environment. Especially in the most recent suburbs, like Tensta and Rinkeby, Northern Botkyrka, and in Haninge municipality, the residents have tended to be very young, often unmarried, with a high percentage of working mothers—social statuses which are associated with lower incomes.[8] The number of households in the newer suburbs with economic problems is apparently quite high, and persons with very low incomes are prone to the social problems with which the suburbs have become identified in the public mind—troubled youth, alcoholism, divorce, and chronic financial difficulties. Further, the newer suburbs are quite homogeneous in class and stage of the life cycle. While the earlier developments contained at the outset a relatively large mix of age and income groups, the newer suburbs house mainly young, working- and lower-middle-class households, a fact which may exaggerate the problems which these households face.[9] Finally, the recent suburbs have become the domicile of most of the foreign workers who have come into the Stockholm area in the 1960s and early 1970s. In some areas of the recent Stockholm suburbs the percentage of residents of non-Swedish birth is as high as 20 or 30, a significant portion of whom are from southern Europe.[10] Though the immigrants are for the most part residentially intermixed and relatively well integrated into Swedish society, problems of prejudice, discrimination, and intergroup conflict are by no means unknown; indeed they have come to be one of the major social concerns in Swedish life in the past decade, although the problems appear to be much less serious than in other European nations.

But the negative image of the newer suburbs does not stem solely from the social characteristics of the residents. The suburbs which followed Vällingby increased in density almost with each successive year, an increase which was dictated by the pressures for housing, the need to keep costs low, the demands of labor unions for full employment, and the interests of commercial and transportation officials in assuring a large and available body of clients for their services. Associated with the rise in density was a change in building type; the three-story walk-up garden apartments, characteristic of Vällingby, were for the most part replaced by six- to eight-story slab buildings with elevators, often a block or more in length. Though efficient in access, and with light and airy dwelling units, this building type has a heavy and stolid appearance—a massive concrete structure whose facade can be softened only with great difficulty and expense.

Sweden has not been willing to incur this expense, and the exterior appearance of these buildings is the subject of well-deserved reproach. In the very recent suburbs an abundance of color has been used to soften the lines and brighten the ambience, but in my opinion this solution has not been a success. The colors are often of poor quality and frequently are intermixed in a way which is almost garish. It is curious that the Swedes, whose use of color in interior design is typically skillful and highly imaginative, should have fallen so flat in the use of exterior colors. Perhaps there was too direct a transmission to the exterior of interior design practices, without realizing the effects of the difference in scale. A touch of orange within the dwelling unit can be pleasing; an entire complex of orange buildings is another matter.

Two additional elements have helped to give the recent suburbs a raw, sterile, uninviting feel and appearance. The introduction of industrial building methods has caused most of the buildings to be constructed in parallel rows. Cranes on long tracks function more efficiently if they can operate on each side of the track, usually at a fixed distance. Thus the staggering of buildings, the surprising angles, and the blending with the natural features of the landscape which one finds in Vällingby are often gone. Instead, one is confronted with long concrete "streets" from which there is no variation, no visual escape.

The feeling of being in a sea of concrete is stimulated further by the way in which many of the suburbs have handled the parking problem. Parking always poses a threat to planners and architects; they want to get vehicles out of the way, yet the cars must be reasonably near the dwelling units. The problem has escalated over the years as the standard of parking spaces has increased from about one per dwelling unit toward two, to allow for second cars and visitors. In Vällingby, which is considered to be underserviced with parking facilities, the lots are at grade but often concealed behind vegetation and often apart from the main "working areas" of the environment. In the later suburbs, the need for most parking spaces has forced the use of multideck parking garages. When put above ground, the result is a massive concrete structure, sometimes as long as a football field; there are many such structures in a single development. When put below grade, the lack of much vegetation on the roof yields a large, dead space which is seldom useful for any kind of social activity.[11] It seems only marginally preferable to the aboveground deck.

The parking situation illustrates a significant feature of the later suburbs: a higher level of facilities and services has been provided to the resident, both inside the dwelling unit and out, but the external environment has been made less desirable than in the earlier suburbs in the eyes of most residents. Thus a move to the newer suburbs involves a trade-off: a larger dwelling unit, with more services and facilities, but in a less desirable location and environment.

Although the combined pressures of labor, industry, housing finance, technology, and housing demand typically are cited as reasons which account for the character of the new suburbs, there has also been some ideological support for these suburbs in architectural and design circles. As explained by Igor Dergalin, one of the principal architects of Järvafältet, a suburb northwest of Stockholm still being developed,[12]

> the layout of these housing blocks does in fact demonstrate a very much more compact and urban type of community than hitherto. The somewhat Utopian proliferation of... flats standing in wide arcadian parklands, which was such a prominent feature of earlier suburban developments, has now disappeared from the plans... the sense of a physical community needs to be actively fostered, especially during the long winter. The compactness of urban-type communities is a strong force to this end. ... We planners aimed at a "concentration of visual order"... generally, the detailing of the whole environment is given the same close attention... as is applied to building design itself. The aim is to insure that within the more concentrated development that has been achieved, the maximum use is made of every square foot of open space throughout the year (for instance in snow) according to use at the time and its potential for recreation.

Thus the new suburbs, in addition to being an economic and technological advance, represent an important architectural and design achievement in the minds of some: the minutely planned, fully built-environment; new pieces of city in the suburbs.

While the completely planned and built-environment may have a natural attraction to architects, however, its appeal to residents is considerably less. Few suburbanites the world over seem to prefer urban and urbane living; they are struggling to get back to the country and only accept the suburb as a halfway measure. The residents of Vällingby value their environment highly because they feel they are living in a parklike setting, close to nature, precisely the qualities which have been left out of the later suburbs. Moreover, the new environments lack many of the features of the city which urban denizens find attractive: the diversity and environmental surprise, the mixture of land uses, the orderly disorder, the greater anonymity and privacy.

In terms of some environmental characteristics, such as visual and aural contacts among residents in and around their dwelling units, the new suburban environments stand in a class by themselves, unlike cities, small towns, and most other suburbs. In the city, most of life takes place either in the intimacy of the apartment, protected for the most part from unwanted visual intrusion and surrounded by the din of background noise, which provides aural privacy, or on the street, where there is privacy through anonymity.[13] In the low-density suburb, privacy is maintained by the distances between the buildings and by the encompassing vegetation which softens the view and the sounds. In the moderate-density suburb, like garden-apartment areas of Vällingby, the buildings are low enough to be below the tree line and are spaced irregularly and far enough apart so that often little aural or visual contact is possible between buildings.

In the newer suburbs, however, built in parallel rows of six-, eight- and even ten-story buildings, with relatively large and usable balconies, the sounds of activities on the ground and in the apartments reverberate back and forth between the buildings as in an echo chamber. Because the height of the buildings is well above the line of even mature trees, the eventual maturity of vegetation will do little to soften the sound; and with the sound presence is a continual visual presence. Yet the developments are typically not large enough to provide the high anonymity of urban life. In these respects the new suburbs are similar to the tenement houses in outlying areas of East Coast cities in the U.S., where people have a continual sense of being crowded and of having insufficient aural and visual privacy.

It is sometimes argued that such sights and sounds are functional for the establishment of "community"; that they will help to bring people together, to make them feel less alone. But this is not the kind of contact people seem to want and need, and there is no evidence that social interaction among residents in the later suburbs is greater than in Vällingby; probably it is less. Paradoxically, social interaction tends to be greater in lower-density areas, where there is a greater assurance of privacy.[14]

For all of the above reasons, therefore, I feel that there is a sharp discontinuity between the suburban environment of Vällingby and the higher-density Stockholm suburbs of recent vintage. Vällingby is an apartment environment which, because of its density, building height, and landscape features is still within a human scale, a scale at which people feel a sense of security, privacy, ease and comfort, and closeness to the natural world. It resembles a small town in these respects, and also in its pedestrian orientation, proximity of services, life-cycle heterogeneity, and low population turnover. The newer suburbs are off the range of this scale; they have a crowded, artificial feel which I believe is intrinsically less desired by most persons. Because of their spacious and well-equipped dwelling units, and the outstanding provision of residential services, it is unlikely that most of these areas will become slums, but it seems equally unlikely that they will ever achieve the degree of resident and public acceptance that has come to Vällingby; many will remain environmental problem-areas for years to come.

While criticism has exaggerated the defects of the new suburbs, then, much of it is not without foundation. Indeed, the suburbs today have few strong supporters among Swedish professionals and officialdom; most, including those responsible for planning and development, are proud that Sweden has solved its urban housing crisis but are somewhat embarrassed about the environmental result.

It is to the relief of many in Sweden, therefore, that the postwar period of urban development has now come to an end. What is probably the last of the large high-density suburbs of Stockholm—Northern Järvafältet—is currently being completed to the northwest of the city.[15] Located on a new link of the city's subway system, it will provide housing for about 30,000 people. The suburb was planned in the late 1960s, and construction began about 1972; there are no other large, high-density suburbs on the planners' drawing boards.

Within the last several years the construction of Northern Järvafältet has been considerably slowed down. Indeed, if the development of this area had come three or four years later it might never have been built, because in the early 1970s the supply of new housing finally caught up with the demand; for the first time in decades the waiting lines for housing became depleted. Sweden's postwar housing program, from a quantitative point of view, was a great success. Possibly it was too successful, for vacancy rates in the newer suburbs increased to alarming levels; Stockholm and the other large cities suddenly found themselves in the position of having overbuilt. Although by 1975 the rise in the vacancy rates had begun to level off, during 1974 some suburban developments around Stockholm and Gothenburg had 20 to 30 percent vacant apartments, a serious financial loss for the municipalities, which typically are the landlords, and for the government agencies that are their financial backers.[16]

The oversupply of apartment units in Sweden's urban areas resulted in part from the economic downturn of the early 1970s, which sent many foreign workers home and cut into the rent-paying ability of the average Swede. But a drop in demand also resulted from growing consumer resistance to apartment living, together with the increasing importance in the housing market of an alternative: the single-family house. In 1970, 34,617 single-family dwellings were built, 32 percent of the Swedish housing starts that year. (Most new single-family houses in Sweden are attached, rather than detached as in the U.S.) The number and percentage of single-family homes being built climbed steadily in the early 1970s; by 1974, 46,563 single-family units were constructed, representing 55 percent of the total Swedish housing production.[17]

Public-opinion polls made over the years have shown that Swedes prefer single-family houses at almost as high a rate as do citizens of other modern nations. Consumer resentment toward the newer apartment suburbs; a strong promotional campaign by banks and savings institutions interested in growth in savings accounts and mortgage lending; and some long-standing tax and

other economic advantages in home ownership similar to those in the U.S., all
spurred demand for the suburban single-family house, which, by 1975, had
become the main focus of the housing industry. Many of the publicly subsidized cooperative and municipal housing corporations have shifted over to
single-family house production. In the far suburbs of Stockholm and other
major cities, beyond the high-density suburbs and the major rapid transit
systems, large tracts of land currently are undergoing low-density, suburban
development.

The rapid increase in single-home demand and production was not planned
by central government housing officials, and it caught many of them by
surprise. This new trend in Sweden, however, appears similar to that which
has long been in evidence in other highly industrialized societies. With rising
incomes, many middle-class families went to live in larger, more spacious
units that they own and can control; and an automobile, or perhaps two,
makes it possible for them to live far from jobs and residential services.

Unfortunately, many of the new low-density developments have the mass-
produced, sterile, architecturally undistinguished look of their higher-density
predecessors. And a growing number share the negative social traits of many
suburbs in North America: isolation from community life; lack of services and
facilities, including jobs and transportation; residential homogeneity of young
families in the early childrearing years; and a clustering of families living at
the economic margin, barely able to make ends meet. These problems, several
of which are new to Sweden, have in the past year overtaken the difficulties of
apartment suburbs as topics of newspaper and magazine interest and debate.[18]

Future Urban Growth in Sweden: A Time of Decision

With the rapid urban growth and housing shortages of the postwar period
behind them, a legacy of high-density suburban residential environments in
which few take much pride, and a demand for single-family houses which
appears to be of landslide proportions, Swedish planners are at another moment of decision comparable to that at the end of World War II. Has the time
come for urban growth in Sweden to make a break with the past and to follow
the route of other affluent Western nations toward the single-family-house
tract development, geared to the automobile and detached from the city?

The Social Democratic government in Sweden maintained officially that the
choice of housing type was a matter to be decided at the local level. But their
policies, particularly in housing finance, were instrumental in fostering
higher-density urban development, and government policies in the next few
years will probably have a marked effect on the shape which Sweden's future

urban areas assume. Though most high party officials themselves apparently resided in single-family homes,[19] the Social Democratic party was known to be concerned about the recent housing trend and to be interested in finding ways to modify it. In a major new housing policy of 1974 the government had already sought to achieve economic equality between renters and home-owners, and thus reduce one of the advantages of a single-family house, by modifying the tax structure in ways which made home ownership eco-nomically less desirable, and by giving subsidies that reduced the level of rents.[20]

The party's concern about single-family housing emanates from two ideological sources. First is the belief that the development of single-family-house areas, because they tend to become stratified by class and stage of the life cycle, retards the achievement of a more egalitarian society. Age and income groups become more geographically separated, which in the long run is potentially devisive for the society as a whole, and the goal of greater equality of housing accommodation is made more difficult to achieve. The experience of the United States seems to support this belief.

Second is a belief, held especially by more doctrinaire socialists, that rental multifamily housing generates feelings of community, brotherhood, and socialist solidarity, whereas privately owned single-family housing breeds individualism and capitalist inclinations. This ideological stand rests on shaky empirical foundations; research into patterns of social interaction in different environments lends little support, and the example of the British new towns, where socialism and ground-level housing seem complementary, is instruc-tive.[21]

Some housing officials feel that the demand for single-family housing will begin to dwindle eventually, regardless of government policies, as home buyers realize that home ownership is costly, requires a great deal of extra effort, and is inconvenient due to commuting distances, lack of nearby part-time jobs (especially for women), and distance from neighborhood services such as shops, schools, and day-care centers. These officials predict high vacancy rates in the outlying single-family-home areas within the next three or four years and even a return by many to closer-in apartment living. The experiences of other countries cast doubt on such predictions; in the U.S., for example, even the dweller in the most underprivileged suburb seemingly will balk at giving up his home for an apartment as long as he is able to meet the housing cost, and most efforts to get residents to return to city apartment living have been notable failures.

Other factors in Swedish society, however, will probably diminish the demand for the single-family house. It has been estimated that by 1980 almost two-thirds of Swedish households will consist of just one or two persons;[22] the figure for the Stockholm region now stands at nearly this level. This means that the market for larger dwelling units in Sweden is not as large as it is in other modern societies. Moreover, the pattern of two-dwelling ownership in Sweden, which is probably more pronounced than anywhere else in the world, indicates that many Swedes may continue to be satisfied with winter apartment living in return for summer ground-level living, if the economics of the situation continue to dictate that kind of a trade-off. Home building in Sweden is expensive; the average new single-family house being built in the Stockholm area in 1975 cost over $60,000 (versus about $40,000 in the U.S.).[23]

The issue of housing type in Sweden, like everywhere else, may be settled mainly by economic realities: how many Swedes will be able to afford a single-family house? What other consumer items will they be willing to give up in order to do so? In the present housing market, not a very large percentage of Swedes have the income necessary to buy a home of their own. The question may soon arise, however, of whether or not to give government subsidies to single-family houses to bring their cost down to a level at which the average urban worker can afford one. This is the policy which, at least indirectly through the guaranteeing of mortgage loans, was followed by the U.S. government. The Social Democratic party steadfastly refused to entertain such a notion. However, with growing public pressure for single houses, and in view of the 1976 shift in government control to the more conservative political parties, the picture could change.

The case for the single-family house rests on strong foundations, starting with the fact that a large majority of Swedes desire to own one sometime during their lifetimes. This desire is based on the comfort and internal convenience of the house, the extra space that it provides, the ease of access to the out-of-doors with the possibility of a private yard and garden, the opportunity which inheres in a private house to mold the dwelling unit in any way one sees fit to suit individual tastes, and, not the least, the added social status which is implied in home ownership. The single, detached home is particularly congruent with the large family, the family with small children, and the family where the woman is a full-time housewife.

These advantages have become highly compelling in the majority of advanced, Western societies, and there are indications that they will rise more into public consciousness in Sweden over the next decade. With increasing affluence, the desire and need for additional private living space rises sharply. This is partly a function of the expansion of material possessions, which require added space for use, display, and storage. With increasing leisure time, the large private home grows in importance as a place of informal socializing and recreation and as an outlet for creative skills and hobby activities. Sweden already has the highest per capita income and the shortest work year among the modern nations, and there is no reason to believe that it will not advance still further in these respects, perhaps promoting changeover to single-family houses in the process.

Another major trend which propels the suburban, single-family house is the rise in automobile ownership and use. The low-density suburb depends on the automobile as modern nations depend on vast energy sources; there is an element of indispensability. As people become car owners, they become dependent on the ease, convenience, and freedom of the automobile for many of their daily activities. The residents of Levittown take recreational driving trips, for example, the way Vällingby dwellers take recreational walks. It is easier and almost as inexpensive for car owners to use their cars than it is for them to take public transportation or to walk; the alternative is to let the cars sit in the garages, where the largest cost of car ownership—depreciation—is incurred no matter what happens. Moreover, once inside the car, people are willing to drive an extra five or ten minutes to get a better buy or to get to a more desired locale. Thus services, especially commercial ones, become more widely distributed and adapted to the automobile, new highway systems are built, public transportation falls into disuse, and low-density residential development becomes, at the very least, a natural element in an emerging sociospatial system of land use and activity patterns. This course of events can be checked—by preventing the ownership of automobiles—but what democratic nation is able politically to do that?

Some Swedish experts suggest a partial way out of the trend to single-family houses. It is argued that if people want and need a house, it is only for a brief period in their lives—the early childrearing years. After that time, the single-family home dweller can be induced to go back to a multifamily dwelling. Thus the actual demand for houses may be far less than it now seems. The experiences of other nations call this line of thinking into question, however.

Many people are willing to leave the single-family house at retirement time, when their income drops, their taste and physical ability for automobile driving declines, and their energy for home maintenance dwindles. Although the information from Levittown indicates that older people will cling to their houses as long as it is physically and economically possible for them, this is largely because they have few good alternatives, and a move would probably shift them to an unknown community far from their friends. But the shift of a significant number of persons out of their private homes in the years before retirement has not happened in any place of which I am aware, and there are several important factors which militate against it. The middle-aged family is at the peak of its earning power; in fact that power is typically much higher at age fifty-five than it is at ages twenty-five or thirty-five. If the young family could afford the extra space, privacy, and convenience of a single-family house, the older family is in an even better position to do so. Further, youth and young adults prize continuity in the residential environments of their childhood, and parents will extend themselves to provide a home, and space, to which their children will enjoy returning. In addition, the parents prize continuity with their own friends and the memories of their early family years. Finally, it is psychologically difficult for a person suddenly to face a sharp decrease in his private space, unless there is a compelling reason for it. All his life has been spent, in a sense, struggling for more space, more freedom, and more personal opportunity. Once a person's life has become "spread out," it is not an emotionally easy task to draw it in, as millions of retired persons have discovered.

Thus the case for the single-family house is a strong one, and indeed the trend toward low-density urban development has an appearance of inevitability. In the current Swedish debate over housing types and urban development alternatives, however, the advantages of the single-family house have been magnified by pitting them against the disadvantages of the high-rise urban apartment environments of recent vintage. Often overlooked in the debate are the many social advantages of low-rise, high-density suburban developments like Vällingby—the residential environments with which Sweden began its postwar urban growth but which were soon overshadowed by their high-density counterparts.

The example of Vällingby indicates that urban dwellers can live comfortably and happily in apartments if they are provided with an abundance of urban services to offset the limited private space, if their residential environments are designed so that there is a feeling of being in a natural rather than a man-made or urban setting, and if they have easy accessibility to both city and countryside. In addition, four major social advantages of the low-rise, high-density suburban environment, in comparison with its lower-density alternative, were highlighted by this inquiry.

First, the low-rise, high-density residential environment offers many advantages to the woman who works, who has many activities outside the home, and who wishes to minimize housekeeping activities. The working women of Vällingby have a far more enviable situation than do those of Levittown because of the larger job market available, public transportation, day care and other services for families with children, and ease of home maintenance.

This advantage has a special significance in view of the high percentage of women in Sweden who work: in 1974, 57 percent of all Swedish women between the ages of sixteen and seventy-four held jobs outside the home; this figure includes 57 percent of Swedish women who have children under seven years of age.[24] The percentage of working women in urban areas is even higher, and these percentages are increasing rapidly year by year. The day may be fast approaching when almost all Swedish women will be working during most of their adult lives, a very marked change from just thirty years ago.

During her childrearing years, the working woman requires a great many services which are difficult to provide in low-density areas. It would be possible for the Swedish working woman to get by in outlying, low-density suburbs if jobs and services were radically decentralized, if the urban system were given over to the automobile, and if she had the income to own and maintain two cars, plus provide herself with other private services as needs arise. This is the situation of many higher-income American women. But these conditions are not likely to occur in Sweden. Business and industry are being discouraged from locating in the suburban areas of the larger cities, in favor of the smaller urban places, and there are real political limitations on the extent to which high-quality neighborhood services can be publicly subsidized in costly low-density arrangements which would favor mostly the well-to-do Swede.

The relative advantages of high-density environments for working women have been pointed out in studies of the situation of women in several of the recently built single-family-house suburbs of Stockholm. In one such study it was found that the percentage of working women in the area was among the lowest in all of Sweden, and the women expressed strong dissatisfaction with their condition.[25] It appears quite possible, as some Swedes have suggested, that the woman's movement in Sweden will lead the fight against single-family houses and work to promote higher-density housing arrangements.

A second advantage of the low-rise, high-density environment over the single-family-house area is in the situation of teenagers. One might speculate that the ideal environment from a teenage perspective is an active, medium-sized town where all aspects of life take place; a town whose scale and density afford ease of movement to both the pedestrian and the bicyclist and is surrounded by open countryside. Here, perhaps, youth would have the greatest sense of completeness, the highest chance of community participation, and the largest number of stimulating environments ranging the scale from urban to rural. Because they are loose-knit, transient, and lacking in self-sufficiency, few suburban environments can match this ideal. But among the suburban types, a low-rise, high-density environment like Vällingby seems to come considerably closer to being a satisfactory environment for teenagers than its low-density counterpart, because it offers an ease of movement, an abundance of youth services, and is near both city and countryside. In contrast, the low-density environment tends to be, as in the case of Levittown, bereft of community life, environmentally dull and listless, and lacking the transportation and other services which teenagers require.

While the youth of a nation have very little say on housing and planning policy and in the decisions which lead to the construction of residential environments, it appears from this inquiry that they are more affected by the characteristics of the environment than almost any other age group. The growing sense of anxiety and even despair about modern youth, especially over the aimlessness, boredom, and often antisocial behavior of youth from relatively privileged homes, lends special significance to the requirement of taking into greater consideration the needs and desires of youth in environmental design.

A third major social advantage of the low-rise, high-density environment is the residential heterogeneity which it promotes. Such environments offer the diversity of housing types, the variety of services, and the range of microenvironments that can bring together people of many walks of life to share a common residential area. It is within an urban network of such heterogeneous local community units that democracy and equality may find their deepest roots in modern societies.

The geographic segregation of people in terms of income, age, and lifestyle is a real and growing problem in societies where the low-density suburb is the main form of urban growth. An argument can be made for moderate residential segregation, in terms of social class, age, and life-style, at the microneighborhood or block levels, so that a maximum of friendly and mutually supportive social interaction is assured.[26] But there are growing indications that the extreme residential segregation by age and class fostered by low-density development in the United States has become a very divisive force in American life, retarding the achievement of a more equal and a more just society.[27]

The segregation of the aged has become an especially vigorous trend in the U.S., a major reason being that low-density suburban communities are not suitable for older people in many ways, such as transportation, housing accommodation, and neighborhood services. In Sweden, on the other hand, a strong public stand has been taken against residential segregation of the aged. The main principles set forth by the government to guide the municipalities are the following:[28]

1. Every individual should, as far as possible, be given the opportunity to live in a normal environment and under as normal conditions as possible.

2. The independence of the individual and his right of self-determination must be respected.

These principles are difficult to achieve in the low-density, automobile-oriented suburb.

A fourth social advantage of low-rise, high-density environments is in the impact which this developmental form has on the central areas of metropolitan regions. If a reasonable level of environmental quality is to be preserved in the inner areas of large cities, so that the option of an urban way of life remains open to those in each society who desire it, it is probably necessary for peripheral urban development to be constructed at a moderately high density. This density involves some suppression of the use of private automobiles and permits the preservation in a natural state of large tracts of centrally located land for urban residents to enjoy.

The association between the decay of central cities and low-density, automobile-oriented suburbs is a close and probably causal one. It is difficult, for example, to find many large metropolitan areas in the U.S. today which have inner-lying residential districts providing even modest levels of environmental amenities. In most metropolitan areas the central districts have been sapped by their peripheral development, which has used up most of the desirable open space, spawned a daily avalanche of automobile traffic, and attracted from the city jobs, resources, and the more affluent citizens.

In view of the substantial relative advantages of low-rise, high-density residential environments, it is difficult not to feel that a serious mistake was made by the larger Swedish cities when this environmental form was passed over, soon after the completion of Vällingby, in favor of projects of higher density and scale, these, in turn, later causing a backlash which spurred the current demand for single-family houses. The end of the housing shortage may have been speeded up by a few years but with negative consequences which will last for decades. This inquiry was initiated by the search for an alternative to the U.S. single-family-house suburb which might have significant lessons for the planning of future urban growth in the U.S. These lessons were found, and the contribution they could make toward a more rational urban growth policy in the United States are discussed below. But perhaps these are not just lessons to be given by Sweden to other countries; do they also have to be relearned, now, in Sweden itself?

Suburban Development in the United States After Levittown

In the almost one-quarter of a century since ground was first broken in the construction of Levittown, Pennsylvania, suburban development in the U.S. has grown rapidly, spurred by economic prosperity and a sharply increasing population. Over one million new housing units have been built each year, a rate unparalleled in the nation's history, and most of these have been single-family homes on large lots.[29] Lot and house sizes in the nation's new suburban tract developments have tended to increase since the early Levittowns, due in part to zoning regulations and stricter utility requirements. This increase in scale, together with the discontiguousness of many developments, gave rise to what is called "spread city" or, more pejoratively, urban sprawl.

While millions of families were provided with good housing, the spread pattern of development came under sharp attack from planners, designers, housing officials, and others as being unaesthetic, costly to service with public facilities, and wasteful of natural resources, especially land and, more recently, gasoline. Urban sprawl is not without its defenders,[30] but the sprawling or scattered form of urban development has become a rallying point around which America's rather powerless corps of planners and urban experts could achieve a consensus of negative opinion.[31]

In the last few years, the negative view of urban sprawl has been given greater currency by proclamations and findings of national and government commissions and research studies. One such study (sponsored by the Department of Housing and Urban Development, the Council on Environmental Quality, and the Environmental Protection Agency) determined that planned, higher-density suburban development can save communities up to 50 percent in land cost, construction cost, energy consumption, air and water pollution, and municipal operating costs. It concluded that, "for a fixed number of households, sprawl is the most expensive form of residential development in terms of economic costs, environmental cost, natural resource consumption, and many types of personal cost."[32]

For most of this quarter-century period, Americans appeared ready to pay this high price. It was a "seller's market," and almost anything with a roof would sell. Americans had rising incomes, there was a high rate of family formation and births, and home ownership had undeniable tax and other personal financial advantages. Further, the cities were deteriorating, and whites were fleeing from high taxes, poor schools, racial strife, and crime. For many, the farther and more insulated from the cities' problems their homes were, the better. They were more than willing to live with the disadvantages of urban sprawl, although most were not fully cognizant of these disadvantages: poor public services, isolation from community life, heavy reliance on the automobile as the only means of transportation, a long journey to work, and heavy home and yard maintenance demands. For much of this period, because of ingrained American preferences in housing, the idea of introducing higher-density, European-type suburban environments to the American scene was simply out of the question. The alternatives discussed by planners and public officials were a more rational ordering of single-family home development, with occasional vague references to new towns.

Yet as the size of new suburban homes and lots was ever increasing, so was the price. In the early 1970s, the Levitt Organization was marketing new single-family homes to sell at close to $40,000; by 1975, the price had jumped to $50,000.[33] By shifting to attached row houses (called town houses in most parts of the U.S.) about $10,000 could be cut from this price, but it was still far beyond the means of the average American. Gradually over these years, the price of new housing had escalated at a steeper rate than personal incomes. As the *New York Times* reported in an editorial in May 1975: "The cost of the American dream—that rose-covered cottage or split level ranch in suburbia— is now $41,300 (new) or $35,000 (used) and is unavailable to anyone with an income of less than $23,300. Since the average family's income is half of that, the average family is just out of luck."[34] A report from the Congressional Joint Economic Committee indicated that, in the mid-1970s, "a new home is unavailable to 85% of all families, and a used home is out of reach for 80%. . . . The American dream is realistic only for the rich and the upper middle class. People at lower economic levels increasingly must settle for rental housing."[35]

As an unplanned, although not in some instances unexpected or undesired consequence of the postwar suburban development pattern in the U.S., the nation's metropolitan areas have become more residentially segregated—in terms of class, race, and age—than probably any other community type in recent history. Suburban life became the privilege, mainly, of the young, the well-to-do, and the white; others were left in the cities or the small towns, or moved to the suburbs at a financial risk.[36] Those low- and moderate-income families who made it to the suburban single-family homes, although better off usually than their city-dwelling cousins, became vulnerable, as our Levittown inquiry showed, to the disadvantages of low-density suburban life, especially the high private costs and lack of public services. Though both were elements of a single urban system, city and suburb became increasingly differentiated from one another in social and cultural structures and values and remained politically disconnected.[37]

It did not take long before some suburban real estate developers and municipalities realized that the number of middle-income families was limited and that it would be necessary, if money was to be made and municipalities were to grow, to build higher-density and thus lower-cost housing. Always fearful of opening up the suburban floodgates to the large, lower-income families of the city who would be unable to pay enough in taxes to cover the added schooling and other essential municipal services which would be required, the suburban municipalities restricted their multifamily housing to middle-income town houses and two- or three-story walk-up "garden" apartments containing small dwelling units. Already by 1960 some 15 percent of suburban units were in multifamily buildings.[38]

In the decade 1960 to 1970 the number of suburban multifamily housing units increased by 96 percent, while single-family units increased by only 17 percent. Yet in 1970, multifamily units made up only 22 percent of the total suburban dwelling units in the nation—still a relatively small proportion.[39] Spurred by such demographic changes as smaller family size, rising age of marriage, and an increase in the elderly population, as well as by the pressures of lower-income families who have been economically shut out of the single-family home market, the construction of multifamily housing starts in the nation as a whole during the 1970s has exceeded that of single-family houses and is increasing each year.

As with the recent swing to single-family housing in Sweden, the rising demand for multifamily suburban housing has caught many municipalities by surprise. Few suburban communities seem to plan positively for such housing in a way which accepts it as a coequal dwelling type with its single-family counterpart and which carefully integrates it into the mainstream of community life. More often than not, multifamily housing is accepted grudgingly and some times only after long zoning-board and court battles; it is restricted to relatively undesirable locations, and it is underserviced. The Swedish tenet that higher-density housing is more desirable because it can more efficiently be provided with public services at a higher quality level, is typically lost on the U.S. scene, where families in multifamily housing are frequently more deprived of services than their home-dwelling counterparts. When the often dismal architectural design and poor landscaping of much of American multifamily housing is added to this picture, one can visualize why multifamily housing is in danger of becoming, in the U.S., the slums of the suburbs. In too many cases this danger seems already to have become a reality.

The negative views of public officials toward multifamily housing are paralleled by those of many residents, both renters and homeowners. Homeowners tend to look with scorn on most multifamily housing developments, partly due to the real or imagined threat of tax increases which these developments represent, a point emphasized by the Levittown families. And the younger renters themselves seldom regard their apartments as a permanent abode, but instead view them as temporary quarters which suffice only until they are able to move to a single-family home. Thus, there has been little public support for the acceptance of multifamily units as serious alternative housing for a large segment of the population.

Yet for a growing number of U.S. citizens, the move to a single-family house no longer is economically possible. The dream of many Americans for a home of their own will not become a reality;[40] their lives are going to be spent not with garage and garden but with parking lot and stairwell. It is due to this stark and generally undesired economic fact that multifamily housing in the U.S. suburbs is going to have to be taken much more seriously in the last quarter of the twentieth century than it has been in the past. The next few decades will see a marked increase in families and other household types *permanently* housed in multifamily structures, a trend opposite to that now underway in Sweden.

There is one alternative to apartment living in the U.S., however, which seldom is found in Sweden: the mobile home. Starting around the time of the Second World War as relatively permanent trailer camps, mobile home parks have become within the last decade one of the fastest growing and most controversial residential environments in America. If the typical suburban municipality looks with disfavor on multifamily housing, it abhors mobile home parks, which pay few real estate taxes and are thought to be a blighting element on the landscape. Consequently, when suburban municipalities permit mobile home developments, they relegate them to the most peripheral and least desired locations, where they typically are cut off almost completely from the main centers of habitation and are often devoid of public services as well.

This treatment by local governments has not slackened the demand for mobile homes, however; it has merely forced mobile-home dwellers to live in some of the most undesirable urban and nonurban residential environments in the country. Mobile home units have proven most attractive to small households, especially young married couples and the elderly, whose alternative is often a garden apartment, a housing form to which mobile-home dwellers express considerable aversion.[41] Between 1960 and 1970 the percentage increase of mobile-home units in the suburbs was 101.5 percent, while the percentage increase nationally was 141 percent.[42] While mobile homes made up in 1970 only 3 percent of the total housing stock both in the suburbs and the nation as a whole, by the mid-1970s the annual production of mobile homes amounted to 28 percent of all new housing units and almost 100 percent of new single-family units selling for under about $20,000.[43] The mobile units themselves range in price from $6,000 or $7,000 to over $30,000 for luxury models. Typically, they are mobile only from factory to site, where their wheels are removed and they remain fixed in position for their lifetime.

It is obvious that the mobile-home boom has been triggered by the grossly inadequate production in the U.S. of other kinds of new housing units in a price range that is within reach of low- and moderate-income families. And the mobile-home dweller's animosity towards his one alternative, garden

235   Implications for Urban
Housing and Development
in Sweden and the U.S.

apartments, is often well founded in reality. Yet many mobile-home communities have a level of environmental amenities that is woefully inadequate;
an isolation from normal community life that is socially regressive, particularly for children and youth; a standard of public service that is shameful; and
a strikingly high degree of age, income, and racial segregation.[44]

Urban Growth in the United States: The Path Ahead

The United States, like Sweden, is at a moment of decision in its policies on
urban growth and development. Economic pressures are forcing an abrupt
change in the postwar pattern of low-density suburbanization for which
America has become known throughout the world. Whether or not this change
can be guided in a direction which leads to a higher quality of residential life
for a broadening spectrum of American people is an open question. Like the
central cities before them, the suburban areas of the nation show signs of
entering a spiral of decay and mismanagement. The combination of large-lot
single-family-house developments, scattered garden apartment projects, and
isolated mobile-home parks does not add up to an urban development pattern
that is economically efficient, environmentally protective, or socially
humane. There must be a better urban growth alternative for what, in general,
is the world's most lavishly housed society. What is this alternative if not the
low-rise, high-density housing, closely integrated into existing communities,
serviced at a high-quality level, designed at a human scale, and in harmony
with the natural environment—in short, the Vällingby model?
   One must look with initial skepticism on the probability of successfully
transplanting a social mechanism which works well in one sociocultural setting to a new and different milieu. The financial, organizational, and planning
problems involved in building developments in the United States on the scale
of Vällingby, with such a high level of public services, would be great; these
problems are more complex in the U.S. than in Sweden. But the task is not
insurmountable, as the recent success of some new towns and other large-
scale developments in the U.S. has proved.[45]
   The difference in city-suburban ties between the U.S. and Sweden also
poses difficulties. The Vällingby model includes a close relationship with an
inner-city area, yet there are few cities in the U.S. any longer with which
suburbanites would want to have such a relationship. The cities have been
allowed to deteriorate to such a degree that the suburbanite lives where he
does precisely because he does not want to have to relate to them.
   While low-rise, high-density suburban housing in the U.S. would have to
compromise some Vällingby attributes, therefore, the compromise might be

less serious than would appear at first glance. The typical Vällingby dweller has surprisingly little contact with the city and no great love for urban living. His main tie to the city is the job; if jobs were more decentralized, his satisfaction would probably increase, for his heart and soul lie outside of Stockholm and not within it. He seems no different from the typical Levittown dweller in this respect. In compromising the close urban relationship of the Vällingby model, some things of importance, such as social diversity, would undoubtedly be lost, but the loss would not do irreparable harm to the idea and ideal of low-rise, high-density housing.

A serious impediment to the development of this kind of housing in the U.S. has been the Americans' apparently intense dislike of garden apartments and high-density living in general. In a recent Gallup Poll, a cross-section of Americans was asked: "In terms of the future growth of housing in this locality or region, which would you prefer—single family dwellings spread more or less evenly over the overall region, or clustered multi-family apartment dwellings with open areas in between?"[46] The result was 75 percent in favor of the single-house alternative and only 13 percent in favor of multifamily housing, with 6 percent favoring both and 6 percent having no opinion. There was little variation in these percentages by sex, race, age, income, political party, or city size. The segments of the population most strongly in favor of the multifamily alternative were nonwhites and young people aged eighteen to twenty-four, but only by 17 percent and 18 percent, respectively, not a very noteworthy difference from the national figure of 13 percent. Thus, even the persons who would most benefit from multifamily housing seemed overwhelmingly negative toward it.

Most Swedes also express opposition to multifamily housing in public opinion polls, yet this has not prevented Sweden from producing, with general public acceptance, except in the case of the recent high-rise projects, more multifamily housing per capita than any other country in the Western world. While this may partially be attributed to the more centralized political decision-making in Sweden, it also suggests that such public opinion questions do not always cut very deeply into the desires, needs, and practical choices of a population. It would be unwise to interpret the Gallup Poll results as more than brief, idealized verbal responses to a question which conjures up all sorts of negative images in the American mind.

Does the great cultural heterogeneity of American society pose difficulties for the successful implementation of low-rise, high-density suburban housing in the U.S.? Part of the smooth functioning of Vällingby may be attributed to the cultural homogeneity of Swedish society. Almost all Vällingby residents share similar values, traditions, and basic patterns of personal behavior; class

237   Implications for Urban
Housing and Development
in Sweden and the U.S.

differences among the residents, insofar as these are reflected in life-style and behavior, are less, for example, than between working- and middle-class subcultures in the U.S. Few urban communities in the U.S. have residents who are culturally as homogeneous as those of Vällingby; even suburbs like Levittown, which are noted for their homogeneity, have a significant amount of ethnic and religious diversity, and there are important differences in values and attitudes between blue- and white-collar workers.

Such cultural diversity in U.S. communities has been instrumental in generating intergroup conflict and social tension, and probably contributes to the spread pattern of U.S. metropolitan development. The residents of metropolitan areas seek, if they can afford it, insulation from persons whom they regard as incompatible. The mechanisms of geographic and functional distance are used to achieve this insulation: fenced-in private yards, detached houses, and the establishment, where possible, of homogeneous blocks and neighborhoods. The U.S. suburban community itself represents an attempt to achieve geographic and functional isolation from center-city dwellers.[47]

This system of sociospatial isolation is difficult to maintain in a low-rise, high-density environment like Vällingby. With minimal geographic distance between neighbors, the substitution of public for private space, and the common usage of neighborhood services and facilities, many Americans in a Vällingby-type environment would find their normal patterns of social interaction subject to serious strains. The low-rise, high-density environments throws people more on top of one another; they must cooperate in the use of public facilities and spaces and to some extent in their maintenance and upkeep; they must achieve, if strife is to be avoided, a higher level of agreement about norms of behavior in public places, teenage disciplinary standards, and approaches to childrearing. Such cooperation and agreement could be enhanced by designing the environment in a way which would foster homogeneous blocks and small neighborhoods and by being careful, especially at the outset, to avoid too wide a class distribution in the development as a whole.

Another impediment to the use of large-scale, low-rise, high-density developments as an urban growth alternative is the suburban American's strong penchant for private space and a house as both material possession and status symbol, a taste which would surely be thwarted in the more egalitarian setting of such an environment. If the Vällingby-type environment were to become a permanent U.S. settlement type, desired by a sizable section of the American population, there would have to be a diminution in the material and status-striving motivations which are so dominant in American life. As a replacement, such an environment could offer greater personal and family security, a slower and more relaxed pace of life, and a greater opportunity to own a summer cottage, attributes which over time may well become more highly valued.

A final problem is the American's utter fascination with the automobile. Is this fascination based on a deep-seated need, as some argue, or merely environmental exigencies? If it is the latter, as seems more probable, the role of the automobile in U.S. life could be expected to change over time; there are signs that this change is already beginning, and a rising chorus of American voices is urging it on.[48]

One cannot be sanguine about prospects in the U.S. for the widespread channeling of urban growth into Vällingby-type environments, yet such a course of action is not unfeasible. Some low-rise, high-density environments, not unlike Vällingby but on a smaller scale and designed mainly for persons of middle income, have already successfully been developed.[49] Public awareness of the negative consequences of the last quarter-century's urban growth pattern heightens each year. That new growth in U.S. metropolitan areas must be channeled into residential environments which are of higher density than those of the past is now accepted reality. What remains to be accepted is the view that the higher-density residential environment is not just a temporary expedient brought about by economic necessity but a positive means through which the nation's urban areas can become more livable at the same time that her citizens are better housed.

Appendix   The British New Towns—A Middle Way?

Let me say in general that I regard the British new towns as a remarkable achievement in the annals of urban planning and development. I am quite cognizant of the criticisms that have been leveled against them over the years: that they are sterile and boring, that they do little to solve London's urban problems, that they represent a misallocation of scarce resources, and so on. Indeed, these criticisms have been commonly heard in the United States in recent years, where the idea of new towns has been held in low repute by many intellectuals. A point too often missed is that the proper focus for the evaluation of new towns is on *other* suburban developments. New growth around cities must take some form or other; the British new towns are clearly preferable to most alternative suburban patterns and especially to the suburban "sprawl" which is so prevalent in the United States.

Further, there is little evidence that the new towns do not "work." The new towns policy has been continued through political administrations of varying persuasions, the people living in the towns seem by outward manifestations to be

These remarks were written in 1972, following a new towns study tour, at the invitation of the director of the Town and Country Planning Association. They first appeared, slightly abridged, in *Town and Country Planning* (London) 41, no. 6 (June, 1973), and are used here with permission.

reasonably content, and the older of the towns have even begun to make something of a financial profit.

I thought it might be useful to discuss my observations of the new towns in terms of seven basic community variables which have emerged in my own work in Sweden and the United States as particularly germane to the *social quality* of residential environments. These variables provide a way to understand and compare residential settlements from a sociological perspective; they also underlie many public-policy and moral discussions about the "good community."

1. What is the best *scale and density* for a residential environment? The "optimum" size of the new towns has been creeping upwards through the years. Though this has been mainly for nonsocial reasons, I have heard few sociological complaints about the increasing scale. Ebenezer Howard himself was in favor of *clustered* smaller towns, bringing to mind the important perspective that the optimum scale for a specific community is greatly dependent upon what is around it. The new communities around Stockholm are about the size of the earliest British new towns, but they are closely tied to Stockholm. The later and larger British new towns tend to be farther from the large cities, especially London. The size of 100,000 to 250,000 seemed to emerge as a generally agreed upon middle-range optimum in our discussions with British planners; this is about the same range that is commonly cited in the U.S.—perhaps it is coming to be an international standard in advanced, industrial societies. Several of the latest new towns in Britain are projected to be well above 250,000, however, and there are always pressures in that direction.

In residential densities, as in the matter of scale, the British may be approaching some international standard of desirability and acceptability. British new-town residential densities are well below those of Sweden and well above the typical American suburb. But densities in the United States are going up, with the rapid emergence of what we call "town houses" and "garden apartments,"—the dwelling types which are most typical of the British new towns. This density seems the most desirable balance-point among such factors as the widespread use of private cars, the desire of families for ground-level dwellings, and a reasonable proximity to services. A strong case can also be made for the social desirability of this level of density in terms of the balance between community and privacy: both the alternative extremes of high-rise flats and single-family detached housing seem to foster excessive privatization.

The lower-density level does economically seem to foreclose good public transportation, however, which was a problem (and consumer complaint) in many of the new towns which we visited. While some very interesting public transportation experiments are under way in Britain (such as the separate roadway for buses at Runcorn), one does get the feeling that the automobile is here to stay, perhaps even to dominate. This is of course the overwhelming feeling in America, and it seems to represent an international expression of consumer demand.

The example of Sweden in this regard must not be overlooked. With the highest level of automobile ownership, personal income, and available land in Western Europe (factors which are closely associated with low densities), Sweden has perhaps the highest Western European densities in its new urban environments. This is the result of many factors, but principally of a decision to make public transportation work. It does work very well indeed in Stockholm, and the resulting high-density settlements have the advantages of being better "serviced" by community facilities, and of being more urbane in character. There is much public discussion in Sweden at the moment in favor of lowering densities, but public policies have not changed substantially. In the long run, however, I think that the density of new development in Sweden will drop, more closely approaching the British level.

Two final points about British new town densities: first, as almost everywhere else, they are closely related to social class. The lower the social-class level of the town, the higher tends to be the density. This fact is sometimes overlooked and is related mainly to the residents' ability to pay for housing. Second, it is interesting to note the shifts over time in thinking about densities among British planners and policymakers. After a "middle period" of experimentation with higher densities (especially Cumbernauld), densities in Milton Keynes, for example, are now back almost to the original garden city level. The reasons for this would be a fascinating subject in the analysis of public policy formation.

2. How much *social and cultural heterogeneity* or diversity should a community have?

The "big three" sociological variables of importance here are class, ethnicity, and stage of the life cycle. I found that the towns were somewhat more class homogeneous than I had anticipated; this generates a rather great diversity among the towns in social-class terms (compare, for example, the overwhelmingly working-class Skelmersdale with Crawley). But they are a long step away from the predominant social-class homogeneity of American suburbs (and even new towns). The degree to which the class level of the towns affects the general ambiance was quite striking, with street litter, poorly maintained private yards and even poorer-quality public services more common in the lower-class towns (and areas within towns).

Another emerging international planning concept in which the British have pointed the way is class homogeneity by block, housing cluster, or neighborhood, yet with overall community heterogeneity. This again seems to be the best balance-point among competing values (and is also a focus of much research), and it was the common pattern in those towns which had a fairly wide class distribution. Further, it seems to work.

One does not get the impression from the new towns that Britain is very diverse ethnically. I recall seeing almost no minority groups in new towns, and I would suspect that ethnic intermixing has not been a major achievement or perhaps even goal of the new-towns program. My information, however, could be quite faulty. The same observation applies to some extent to stage of the life cycle. The British have made no breakthroughs in this regard; the mixing of age groups and persons with different family statuses is considerably less than in Sweden (though well ahead of the American pattern).

Many new towns were concerned about this, however, and seemed to be making serious (and often successful) attempts to bring in older people especially, and even a few singles (though it must be admitted that a new town is not always the habitat most preferred by young, single adults, many of whom want more anonymity and excitement than any new suburban environment can offer).

Of course the central issue here is to what degree a community should be balanced in terms of different types of people. The goal of social balance has been continuously maintained as a central tenet of urban development policy in Britain, although the actual new-towns experience has not brought us much closer to an understanding of the level and kinds of social heterogeneity in residential environments that are most desirable.

3. What level of *political autonomy* should a local community have, as distinct, for example, from the region and the national state?

Local self-government is often regarded as basic to the good community, especially in the United States. Yet the key to the good new town is quite obviously national power, as expressed through the local development corporation. As an American I found the attainments of public planning in Britain quite remarkable. I am used to seeing many fine plans, but I am unused to seeing them carried out; it is virtually impossible in the United States actually to see a town *completed* according to a plan.

The citizens of Britain seem to have adjusted quite well to the loss of local autonomy, although I am not unmindful of the many battles which have taken place (and which will take place). Britain still has retained more local autonomy than Sweden, where the frictions, if anything, are even less and the accomplishments as great. The belief in political decentralization and local autonomy has become something of a fad in some American intellectual circles in recent years, and there are strong political pressures in this direction from many fronts. The British new-towns experience must be, I believe, a major contribution to that debate.

4. How much *functional self-sufficiency* should a community have?

British planners have kept continuously in the forefront the goal of creating communities which are not heavily dependent upon other settlements in such matters as work, shopping, recreation, and education—the major community functions. In the achievement of this goal there has been a very high degree of success. The fact that only 6 percent of the workers of Welwyn Garden City commute to London must be regarded almost with awe. This degree of self-containment is markedly different from both the Swedish and the American patterns, and it seems to work well economically (it has not stood the test of a serious recession, I believe). Socially, its main consequence is to reduce the journey to work, an accomplishment that is important in bringing working members of the family home earlier and in providing job opportunities for those with low mobility (for example, housewives). More generally, it concentrates around the residential environment the major functions of life; this is especially important, perhaps, for growing children and the elderly. We can look to the British experience to throw much more light on the extent to which self-containment does in fact yield social benefits such as these.

Another aspect of this self-sufficiency is the internal self-containment of functional areas. There is general agreement that employment areas should be separated from residential areas, but an interesting debate is emerging over the separation of residential from commercial areas. In almost all earlier forms of human settlement these functions were geographically united to a very large extent. The British new towns have followed the American suburban pattern of residential areas which are dead by day and shopping areas which are dead by night (in the United States many central-city areas have become virtually lifeless at night). In one town we were told that the new hotel would not be put in the town center (it would go on the edge of a golf course, instead), an implicit reason being that the town center has few nighttime attractions for guests. Harlow's town center is completely cut off from the residential areas by green belts, traffic ways, and parking areas. There are no clear answers to this problem (the two solutions of putting a few community facilities on the edge of the town center and decentralizing some stores to the neighborhoods do not seem to change the basic situation very much); it is surely an area where more experimentation is needed, the desired goal being more "urban vitality."

5. What level of *diffuse solidarity* should a community have?

6. What level of *primary relationships* should a community have?

These variables have long been a fundamental focus of sociological interest in new towns. Diffuse solidarity is a technical sociological term meaning the "sense of community" in a town—feelings of identity, loyalty, solidarity. This is affected to some extent by how many friends or primary relationships one has in a local area but also by such things as political autonomy, community-wide communication systems, school athletic teams, and architectural design (such as the use of focal points and the hierarchical nesting principle in neighborhood planning). Conventional wisdom holds that it is good for communities to be "close-knit" in this respect, and it has long been a prominent goal of architects and planners. Yet local community solidarity has been in rapid decline in advanced countries, being replaced by interest- and occupational-group loyalties, and national loyalties: perhaps there is even a general weakening of feelings of solidarity toward all social groupings.

Planners in the older new towns seemed to show more interest in this variable than those in the newer towns, one of whom spoke of it as "that sociological crap." Residents in new areas have less community solidarity than might be desired because diffuse solidarity is affected enormously by the length of time people have lived together (as well as by how homogeneous they are); this suggests that the planners in the newer towns are merely being realistic about what they can accomplish.

Community solidarity in the new areas of Sweden seems to be much less than in Britain (there are almost no local community newspapers, for example). I think it is reasonable to conclude that a rather low level of diffuse solidarity in residential environments is almost inevitable in advanced industrial societies and probably not as undesirable as much traditional planning ideology would have us believe.

Of much greater importance is the chance to make and hold close friends in a community and the tone of interpersonal relationships. I wish I had been able to learn more in this regard. The ability of planners and architects to affect social interaction has sometimes been overstated (the doctrine of architectural determinism). This has helped to generate a view which is not uncommon in the United States (especially among sociologists) that the physical form of the environment has almost no effect whatsoever on social behavior. There is a growing body of research findings which is helping us to assess cause and effect in this area, and the social consequences of physical form appear to be not inconsiderable. The physical arrangement of housing clusters, the location of social facilities and public spaces, and perhaps also the arrangement of neighborhoods and neighborhood functions, for example, seem tangibly to be related to the formation of friendships. One of the most exciting things we observed on the new towns tour was the experimentation along these lines, some of which were much more successful, of course, than others. For instance, the use of public spaces in housing developments is related to social-class levels; the lower the class level, the more the public space tends to be used. This fact presented problems in several of the middle-class areas which we visited. Here the architects had provided a great deal of public space, but it appeared seldom to be used. We had the feeling that it would have been put to better use as private yards, although the public space was quite important to the area's aesthetic quality.

7. What *social and cultural facilities* should be available?

This variable presents fewer basic policy issues; the experts all feel that there should be more facilities in the areas of health, recreation, welfare, education, although there is much to debate in terms of type and distribution. The British set a high standard in this field, though not as high as the Scandinavian countries. Several of the new towns were quite late in the provision of basic social facilities (a major source of residents' complaints), and we got a strong impression that the working-class towns tended to have fewer facilities, and to have them much later, than the towns of higher social standing. This is unfortunate—because the working-class towns need them more—though not unexpected. The same seemed to be true of expenditure of time and effort in "social development" functions.

Again, the amount of experimentation was of great interest. Some communities had centralized "amenities centers"; in others the amenities were more decentralized. Some towns were trying out large youth centers and old-age centers. The variety of neighborhood-center arrangements was fascinating: some connected to shopping, some to pubs, some to sports facilities, and some to schools.

There is one international community problem in which the British seem not to have made any significant advances. Every town which had teenagers had a teenage problem: "They have nothing to do!" A major international award should await the person who can find a solution to this one.

The continuation of the new towns program in Great Britain is surely to be desired. It provides an almost unparalleled laboratory for the study of human settlements, at the same time that it is a significant contribution to human welfare. There is also little doubt that it has had a major impact on urban development in other countries, especially through the work of the Town and Country Planning Association.

Notes

Chapter 1

1 Lewis Mumford, *The City in History* (New York: Harcourt, Brace & World, 1961), p. 487.
2 Ibid., p. 484.
3 See Sam B. Warner, *Streetcar Suburbs* (New York: Atheneum, 1970), and Janet Roebuck, *The Shaping of Urban Society* (New York: Charles Scribner's Sons, 1974).
4 Mumford, *The City in History,* p. 486.
5 In 1970, about 36 percent of Americans were classified by the U.S. census as suburban residents, but many not so classified, especially those in Western cities inhabit environments which are similar in character to the suburbs.
6 Wilbur C. Hallenbeck, *American Urban Communities* (New York: Harper and Brothers, 1951), p. 202.
7 New York: The Century Co.
8 Hallenbeck, *American Urban Communities,* p. 207.
9 Svend Reimer, *The Modern City* (Englewood Cliffs, N.J.: Prentice-Hall, 1952).
10 Especially by ecological sociologists at the University of Chicago.
11 Small towns were the favorite research habitat of anthropologically oriented sociologists.
12 See Morton White and Lucia White, *The Intellectual Versus the City* (New York: Mentor Books, 1964).
13 Scott Donaldson, *The Suburban Myth* (New York: Columbia University Press, 1969), p. 1.
14 William H. Whyte, Jr., *The Organization Man* (New York: Simon and Schuster, 1956); John Keats, *The Crack in the Picture Window* (Boston: Houghton Mifflin, 1956); R. Gordon, K. Gordon, and M. Gunther, *The Split-Level Trap* (New York: Geis, 1961).
15 See Donaldson, *The Suburban Myth,* chap. 1.
16 Walter Martin, *American Sociological Review* 21 (August 1956).
17 S. F. Fava, *American Sociological Review* 21 (February 1956).
18 Fall 1957, pp. 123–46. The article was later rewritten as "The Suburban Sadness" for William Dobriner, ed., *The Sub-*

247

urban Community (New York: G. P. Putnam's Sons, 1958), pp. 375–408.

19 Ibid., p. 375.

20 J. Seeley, R. Sim, E. Loosley, *Crestwood Heights* (New York: Basic Books, 1956).

21 These factors are further embellished in the interpretation of this book by Maurice Stein in *The Eclipse of Community* (New York: Harper Torchbooks, 1964).

22 Berkeley: University of California Press, 1960; paperback edition, 1968.

23 Ibid., p. 91.

24 Ibid., p. xiv.

25 Ibid., p. xvi.

26 Ibid.

27 For example, "Suburbia and the American Dream," *The Public Interest* 2 (Winter 1966), and "Suburbs, Subcultures and Styles of Life," in Berger, *Looking for America* (Englewood Cliffs, N.J.: Prentice-Hall, 1971).

28 New York: Pantheon, 1967.

29 Levittown, New Jersey, now called Willingboro, was built several years after Levittown, Pennsylvania, the subject of the present inquiry, and is located across the Delaware River from it.

30 Gans, *The Levittowners*

31 Ibid., p. 288.

32 Ibid. Gans developed this point of view much further in his now classic "Urbanism and Suburbanism Reconsidered," in R. Gutman and D. Popenoe, eds., *Neighborhood, City, and Metropolis* (New York: Random House, 1970).

33 Gans, *The Levittowners,* pp. 289–90.

34 Gans modified his views somewhat in later writings; see his *People and Plans* (New York: Basic Books, 1968).

35 *Levittowners,* p. 413.

36 Ibid., p. 432.

37 Ibid.

38 The major works were Scott Greer, *The Emerging City* (New York: The Free Press, 1962). S. D. Clark, *The Suburban Society* (Toronto: University of Toronto Press, 1966), and William Dobriner, *Class in Suburbia* (Englewood Cliffs, N.J.: Prentice-Hall, 1963).

39 See, for example, R. C. Wood, *Suburbia, Its People and Their Politics* (Boston: Houghton Mifflin, 1958), and Benjamin Chinitz, *City and Suburb: The Economics of Metropolitan Growth* (Englewood Cliffs, N.J.: Prentice-Hall, 1964).

40 Almost no major suburban studies were published between 1968 and 1974.

41 See Blake McKelvy, *The Emergence of Metropolitan America* (New Brunswick, N.J.: Rutgers University Press, 1968), chap.

6, and David Popenoe, ed., "The University and the City," special issue of *Urban Education* 6, no. 1 (April 1971).

42 Charles M. Haar, ed., *The End of Innocence: A Suburban Reader* (Glenview, Ill.: Scott, Foresman, 1972); John Kramer, ed., *North American Suburbs* (Berkeley, Calif.: Glendessary Press, 1972); L. H. Masotti and J. K. Hadden, eds. *Suburbia in Transition* (New York: Franklin Watts, 1974), also, *The Urbanization of the Suburbs* (Beverly Hills: Sage, 1973); Frederick M. Wirt et al., *On the City's Rim: Politics and Policy in Suburbia* (Lexington, Mass.: D. C. Heath, 1972).

43 New York: David McKay, 1972.

44 See, for example, the review symposium in *American Journal of Sociology* 79 (1) (July 1973): 165–75.

45 See n. 42 above.

46 The title of volume 7 of the Urban Affairs Annual Review is *The Urbanization of the Suburbs* (1973).

47 In a 1971 Gallup poll the question was asked, "If you could live anywhere in the U.S. that you wanted to, would you prefer a city, suburban area, small town, or farm?" Of those persons living in cities of over 50,000 population, only about 25 percent chose "city," while approximately 37 percent picked "suburb." *The Gallup Opinion Index,* no. 74 (Princeton, N.J., August 1971).

48 See L. Schnore, "The Socioeconomic Status of Cities and Suburbs," *American Sociological Review* 28, no. 1 (February 1963): 76–85; and Norval D. Glenn, "Suburbanization in the U.S. since World War II," in Masotti and Hadden, *The Urbanization of the Suburbs.*

49 R. Gutman, "Site Planning and Social Behavior," *Journal of Social Issues* 22, no. 4 (October 1966), 103–15.

50 Quoted in D. P. Warwick and S. Osherson, *Comparative Research Methods* (Englewood Cliffs, N.J.: Prentice-Hall, 1973), p. vi.

51 Ibid., p. 8.

52 See "Studies of the American Suburb" section above.

53 *The Housing Environment and Family Life* (Baltimore: Johns Hopkins University Press, 1962).

54 R. N. Morris and J. Mogey, *The Sociology of Housing* (London: Routledge and Kegan Paul, 1965).

55 Ibid., p. 163.

56 There is a good discussion of the newcomer effect on neighboring in S. Keller, *The Urban Neighborhood* (New York: Random House, 1968), pp. 67–72; see also Morris and Mogey, *Sociology of Housing,* chap. 3.

57 London: Routledge and Kegan Paul, 1963.

58 The changes in the second generation were more significant than those in the first.

59 Leo Kuper, ed., *Living in Towns* (London: Cresset, 1953).

60 S. F. Fava, "Contrasts in Neighboring: New York City and a Suburban County," in Dobriner, *Suburban Community*, pp. 122–31; H. Laurence Ross, "Uptown and Downtown: A Study of Middle Class Residential Areas," *American Sociological Review* 30 (1965): 255–59.

61 See, for example, S. Greer and E. Kube, "Urbanism and Social Structure: A Los Angeles Study," M. Sussman, ed., *Community Structure and Analysis* (New York: Thomas Y. Crowell, 1959), and Wendell Bell and M. T. Force, "Urban Neighborhood Types and Participation in Formal Associations," *American Sociological Review* 21 (1956): 25–34.

62 See S. Greer, "Urbanism Reconsidered: A Comparative Study of Local Areas in a Metropolis," in Gutman and Popenoe, eds., *Neighborhood, City, and Metropolis*.

63 T. Caplow, S. Stryker, and S. E. Wallace, *The Urban Ambience* (Totowa, N.J.: The Bedminster Press, 1964).

64 Baltimore: Penguin Books, 1962; first published in 1957 by Routledge and Kegan Paul.

65 P. Willmott and M. Young, *Family and Class in a London Suburb* (London: Routledge and Kegan Paul, 1960). See also M. Young and P. Willmott, *The Symmetrical Family* (New York: Pantheon, 1973).

66 Willmott and Young, *Family and Class,* p. 123.

67 New York: The Free Press, 1961.

68 New York: Oxford University Press, 1971.

69 Clark, *Suburban Society,* p. 144.

70 Ibid., p. 148.

71 L. Carey and R. Mapes, *The Sociology of Planning* (London: B. T. Batsford, 1972).

72 J. B. Lansing, R. W. Marans, and R. B. Zehner (Ann Arbor: Survey Research Center, University of Michigan, 1970).

73 The results of this research project are reported in William Michelson, *Environmental Choice, Human Behavior, and Residential Satisfaction* (New York: Oxford University Press, 1976).

74 W. Michelson, "Environmental Change" (Toronto: Centre for Urban and Community Studies, University of Toronto, 1973).

75 Baton Rouge: Louisiana State University Press, 1964.

76 For example, a study entitled *The Costs of Sprawl: Environmental and Economic Costs of Alternative Residential Development Patterns on the Urban Fringe* (Washington, D.C.: Government Printing Office, 1974), commissioned by the Council on Environmental Quality, the Environmental Protection Agency, and the Department of Housing and Urban Development, argues forcefully for suburban alternatives, and has been well received and widely discussed by influential government officials.

77 Calculated from summary report of 1970 census.

78 See George Sternlieb, "Death of the American Dream House," *Society* 9 (February 1972): 39–42.

79 E.g., R. W. Burchell, *Planned Unit Development: New Communities American Style* (New Brunswick, N.J.: Rutgers University Center for Urban Policy Research, 1972); James A. Clapp, *New Towns and Urban Policy* (New York: Dunellen Publishing Co., 1971); Royce Hanson, *New Towns: Laboratories for Democracy* (New York: The Twentieth Century Fund, 1971); and Lansing et al., *Planned Residential Environments*.

80 See Lansing et al., *Planned Residential Environments*, chap. 2. Similar upper-middle-class characteristics were found in the residents of one of New Jersey's first planned unit developments, which has been under investigation by a team of social scientists and architects from Princeton Universtiy. See Burchell, *Planned Unit Development*, chap. 4.

81 "The Methodology of Comparative Analysis," in Warwick and Osherson, *Comparative Research Methods*, p. 75.

82 A purposive sampling procedure was used in selecting the households, designed to secure cases reasonably representative of the range of life stages, life styles, and social classes in each environment. The bulk of the twenty-five households was selected systematically from housing lists in Sweden and the telephone book in the U.S. These households were supplemented by cases selected to achieve a sample roughly proportional to each community's social class and life-stage distribution, though with a heavier weight given to working-class families in the middle stages of the life cycle, which demographic data had indicated were most typical of the two environments. In addition, several known problem-families were included in the sample so as to have access to a wide range of environmental adaptations. Household heads were phoned, and in Levittown also written, in advance to arrange the interview; the refusal rate was 35–40 percent in each community.

The household interviews were conducted by me alone in the United States. In Sweden, I had the assistance of a translator, feeling that my knowledge of spoken Swedish was not yet adequate to the task. The translator was a person trained in sociology, knowledgeable about this particular field, and herself a resident of Vällingby. In addition to the formal household interviews, many other residents in each community, both teenagers and adults, were interviewed casually over the three-year period of the study.

83 William Michelson has labeled this the ego-oriented approach. *Man and His Urban Environment* (Reading, Mass.: Addison-Wesley, 1970), pp. 44–50.

84 In a recent bibliography in this field, it was noted in regard to teenagers that "very little seems to be written about this

252 Notes to Chapter Two

group." Gwen Bell, Edwina Randall and Judith E. R. Roeder, eds. *Urban Environments and Human Behavior* (Stroudsburg, Pa.: Dowden, Hutchinson and Ross, 1973), p. 11.

85 The wide-ranging life-styles of some upper-middle-class members have given rise to the concept of "community without propinquity," and the judgment that the geographic community is no longer of much importance. See Melvin Webber, "Order in Diversity: Community without Propinquity" in Gutman and Popenoe, eds. *Neighborhood, City, and Metropolis*, pp. 791–811.

86 As was noted above, however, many sociologists are not concerned directly with the individual in any of these dimensions but rather with the social system.

87 For example, Carey and Mapes, *The Sociology of Planning*, and Young and Willmott, *The Symmetrical Family*.

Chapter 2

1 See "The World's Richest Nation," *The Economist* (April 1974).

2 For an interesting discussion of Swedish cultural and personality traits, see Paul Britton Austin, *On Being Swedish* (Coral Gables, Fla.: University of Miami Press, 1968).

3 The best book on Swedish society from a sociological point of view is Richard F. Tomasson, *Sweden: Prototype of Modern Society,* (New York: Random House, 1970).

4 In a recent survey of Americans' "Knowledge of and attitudes toward Sweden," commissioned by the Swedish Information Service, a high pecentage of respondents felt that "in Sweden, the government owns most of the industry." Forty-one percent of "elite" respondents felt this was true, for example, versus 30 percent "not true" and 29 percent "don't know" (Princeton, N.J.: Response Analysis Corporation, June 27, 1973).

5 The industrial field that has the largest percentage of government ownership is mining. A state company mines about 70 percent of Sweden's rich deposits of iron ore.

6 See Joseph B. Board, Jr., *The Government and Politics of Sweden* (Boston: Houghton Mifflin, 1970).

7 The political makeup of the Swedish parliament from 1973 to 1976, in terms of percentage of seats, was: Social Democrats (45 percent) and Communists (5 percent); Center party (26 percent), Conservative party (14 percent), and Liberal party (10 percent), thus giving the leftist parties and the rightist parties each 50 percent of the vote.

8 Information from Statens Invandrarverket. The only comparable homogeneous nations are the other Scandanavian countries, plus Japan.

9 S. M. Lipset, *The First New Nation* (New York: Basic Books, 1963).

10 Tomasson, *Sweden,* p. 7; also, S. Carlsson and S. Rosén,

Svensk Historia (Stockholm: Svenska bokförlaget, 1962), pt. 1, pp. 290ff.

11 See Kurt Samuelsson, *From Great Power to Welfare State* (London: Ernest Benn, 1972).
12 See Introduction, by Michael Roberts, Ingvar Andersson, *A History of Sweden* (Stockholm: Natur och Kultur, 1955).
13 John S. Lindberg, *The Background of Swedish Emigration to the U.S.: An Economic and Sociological Study in the Dynamics of Migration* (Minneapolis, 1930).
14 See *Urbanization and Planning in Sweden* (Stockholm: Royal Ministry for Foreign Affairs, 1972), pp. 14–18.
15 Ella Ödmann and Gun-Britt Dahlberg, *Urbanization in Sweden* (Stockholm: Allmänna Förlaget, 1970), pp. 49–53.
16 "The Swedish Population," *Fact Sheet on Sweden* (Stockholm: Swedish Institute, 1973).
17 Ödmann and Dahlberg, *Urbanization in Sweden,* p. 37.
18 International Urban Research, *The World's Metropolitan Areas* (Berkeley: University of California, 1959), p. 25.
19 *Urbanization and Planning in Sweden,* p. 19.
20 Ibid., p. 21.
21 For brief accounts of the history of Stockholm see W. William-Olsson, *Stockholm—Structure and Development* (Stockholm: Almqvist and Wiksell, 1961), and Kell Åström, *City Planning in Sweden* (Stockholm: Swedish Institute, 1967). See also W. William-Olsson, *Huvuddragen av Stockholms geografiska utveckling 1850–1930* (Stockholm, 1937).
22 Per Holm, *Swedish Housing* (Stockholm: The Swedish Institute, 1957), p. 10.
23 See David Popenoe, "Urban Residential Differentiation," in M. Effrat, ed., *The Community: Approaches and Applications* (New York: The Free Press, 1974), pp. 46–48.
24 Åström, *City Planning in Sweden,* p. 29.
25 See Holm, *Swedish Housing,* p. 10, and Per Holmgren, "The Planned Development of Stockholm" (Department of Planning and Control, City of Stockholm, 1970), mimeo.
26 Åström, *City Planning in Sweden,* chap. 2.
27 A pioneering sociological investigation of a prewar suburb is Edmund Dahlström, *Trivsel i Söderort* (Stockholm: Esselt Aktiebolag, 1951).
28 For further discussion of building in the 30s and 40s, see *Swedish Housing of the 40's,* Sven Backström and Stig Ålund, eds. (Stockholm: Tidskriften Byggmästaren, 1950), and Åström, *City Planning in Sweden,* chap. 2.
29 Göran Sidenbladh, "Stockholm: A Planned City," in *Cities: Their Origin, Growth and Human Impact* (readings from *Scientific American*) (San Francisco: W. H. Freeman, 1973), p. 193.
30 National Housing Board, Stockholm, *Housing in the Nordic Countries* (Copenhagen: S. L. Møllers Bogtrykkeri, 1968), p. 185.

Notes to Chapter Two

31 Ibid.
32 Figures from Erland von Hofsten, "Town Planning in Stockholm—Some Statistics," in Svenska Arkitekters Riksförbund, *Ten Lectures on Swedish Architecture* (Stockholm, Victor Pettersons Bokindustriaktiebolag, 1949), pp. 56–57.
33 The best discussion in English of these Swedish planning principles is Åström, *City Planning in Sweden,* chap. 3. See also David Pass, *Vällingby and Farsta: From Idea to Reality* (Cambridge, Mass.: M.I.T. Press, 1973).
34 Stockholm's Stadsbyggnadskontor, *Stockholm—Urban Environment,* (Stockholm: Almqvist and Wiksell, 1972), p. 11.
35 Ibid.
36 The actual process of development of Vällingby, with the day-to-day decisions which led-up to it, are summarized in Pass, *Vällingby and Farsta.* For a general discussion of the planning process in Sweden see Ödmann, *Urbanization in Sweden;* and *Urbanization and Planning in Sweden.*
37 *Trafikundersökningar: Stockholmsregionen—Hösten 1971: Resultatrapport #1* (Stockholm: Trafiknämden, Stockholms Läns Landsting, 1971), p. 16. Only 17 percent dwell in single-family *detached* houses.
38 "Statistical Material of Greater Stockholm" (Stockholm: Department of Planning and Building Control, 1970), mimeo.
39 *Trafikundersökningar.*
40 Ibid.
41 Ödmann, *Urbanization in Sweden,* p. 71.
42 Ibid., p. 74.
43 For an interesting discussion of the downtown renewal efforts, see Peter C. Glyer, "Urban Renewal That Works: A Survey of a Changing City" (Stockholm: Department of Planning and Building Control, 1970), mimeo.
44 *Urbanization and Planning in Sweden,* p. 23.
45 Ibid.
46 *Trafikundersökningar*
47 Ibid.
48 S. Markelius and G. Sidenbladh, "Town Planning in Stockholm—Housing and Traffic," in *Ten Lectures on Swedish Architecture,* p. 73.
49 Ibid., p. 77.
50 Reported in *General Plan of Stockholm—1952,* p. 167.
51 Ibid.
52 Ibid., p. 73.
53 *Stockholm—Urban Environment,* pp. 52, 60.
54 Ödmann, *Urbanization in Sweden,* p. 171.
55 *Urbanization and Planning in Sweden,* p. 31. Figures for period 1963–68.
56 *Stockholm—Urban Environment,* pp. 68, 76.
57 1970 data from *Trafikundersökningar,* p. 16.
58 *General Plan of Stockholm—1952,* p. 47.

59 Pass, *Vällingby and Farsta*, p. 174. Information contained in a
letter by Yngve Larsson, who was in charge of public transportation in Stockholm during the late 30s and early 40s.
60 Pass, *Vällingby and Farsta*, p. 130.
61 Ibid., p. 174; also in letter from Yngve Larsson.
62 This is surmised from the writing and statements of the major
planners of the time.
63 S. Markelius and G. Sidenbladh, "Town Planning in Stockholm," p. 73.
64 Pass, *Vällingby and Farsta*, p. 122.
65 This conclusion is discussed in ibid., pp. 122–23.
66 *General Plan of Stockholm—1952*, p. 123.
67 Pass, *Vällingby and Farsta*, p. 157.
68 See especially *Vällingby and Farsta*, Appendix 1, pp. 141–58.
69 *Urbanization and Planning in Sweden*, p. 31.
70 See Bertil L. Hanson, *Stockholm Municipal Politics* (Cambridge, Mass.: Joint Center for Urban Studies, M.I.T., and
Harvard, 1960). Pass states: "Seldom did the public or the
ordinary citizen directly participate in the process. (Indeed, no
mechanism existed for such direct participation.)," *Vällingby
and Farsta*, p. 2. This characteristic of the Swedish political
process has since become a major target of criticism by scholars,
intellectuals, and political activists. See, for example, T. Anton,
Myth and the Politics of Change in Modern Sweden (forthcoming), and idem, *Governing Greater Stockholm* (Berkeley:
University of California Press, 1975).
71 "The Structure of the Town of Stockholm," *Byggmästaren* 35
(1956), no. A3, pp. 71–76.
72 *General Plan of Stockholm—1952*, pp. 113–15.
73 Markelius and Sidenbladh, "Town Planning in Stockholm,"
p. 72.
74 Ibid., p. 73.
75 Ibid.
76 Ibid., p. 75.
77 Quoted in Pass, *Vällingby and Farsta*, p. 116.
78 Ibid.
79 Ibid., pp. 56–61, and 171–72, n. 20. Industrial location in
Vällingby was also not favored by the national government,
which preferred more decentralized locations outside of the
Stockholm area.
80 Markelius, "Town Planning Stockholm," p. 74.
81 Ibid.
82 This kind of criticism is reflected in much of Kell Åström's *City
Planning in Sweden*.
83 Markelius, "Town Planning in Stockholm," p. 74.
84 Ibid., p. 76.
85 Quoted in Pass, *Vällingby and Farsta*, p. 114.
86 Ibid., p. 113.
87 Hanson, *Stockholm Municipal Politics*, pp. 200–201.

Chapter 3

1 Population and dwelling unit data are from *Statistisk årsbok för Stockholm* (*Statistical Yearbook of Stockholm*), 1973, table 87.

2 A seventh city district—Johannelund—is often included as a part of the Vällingby development area; but because it is industrial, having almost no residential units, consideration will be given to it only in the section on employment structure.

3 Based on data from the Grimsta district, discussed below.

4 Age data are from *Statistisk årsbok för Stockholm,* 1971, table 19.

5 See Ruth Shonle Cavan, *Marriage and Family in the Modern World* (New York: Thomas Y. Crowell, 1974), chap. 13.

6 Calculated from table 90, *Statistisk årsbok för Stockholm,* 1973.

7 Ibid.

8 The two other major indicators of class—education and income—are not used in this inquiry because of serious problems of data comparability between the two societies.

9 *Statistisk årsbok för Stockholm,* 1968, table 281.

10 Ibid. Data on "Sweden" are from Nordal Åkerman, *Klassamhället i siffror* (Stockholm: Bokförlaget Prisma, 1973), p. 11. Based on 1968 data from national Low Income Investigation, and includes all persons fifteen to seventy-five years of age.

11 See Popenoe, "Urban Residential Differentiation," pp. 46–48.

12 *Statistisk årsbok för Stockholm,* 1968.

13 According to the head religious leader of Vällingby parish, only 1,000 out of 27,000 people in the parish formally have left the state church since 1954, when the law permitting this action was established. Ninety percent of those were young people with antireligious views. Personal interview, August 1974.

14 Figures secured during personal interview with an official of the Stockholm Statistical Office.

15 Ibid.

16 1970 data from "Transport Policy and Traffic Trends in Sweden" (Stockholm: Swedish Institute, 1971).

17 For 1971—figure secured from Stockholm City Statistical Office.

18 *Trafikundersökningar,* p. 16.

19 Data in this section, unless otherwise indicated, are from the 1971 and 1961 *Statistisk årsbok för Stockholm.*

20 *Statistisk årsbok för Stockholm,* 1963, table 124, pp. 133–34, and 1973, table 90, p. 118.

21 Ulla Bergström, *Ungdomsgårdar* (Stockholm: Generalplanearbete, 1971), pp. 45–50.

22 *Statistisk årsbok för Stockholm,* 1968, table 281, pp. 318–20.

23 Data secured from Stockholm Statistical Office.

24 Ibid.

25 Figures from Pass, *Vällingby and Farsta,* pp. 20–21.
26 Ibid.
27 Gunnar Åsvärn, *Mark, Lokaler, Arbetskraft, Kostnader: en inventering* (Stockholm: Generalplanearbete, 1971), p. 103.
28 Data secured from the Stockholm Statistical Office.
29 *Governing Greater Stockholm,* p. 5.
30 Stockholm: Generalplanearbete, various dates.
31 Åsvärn, *Mark, Lokaler, Arbetskraft,* p. 105.
32 Ibid., p. 50.
33 *Vällingby,* (Stockholm: Svenska Bostäder, n.d.), p. 2.
34 For further information on the Swedish educational system, see Tomasson, *Sweden: Prototype of Modern Society,* chaps. 4, 5; and Britta Stenholm, *Education in Sweden* (Stockholm: The Swedish Institute, 1970).
35 A recently completed investigation by a Swedish Royal Commission makes very strong proposals along these lines and is currently the subject of a national debate.
36 Ulla Bergström, *Fritid Utomhus* (Stockholm: Generalplanearbete, 1973), p. 39. The data in this section come from this monograph.
37 Lillemor Landström and G. Åsvärn, *Fritid i Vällingby* (Stockholm: Generalplanearbete, 1970). Data in this section are from this monograph.
38 Data in this section, unless otherwise noted, are from Bergström, *Ungdomsgårdar.*
39 This information on recent activities in the Vällingby Youth Centers is based on an interview with the manager of youth centers in Stockholm's western suburbs, August 1974.
40 Ibid.
41 Ibid.
42 Data in this section are from Ulla Bergström and Birgit Weimer, *Folkbibliotek* (Stockholm: Generalplanearbete, 1973).
43 See Tomasson, *Sweden: Prototype of Modern Society,* chap. 3.
44 Information from interivew with the head of Vällingby parish, August 1974.
45 Information from "Så här långa är daghemsköerna i Stockholms Iän," *Expressen* (June 26, 1974).
46 This was a major finding of a study of Vårberg, which was built in the late 1960s. Morgan Davies, *Suburban Folk: A Study of Vårberg, Stockholm* (Aberystivyth, Wales: Department of Geography, University College of Wales, 1973).
47 *Barnstugor i Vällingby* (Stockholm: Generalplanearbete, 1970).

Chapter 4

1 William H. Ittelson et al., *An Introduction to Environmental Psychology* (New York: Holt, Rinehart and Winston, 1974).
2 Louis Wirth, "Human Ecology," in Richard Sennett, ed.,

Classic Essays on the Culture of Cities (New York: Appleton-Century-Crofts, 1969), p. 177.

3 Michelson, *Man and His Urban Environment,* p. 26.

4 Roger Barker, *Ecological Psychology* (Stanford, Calif.: Stanford University Press, 1968); and Paul V. Gump, "Milieu, Environment and Behavior," *Design and Environment* 2, no. 4 (1971): 48–52.

5 See, for example, Christopher Alexander, "The Goodness of Fit and Its Sources," in Harold Proshansky, William H. Ittelson, and Leanne G. Rivlin, *Environmental Psychology: Man and His Physical Setting* (New York: Holt, Rinehart & Winston, 1970), pp. 42–56.

6 Michelson, *Man and His Urban Environment,* pp. 30, 31.

7 Ibid., p. 31.

8 Max Weber, *The Theory of Social and Economic Organization* (Edinburgh: W. Hodge & Company, 1947).

9 See W. Michelson and P. Reed, *The Theoretical Status and Operational Usage of Life Style in Environmental Research,* Research Paper no. 36 (Toronto: Centre for Urban and Community Studies, University of Toronto, 1970).

Chapter 5

1 The brochure was distributed by the Levittown Public Recreation Association.

2 This has been the subject of several scholarly works over the years. See especially W. Dobriner, *Class in Suburbia;* John T. Liell, "Levittown: A Study in Community Development and Planning" (Ph.D. diss., Department of Sociology, Yale University, 1952); Louis H. Orzack and Irwin T. Sanders, *A Social Profile of Levittown, New York* (Boston, Mass: The Research Institute, Department of Sociology and Anthropology, Boston University, 1961); and Harold Wattel, "Levittown: A Suburban Community," in Dobriner, *The Suburban Community.*

3 Interview with Alfred Levitt, *Bucks County Courier Times,* June 19, 1972.

4 Quoted in *Fortune,* October 1952, p. 150.

5 This is mentioned several times in the newspaper and magazine material written for Levittown's twentieth anniversary.

6 Some elements of this physical form can be found in many British new towns, and in the new towns built in the U.S. in the 1960s and 1970s.

7 Levitt interview, *Courier Times.*

8 For further information on the history of Levittown, see the special issue of the *Bucks County Courier Times* and the *Trenton Times Advertiser,* June 18, 1972. Also, David Bittan, "Levitt or Leave It," *Philadelphia Magazine,* September 1972.

9 See "Growing Pains of a Brand New City," *Saturday Evening Post,* August 7, 1954, and "Dream Town: Large Economy Size," *New York Times Magazine,* December 14, 1952.

10 See "Levitt Home Price Triples Since 50's," *Philadelphia Evening Bulletin,* April 12, 1973.

11 The township in which these properties are located has recently begun a campaign to clean up the situation, assisted by private wreckers who will now come and dispose of abandoned cars, paying $20 for their scrap value.

12 *Homeowners Guide,* "Some Information for Residents of Levittown to Help Them Enjoy Their New Homes" (The Levitt Organization, n.d.).

13 David Bittan says, "Levittown is, after all, the town that made Reedman's the world's largest car dealer" ("Levitt or Leave It," p. 81).

14 Ibid.

15 Levitt interview, *Courier Times.*

16 Estimate by the director of the Levittown Public Recreation Association, in *Bucks County Courier Times.*

17 Levitt interview, *Courier Times.*

18 *Fortune,* October 1952.

19 The two main sources of information for this section are *1960 U.S. Census of Population and Housing: Census Tracts, Philadelphia, Pa.-N.J. Standard Metropolitan Statistical Area* (Washington, D.C.: U.S. Bureau of the Census, 1962). Referred to below as 1960 Census; and *1970 U.S. Census of Population and Housing: Census Tracts, Philadelphia, Pa.-N.J. Standard Metropolitan Statistical Area* (Washington, D.C.: U.S. Bureau of the Census, 1972). Referred to below as 1970 Census.

The Levittown Census tracts are as follows:

	1960	*1970*
Bristol Township	B-0004-A	1004.01
	B-0004-B	1004.02
	B-0004-D	1004.04
	B-0004-E	1004.05
Falls Township	B-0058-C	1058.03
Middletown Township	B-0008-C	1008.03
	B-0008-D	1008.04
	B-0008-E	1008.05
Tullytown Borough	B-0059-A	1059.01

20 1970 Census, table P-1.

21 1960 Census, table H-1; and 1970 Census, table H-2.

22 Bristol Township tract B-0004-E (1004.05).

23 1970 Census, table P-1.

24 Ibid.

25 The data in this paragraph come from 1970 Census, tables P-1 and P-2.

26 1960 Census, table P-3.

27 1970 Census, table P-3.
28 Tracts B-0008-D and B-0004-E.
29 1970 Census, tracts 1004.04 and 1008.04, table P-4.
30 Price data from *Philadelphia Evening Bulletin,* April 12, 1973, plus discussions with Levittown realtors.
31 All nine tracts included in the calculations. 1970 Census, table P-2.
32 Tracts 1004.05 and 1008.04.
33 Quoted in *New York Times,* July 29, 1967, p. 11, article on Levittown, Long Island, after twenty years.
34 Ibid.
35 See M. Bressler, "The Myers Case: An Instance of Successful Racial Invasion," *Social Problems* 8 (Fall 1960): 126–42.
36 Estimate made in *Bucks County Courier Times,* June 19, 1972.
37 1970 Census, table P-1.
38 Ibid.
39 Willingboro, N.J., Planning Board Report, 1973.
40 Estimate by a Levittown realtor.
41 Philadelphia Council of Churches, 1953, mimeo.
42 Based on informal, unpublished surveys and estimates of religious leaders.
43 1960 Census, table P-1.
44 Ibid.
45 1960 Census, table P-1.
46 1970 Census, table P-2.
47 Estimate from the director of the Levittown Public Recreation Association.
48 1970 Census, table P-2. Calculation based on all nine census tracts.
49 Estimate in *Bucks County Courier Times,* June 18, 1972.
50 1970 Census, table H-2.
51 See the discussion of this for the New Jersey Levittown in Gans, *The Levittowners,* chap. 2.
52 There was a 1 percent increase, due mostly to the few non-Levitt units which were added.
53 1960 Census, table P-2; and 1970 Census, table P-1.
54 The percentage of persons in households, other than husband and wife, who were not children under eighteen, increased from 8 percent to 16 percent, a small portion of which may consist of adult relatives such as grandparents.
55 1960 Census, table P-3.
56 1970 Census, table P-3.
57 1960 Census, table P-1; 1970 Census, table P-2.
58 1960 Census, table P-3; 1970 Census, table P-2. The percentage of working women with children under six decreased from 27 to 18 percent, however, due to the later stage of the life cycle in 1970.
59 1960 Census, table P-3; 1970 Census, table P-2.
60 1960 Census, table P-1; 1970 Census, table P-2.

61 Ibid.
62 1960 Census, table P-3; 1970 Census, table P-2.
63 1960 Census, table P-3; 1970 Census, table P-2. Eighty-seven percent of 1970 automobile users were drivers while 13 percent were passengers.
64 1960 Census, table H-2; and 1970 Census, table H-2.
65 1960 Census, table H-2; and 1970 Census, table H-2.
66 Reported in E. J. Kahn, Jr., *The American People* (Baltimore: Penguin Books, 1975), p. 7.
67 Prepared by the Incorporation Study Committee of the Levittown Civic Association, March 1954, mimeo.
68 By the Bucks County Development Commission.
69 1970 Census, table P-2.
70 Ibid.
71 Data reported in *Bucks County Courier Times,* June 18, 1972.
72 1970 Census, table H-2.
73 The United Fund does have a guide for the services it supports.
74 Based on information from the household interviews.
75 Based on information collected through interviewing by students of anthropology, sponsored by Princeton University and the U.S. Office of Education, 1969.
76 According to school official interviewed.
77 Estimates by police and school officials.
78 Estimate by school and church officials.
79 The term "church" is used here to refer to all established religious institutions.
80 Based on my household interviews. Eighty percent of the adult respondents were church members; of these, 63 percent were regular attenders. In the U.S. as a whole, 40 percent of adults attended church in a typical week in 1971.
81 Based on international Gallup polls.
82 Data from the director of the LPRA.
83 This assessment of the situation was made by the director of the LPRA.
84 Levittown Community Survey, conducted by the LPRA, April 1959.

Chapter 6

1 These differences were fully described and analyzed for Levittown, N.J., by Gans in *The Levittowners,* chap. 2.
2 John McKinney defines a constructed type as "a purposive, planned selection, abstraction, combination and (sometimes) accentuation of a set of criteria with empirical referents that serves as a basis for comparison of empirical cases." John C. McKinney, *Constructive Typology and Social Theory* (New York: Appleton-Century-Crofts, 1966), p. 3.
3 Ibid., p. 11.

4 This is quoted in Bitten, "Levitt or Leave It," p. 83.
5 *Bucks County Courier Times,* February 10, 1974, p. A-1.
6 Bristol Township. Figures from township police records.
7 *Emerging Adults: A Study of Youth in Lower Makefield Township, Falls Township, Yardly Borough and Morrisville Borough in Pennsylvania* (Falsington, Pa.: William Penn Center, 1969), p. 2.

Chapter 7

1 Unless otherwise noted, the data used in this chapter are drawn from chapters three and five, where the sources are given. These sources have not been repeated here.
2 Kingsley Davis, *World Urbanization: 1950–1970,* vol. 1, *Basic Data for Cities, Countries and Regions.* Population Monograph Series no. 4 (Berkeley, Calif.: Institute of International Studies, 1970). 1970 urbanized area figures are based on projections.
3 The number of households in Levittown with no more than two persons is not known, but a related statistic is that 73 percent of Levittown households contained children under eighteen (1970), the great majority of which are households containing at least three persons.
4 Thirty-three percent of Vällingby's population was in the forty-five-to-sixty-four age group, compared to 17 percent in Levittown; and 7 percent were over sixty-five versus Levittown's 2 percent (1970).
5 The problems of comparability between the systems of occupational classification used in the U.S. and Swedish censuses are discussed in Marvin E. Olsen, "Social Classes in Contemporary Sweden," *The Sociological Quarterly* (Summer 1974): 323–40.

Chapter 8

1 Quoted by Robert K. Merton in "The Social Psychology of Housing," in Wayne Dennis, ed., *Current Trends in Social Psychology* (Pittsburgh, Pa.: University of Pittsburgh Press, 1948), p. 204.
2 Ittelson, *Environmental Psychology,* p. 351.
3 Dobriner, *Class in Suburbia,* pp. 9–11.
4 This same decline was found in the first three years of Levittown, N.J.: by Herbert Gans. See his "Planning and Social Life: Friendship and Neighbor Relations in Suburban Communities," *Journal of the American Institute of Planners* 27 (1961): 134–40; also Keller, *The Urban Neighborhood,* chap. 1.

5 A recent, carefully controlled Swedish study found substantial evidence that neighbor interaction is less in apartment buildings that in housing of lower densities. Linnea Gillvik, "Bostadsområdets Utformning och de Boende. En Undersökning i Göteborg," in Solidarisk Bostadspolitik vol. 18 (Stockholm: Bostadsdepartementet, 1974), chap. 12, pp. 1–175.

6 This was a finding of an early study of Vällingby. Edmund Dahlström, Barnfamiljer i Höghus och Trevånings Låghus i Vällingby Report 38 (Stockholm: Statens Institutet för Byggnadsforskning, 1957). This study was repeated in other environments with similar findings. Lillemor Landström, Höghus och Låghus i Småstadsmiljö Report 48 (Stockholm: Statens Institutet för Byggnadsforskning, 1958). In a major study of the Stockholm suburb of Vårberg, built fifteen years after Vällingby, Åke Daun found that "interaction between neighbors in the larger family apartment houses was insignificant" (Förortsliv [Stockholm: Bokförlaget Prisma, 1974], p. 305–6).

7 For an excellent discussion of neighboring, see Keller, The Urban Neighborhood.

8 See, for example, Charles R. Wright and Herbert H. Hyman, "Voluntary Association Membership of American Adults," American Sociological Review 23 (1958): 284–94; and Arthur B. Shostak, Blue Collar Life (New York: Random House, 1969).

9 The same behavioral effects were found in a comparison among residential environments in the U.S.: the inclusion of walkways in a residential area significantly encourages walking. John B. Lansing et al., Planned Residential Environments (Ann Arbor: Institute for Social Research, 1970), pp. 86–88.

10 Åke Daun found that the summer cottage played an equally important role in the lives of many of the families he interviewed in the suburb Vårberg. Förortsliv.

11 Trafikundersökningar.

12 Stina Sandels, Små barn i trafiken, 2d ed. (Stockholm: Läromedelsförlaget, 1972).

13 This impression is supported by studies reported in Urie Bronfenbrenner, Two Worlds of Childhood (New York: Basic Books, 1970), p. 98, which show that American parents spend significantly less time with their children than European parents.

14 Great assistance was given to me in the preparation of this section by my undergraduate students at Rutgers University. Over the years they have written about their own teenage experiences in the Levittown-like suburbs of New Jersey, providing rich insight and valuable information.

15 Some students of the subject suggest that further delays in the achievement of adult status have led to a new life-stage between adolescence and adulthood, labled "transadulthood." This post-

adolescent phase sometimes extends into the thirties. Carl Danzinger and Mathew Greenwald, *Alternatives* (New York: Institute of Life Insurance, 1973).

16 Denise B. Kandel and Gerald S. Lesser, *Youth in Two Worlds* (San Francisco: Jossey-Bass, 1972), p. 177.

17 Ibid., p. 179.

18 Ibid., p. 178.

19 In his study of the early Levittown, N.J., Herbert Gans also found that teenagers were the least satisfied environmental users. In one of his samples, only 37 percent of tenth-graders "liked" Levittown (*The Levittowners*, pp. 206–12).

20 Kandel and Lesser, *Youth in Two Worlds*, p. 90.

21 An important investigation of this issue is James C. Hackler, Kwai-Yiu Ho, and Carol Urquhart-Ross, "The Willingness to Intervene: Differing Community Characteristics," *Social Problems* 21, no. 3 (1974): 328–44.

22 A useful discussion of this topic is James S. Coleman, "Community Disorganization and Conflict," in Robert K. Merton and Robert Nisbet, *Contemporary Social Problems* (New York: Harcourt Brace Jovanovich, 1971), pp. 690–91.

23 The importance of community differences in accounting for variations in adolescent value patterns and deviance is explored in Coleman, *The Adolescent Society*, chap. 10.

24 A good example is the article "The City as a Mechanism for Sustaining Human Contact," by Christopher Alexander, in Robert Gutman, ed., *People and Buildings* (New York: Basic Books, 1972), pp. 406–34.

25 For a general discussion of this topic, see chap. 8 in W. Michelson, *Man and His Urban Environment*.

26 See David Popenoe, *Sociology* (Englewood Cliffs, N.J.: Prentice-Hall, 1977), chap. 2.

27 Robert S. Weiss, "The Fund of Sociability," *Transaction* (July–August 1969). Weiss works with two other functions which are not as relevant for our purposes: opportunity for nurturant behavior and need for guidance. His basic functions are quite similar to Abraham Maslow's "basic human needs," but I believe that they are more empirically grounded than Maslow's. Maslow's four basic needs are safety and security; belongingness and identification; close love-relationships; and respect, prestige, and self-esteem. See his *Toward a Psychology of Being* (Princeton, N.J.: D. Van Nostrand, 1962).

28 An interesting recent book on this topic is Carol B. Stack, *All Our Kin* (New York: Harper and Row, 1974).

29 One of the best studies of this relationship is Lord Taylor and Sidney Chave, *Mental Health and Environment* (London: Longmans Green, 1964). See also E. H. Hare and G. K. Shaw, *Mental Health on a New Housing Estate* (London: Oxford University Press, 1965).

30 Support for this finding is provided by another recent study of working-class women in the suburbs. Irving Tallman, ''Working-Class Wives in Suburbia: Fulfillment or Crisis,'' *Journal of Marriage and Family* 31, no. 1 (February 1969): 65–72.

31 There is some evidence, however, that Swedish mothers in the more recently built apartment suburbs of Stockholm who are forced to be full-time housewives due to lack of work or suitable child-care arrangements feel more deprived and bored than the working mothers of Vällingby. See Morgan Davies, *Suburban Folk*, p. 93. Davies found many young, nonworking mothers to be unhappy and disgruntled.

32 The best general discussion of the social functions of neighborhoods is Keller, *The Urban Neighborhood*. See also Terence Lee, ''Urban Neighborhood as a Socio-Spatial Schema'' in *Human Relations* 21 (1968): 241–68.

33 This was a principal conclusion of several unpublished studies of living patterns in the new town of Columbia, Maryland, which has a well-defined neighborhood pattern not unlike Levittown's.

34 In discussions with social planners in Great Britain this was also raised as a problem in some British new towns, where residential areas are separated from centralized shopping and cultural facilities by a large green belt, protecting the residents from a mixture of land uses but at the same time inhibiting social interaction by spreading people and facilities farther apart.

35 A methodologically sophisticated empirical investigation of this topic is Carey and Mapes, *The Sociology of Planning*.

36 In a comparison of two new housing developments, one of which was specially designed to promote social contact, a Danish study found little association between physical form and the development of social relationships. Jens Schjerup Hansen and Mogens Holm, *Vaerebro Park* (Copenhagen: Statens Byggeforskningsinstitut, 1972).

Chapter 9

1 In 1967, for example, Sweden produced 12.7 dwelling units per 1,000 persons. The nearest rival, the Netherlands, produced 10.2 while the figure for the U.S. was 6.7. Ödmann and Dahlberg, *Urbanization in Sweden*, p. 163.

2 *Housing, Building and Planning in Sweden*. A report prepared by the Swedish Ministry of Housing and Physical Planning, together with other government agencies, for the ECE Committee on Housing, Building and Planning (Stockholm, 1974), p. 13.

3 Ibid., p. 11.

266   Notes to Chapter Nine

4 *Fakta i Bostadsfrågan* 1975 (Stockholm: Riksbyggen, 1975), p. 14.
5 For example, Daun, *Förortsliv*, and Davies, *Suburban Folk*.
6 The most widely discussed of the critical books are Hans Gordon and Peter Molin, *Man Bara Anpassar Sig Helt Enkelt* (Stockholm: Bokförlaget Pan/Norstedts, 1972); Olle Bengtzon, Jan Delden and Jan Lundgren *Rapport Tensta* (Stockholm: Bokförlaget Pan/Norstedts, 1970); and Carin Flemström and Alf Ronnby, *Fallet Rosengård* (Stockholm: Bokförlaget Prisma, 1972) (on a suburb of Malmö).
7 Based on discussions with the former city planning director of Stockholm.
8 See, for example, Gunnar Åsvärn and Helena Altvall, *At Bo i Handen* (Stockholm: A. B. Svensk Byggtjänst, 1970), and Birgitta Lundberg and Karin Wiklund, *Enkät om Förvärvsfrekvens och barntillsyn i Norra Botkyrka år 1971* (Stockholm: A. B. Svensk Bostäder, 1972), mimeo.
9 Ibid.
10 Information from housing official at Svenska Bostäder.
11 The lack of children's play in these areas is discussed in Eva Insulander, *Barnen och Betongen* (Stockholm: Liber Förlag, 1975).
12 Igor Dergalin, "Plan for the Suburban Group of Southern Järvafält: Rinkeby and Tensta" (Stockholm City Planning Office, 1970) pp. 2–3, mimeo.
13 An interesting discussion of the relationship between the environment and privacy is contained in Barry Schwartz, "The Social Psychology of Privacy," *American Journal of Sociology* 72 (May 1968): 741–52.
14 The relationship between density and social interaction is summarized in Michelson, *Man and His Urban Environment*, chap. 8.
15 This development is briefly described in *Stockholm–Urban Environment*, pp. 83–86.
16 Information from officials at the Swedish National Housing Board.
17 *Fakta i Bostadsfrågan 1975*.
18 In 1975 one of the most widely discussed new suburban developments of Stockholm which had these problems was in Bålsta. See "Hur skall det gå i Bålsta?" *Dagens Nyheter* (April 16, 1975), p. 29; and "Småhus—Idyll eller Fängelse?" *Vi*, no. 21 (May 24, 1975), p. 4.
19 This is an impression based on numerous discussions and interviews with government officials in the housing field.
20 This has been published in English: *Towards a New Swedish Housing Policy: The Housing Bill 1974:150* (Stockholm: Ministry of Housing and Physical Planning, January 1975).
21 See Appendix.

22 From discussions with Swedish population experts.

23 Estimate of a Stockholm housing official.

24 Rita Liljeström et al., *Sex Roles in Transition* (Stockholm: Swedish Institute, 1975), p. 14.

25 This situation, in Åkersberga, was reported to me by a Stockholm housing investigator.

26 Discussed above in chapter 8, "The Social Functions of the Neighborhood."

27 See Popenoe, "Urban Residential Differentiation," pp. 48–53.

28 *Housing, Biulding and Planning in Sweden,* p. 40.

29 See Marion Clawson and Peter Hall, *Planning and Urban Growth: An Anglo-American Comparison* (Baltimore: The Johns Hopkins Press, 1973), pp. 14–18.

30 The defense is often on economic grounds. See, for example, Jack Lessinger, "The Case for Scatteration," *Journal of the American Institute of Planners* 28 (August 1962): 159–69.

31 One of the most outspoken opponents of urban sprawl has been Lewis Mumford, *The City in History,* pp. 503–24; and *The Urban Prospect* (New York: Harcourt, Brace & World, 1968), pp. 3–23, 128–41. See also Editors of Fortune, *The Exploding Metropolis* (New York, 1958).

32 Reported in the *New York Times,* October 22, 1974, p. 21.

33 Ibid., October 25, 1974.

34 May 8, 1975, p. 38.

35 Reported in the *New York Times,* May 11, 1975.

36 See J. Fine, N. D. Glenn, and J. K. Monts, "The Residential Segregation of Occupational Groups in Central Cities and Suburbs," *Demography* 8 (February 1971): 91–101; N. D. Glenn, "Suburbanization in the United States Since World War II," in Masotti and Hadden, *The Urbanization of the Suburbs,* pp. 51–77; and Schnore, "The Socioeconomic Status of Cities and Suburbs," pp. 76–85.

37 Two early books on this topic, still worthwhile reading, are Robert Wood, *1400 Governments* (Garden City, N.Y.: Doubleday, 1961), and idem, *Suburbia: Its People and Their Politics* (Houghton Mifflin, 1958).

38 Jack Rosenthal, "The Suburban Apartment Boom," in Masotti and Hadden, eds., *Suburbia in Transition,* p. 29.

39 Ibid.

40 See Sternlieb, "Death of the American Dream House," pp. 39–42.

41 An interesting anthropological study of a mobile-home community inhabited mainly by the elderly is Sheila K. Johnson, *Idle Haven* (Berkeley: University of California Press, 1971).

42 Rosenthal, "The Suburban Apartment Boom."

43 *New York Times,* May 8, 1975, p. 38.

44 The Center for Auto Safety, *Mobile Homes: The Low Cost Housing Hoax* (New York: Grossman Publishers, 1975).

45 See Gurney Breckenfeld, *Columbia and the New Cities* (New York: Ives Washburn, 1971); and Clapp, *New Towns and Urban Policy.*

46 *The Gallup Opinion Index,* no. 110, August 1974.

47 This system, and the strategies for changing it, are explored in Anthony Downs, *Opening Up the Suburbs* (New Haven: Yale University Press, 1973).

48 See, for example, Ronald A. Buel, *Dead End* (Baltimore: Penguin Books, 1973).

49 See Burchell, *Planned Unit Developments,* and idem, *Frontiers of Planned Unit Development* (New Brunswick, N.J.: Rutgers University Center for Urban Policy Research, 1973).

Index